Introducing Translation Studies

'Jeremy Munday's book presents a snapshot of a rapidly developing discipline in a clear, concise and graphic way. This is a book which raises strong awareness of current issues in the field and will be of interest to translation trainers and trainees alike.'

Basil Hatim, Heriot-Watt University

Introducing Translation Studies is an introductory textbook providing an accessible overview of the key contributions to translation studies.

Munday explores each theory chapter by chapter and tests the different approaches by applying them to texts. The texts discussed are taken from a broad range of languages – English, French, German, Spanish, Italian, Punjabi, Portuguese and Spanish – and English translations are provided.

A wide variety of text types is analyzed, including a tourist brochure, a children's cookery book, a Harry Potter novel, the Bible, literary reviews and translators' prefaces, film translation, a technical text and a European Parliament speech.

Each chapter includes the following features:

- a table presenting the key concepts;
- an introduction outlining the translation theory or theories;
- illustrative texts with translations;
- a chapter summary;
- discussion points and exercises.

Including a general introduction, an extensive bibliography and internet sites for further information, this is a practical, user-friendly textbook that gives a balanced and comprehensive insight into translation studies.

Jeremy Munday is Lecturer in Spanish Studies at the University of Surrey and is a freelance translator, lexicographer and materials writer. He has a Doctorate in Translation Studies and his publications include a wide range of papers in the field, as well as translations of Latin American fiction.

Introducing Translation Studies

Theories and applications

Jeremy Munday

London and New York

First published 2001
by Routledge
11 New Fetter Lane, London EC4P 4EE

Simultaneously published in the USA and Canada
by Routledge
29 West 35th Street, New York, NY 10001

Routledge is an imprint of the Taylor & Francis Group

© 2001 Jeremy Munday

The right of Jeremy Munday to be identified as the Author
of this Work has been asserted by him in accordance
with the Copyright, Design and Patents Act 1988

Typeset in Gill Sans and Goudy Old Style by
RefineCatch Limited, Bungay, Suffolk
Printed and bound in Great Britain by
TJ International Ltd, Padstow, Cornwall

British Library Cataloguing in Publication Data
A catalogue record for this book is available from the British Library

Library of Congress Cataloging in Publication Data
Munday, Jeremy.
      Introducing translation studies / Jeremy Munday.
         p.   cm.
      Includes bibliographical references and index.
         1. Translating and interpreting.   I. Title.
      P306 .M865   2001
      418′.02 – dc21   00–045935

ISBN 0-415-22926-X (hbk)
ISBN 0-415-22927-8 (pbk)

Para Cristina,
que me ha hecho feliz.

Contents

List of figures and tables

Figures

Tables

Acknowledgements

I would like to thank the following copyright holders for giving permission to reproduce the following: Figure 1.1, reproduced from G. Toury, *Descriptive Translation Studies – And Beyond*, copyright 1995, Amsterdam and Philadelphia, PA: John Benjamins. Figure 3.1, reproduced from E. Nida and C. R. Taber, *The Theory and Practice of Translation*, copyright 1969, Leiden: E. J. Brill. Figure 5.1, reproduced from A. Chesterman (ed.), *Readings in Translation Theory*, copyright 1989, Helsinki: Finn Lectura; based on a handout prepared by Roland Freihoff; permission kindly granted by the author. Table 5.1, adapted from K. Reiss, *Möglichkeiten und Grenzen der Übersetzungskritik*, copyright 1971, Munich: M. Hueber. Figure 6.2, reproduced from J. House, *Translation Quality Assessment: A Model Revisited*, copyright 1997, Tübingen: Gunter Narr. Figure 11.1, reproduced from M. Snell-Hornby, *Translation Studies: An Integrated Approach*, copyright 1995, Amsterdam and Philadelphia, PA: John Benjamins.

The case study in chapter 8 is a revised and abridged version of an article of mine: 'The Caribbean conquers the world? An analysis of the reception of García Márquez in translation', published in *Bulletin of Hispanic Studies*, 75.1: 137–44.

I am sincerely indebted to Professor Lawrence Venuti for his encouragement with this project and for his detailed comments and suggestions on earlier drafts of the book. He has assisted considerably in sharpening and strengthening the focus and in pointing out errors and inaccuracies. Responsibility for the final version is, of course, mine alone.

My thanks also go to Dr Rana Nayar (Reader, Department of English at Panjab University, Chandigarh, India) for his assistance with the case study in chapter 9, to my colleagues at the Universities of Bradford and Surrey for their support during the writing of this book, and to my students at Bradford, on whom some of the materials in this book have been 'tested'.

I would also like to express my gratitude to Louisa Semlyen and Katharine Jacobson at Routledge, who have been very supportive and professional both in the early stages of the project and throughout the writing and editing process.

Finally, warm thanks to my family and friends who have had to put up with me writing away on the computer instead of relaxing with them, especially to my brother Chris in France and everyone in Madrid and Mallorca. Most of all, thanks to Cristina, whose love and help were so important during the writing of this book.

Jeremy Munday
London, September 2000

List of abbreviations

BCE   Before Common Era
CE   Common Era
DTS   descriptive translation studies
SL   source language
ST   source text
TL   target language
TT   target text

Introduction

Translation studies is the new academic discipline related to the study of the theory and phenomena of translation. By its nature it is multilingual and also interdisciplinary, encompassing languages, linguistics, communication studies, philosophy and a range of types of cultural studies.

Because of this diversity, one of the biggest problems in teaching and learning about translation studies is that much of it is dispersed across such a wide range of books and journals. Hence there have been a number of 'readers' of key writings on the subject; these include Hans-Joachim Störig's *Das Problem des Übersetzens* (1963), Andrew Chesterman's *Readings in Translation Theory* (1989), André Lefevere's *Translation/History/Culture: A Sourcebook* (1992b), Rainer Schulte and John Biguenet's *Theories of Translation: An Anthology of Essays from Dryden to Derrida* (1992), Douglas Robinson's *Western Translation Theory from Herodotus to Nietzsche* (1997b) and Lawrence Venuti's *The Translation Studies Reader* (2000). Others, such as *The Routledge Encyclopedia of Translation Studies* (Baker 1997a) and *The Dictionary of Translation Studies* (Shuttleworth and Cowie 1997), have attempted to bring together the main concepts and give a description of the field.

The present book aims to be a practical introduction to the field. It sets out to give a critical but balanced survey of many of the most important trends and contributions to translation studies in a single volume, written in an accessible style. The different contemporary models are applied to illustrative texts in brief case studies so that the reader can see them in operation. The new research contained in these case studies, together with the 'discussion and research points' sections, is designed to encourage further exploration and understanding of translation issues.

The book is thus designed to serve as a coursebook for undergraduate and postgraduate translation, translation studies and translation theory, and also as a solid theoretical introduction to students, researchers, instructors and professional translators. The aim is to enable the readers to develop their understanding of the issues and associated metalanguage, and to begin to apply the models themselves. It is also hoped that a closer examination of specific issues and further reading in those areas that are of greatest interest to the individual student will be encouraged. In this way, the book can provide a stimulating introduction to a range of theoretical approaches to translation that are relevant both for those engaged in the academic study of translation and for the professional linguist.

Each of the chapters surveys a major area of the discipline. They are designed to be self-standing, so that readers with a specific focus can quickly find the descriptions that are of most interest to them. However, conceptual links between chapters are cross-referenced and the book has been structured so that it can function as a coursebook in translation, translation studies and translation theory. There are eleven chapters, each of which might be covered in one or two weeks, depending on the length of the course, to fit into a semesterized system. The discussion and research points additionally provide substantial initial material for students to begin to develop their own research. The progression of ideas is also from the introductory (presenting the main issues of translation studies in chapter 1) to the more complex, as the students become more accustomed to the terminology and concepts. In general, the progression is chronological, from pre-twentieth century theory in chapter 2 to linguistic-oriented theories (chapters 3–6 passim) and to recent developments from cultural studies such as postcolonialism (chapter 8).

Clarity has been a major consideration, so each chapter follows a similar format of:

- an introductory table clearly presenting key terms and ideas;
- the main text, describing in detail the models and issues under discussion;
- an illustrative case study, which applies and evaluates the main model of the chapter;
- suggestions for further reading;
- a brief evaluative summary of the chapter;
- a series of discussion and research points to stimulate further thought and research.

Just like the readers listed above, this volume has had to be selective. The theorists and models covered have been chosen because of their strong influence on translation studies and because they are particularly representative of the approaches in each chapter. Exclusion of much other worthy material has been due to space constraints and the focus of the book, which is to give a clear introduction to a number of theoretical approaches.

For this reason, detailed suggestions are given for further reading. These are designed to encourage students to go to the primary texts, to follow up ideas that have been raised in each chapter and to investigate the research that is being carried out in their own countries and languages. In this way, the book should ideally be used in conjunction with the readers mentioned above and be supported by an institution's library resources. An attempt has also been made to refer to many works that are readily available, either in recent editions or reprinted in one of the anthologies. A comprehensive bibliography is provided at the end of the book, together with a small list of useful websites, where up-to-date information on translation studies confer-ences, publications and organizations is to be found. The emphasis is on encouraging reflection, investigation and awareness of the new discipline, and on applying the theory to both practice and research.

A major issue has been the choice of languages for the texts used in the illustrative case studies. There are examples or texts from English, French, German, Italian, Portuguese and Spanish. Some additional examples are given from Dutch, Punjabi and Russian. Yet the case studies are written in such a way as to focus on the theoretical issues and should not exclude those unfamiliar with the specific language pairs. A range of text types is offered, including the Bible, *Beowulf*, the fiction of García Márquez and Proust, European Union and Unesco documents, a travel brochure, a children's cookery book and the translations of Harry Potter. Film and dialect transla-tion, in French, German and Punjabi, are also covered. In addition, the inten-tion is for some short supplementary illustrative texts, in other languages, to be available on the Routledge internet site for the use of students studying other languages.

(see http://www.routledge.com/textbooks/its.html). Above all, my hope is that this book will contribute to the continued development of translation studies by helping and encouraging readers new to the field to pursue their interest in this dynamic discipline.

▌ Main issues of translation studies

Key concepts

- The practice of translating is long established, but the discipline of translation studies is new.
- In academic circles, translation was previously relegated to just a language-learning activity.
- A split has persisted between translation practice and theory.
- The study of (usually literary) translation began through comparative literature, translation 'workshops' and contrastive analysis.
- James S. Holmes's 'The name and nature of translation studies' is considered to be the 'founding statement' of a new discipline.
- The present rapid expansion of the discipline is important.

Key texts

Holmes, J. S. (1988b/2000) 'The name and nature of translation studies', in L. Venuti (ed.) (2000), pp. 172–85.

Jakobson, R. (1959/2000) 'On linguistic aspects of translation', in L. Venuti (ed.) (2000), pp. 113–18.

Leuven-Zwart, K. van and **T. Naaijkens** (eds) (1991) *Translation Studies: State of the Art*, Amsterdam: Rodopi.

Toury, G. (1991) 'What are descriptive studies in translation likely to yield apart from isolated descriptions?', in K. van Leuven-Zwart and T. Naaijkens (eds) (1991), pp. 179–92.

1.1 The concept of translation

The main aim of this book is to introduce the reader to major concepts and models of translation studies. Because of the rapid growth in the area, particularly over the last decade, difficult decisions have had to be taken regarding the selection of material. It has been decided, for reasons of space and consistency of approach, to focus on written translation rather than oral translation (the latter is commonly known as **interpreting** or **interpretation**).

The term **translation** itself has several meanings: it can refer to the general subject field, the product (the text that has been translated) or the process (the act of producing the translation, otherwise known as **translating**). The **process of translation** between two different written languages involves the translator changing an original written text (the **source text** or ST) in the original verbal language (the **source language** or SL) into a written text (the **target text** or TT) in a different verbal language (the **target language** or TL). This type corresponds to 'interlingual translation' and is one of the three categories of translation described by the Czech structuralist Roman Jakobson in his seminal paper 'On linguistic aspects of translation' (Jakobson 1959/2000: 114). Jakobson's categories are as follows:

1 **intralingual** translation, or 'rewording': 'an interpretation of verbal signs by means of other signs of the same language';
2 **interlingual** translation, or 'translation proper': 'an interpretation of verbal signs by means of some other language';
3 **intersemiotic** translation, or 'transmutation': 'an interpretation of verbal signs by means of signs of non-verbal sign systems').

Intralingual translation would occur, for example, when we rephrase an expression or text in the same language to explain or clarify something we might have said or written. Intersemiotic translation would occur if a written text were translated, for example, into music, film or painting. It is interlingual translation which is the traditional, although by no means exclusive, focus of translation studies.

1.2 What is translation studies?

Throughout history, written and spoken translations have played a crucial role in interhuman communication, not least in providing access to important texts for scholarship and religious purposes. Yet the study of translation as an academic subject has only really begun in the past fifty years. In the English-speaking world, this discipline is now generally known as 'translation studies', thanks to the Dutch-based US scholar James S. Holmes. In his key defining paper delivered in 1972, but not widely available until 1988 (Holmes 1988b/2000), Holmes describes the then nascent discipline as being concerned with 'the complex of problems clustered round the phenomenon of translating and translations' (Holmes 1988b/2000: 173). By 1988, Mary Snell-Hornby, in the first edition of her *Translation Studies: An Integrated Approach*, was writing that 'the demand that translation studies should be viewed as an independent discipline . . . has come from several quarters in recent years' (Snell-Hornby 1988). By 1995, the time of the second, revised, edition of her work, Snell-Hornby is able to talk in the preface of 'the breathtaking development of translation studies as an independent discipline' and the 'prolific international discussion' on the subject. Mona Baker, in her introduction to *The Routledge Encyclopedia of Translation* (1997a), talks effusively of the richness of the 'exciting new discipline, perhaps *the* discipline of the 1990s', bringing together scholars from a wide variety of often more traditional disciplines. Now, at the beginning of the twenty-first century, the discipline of translation studies continues to develop from strength to strength across the globe.

There are two very visible ways in which translation studies has become more prominent. First, there has been a proliferation of specialized translating and interpreting courses at both undergraduate and postgraduate level. In the UK, the first specialized university postgraduate courses in interpreting and translating were set up in the 1960s. In the academic year 1999/2000, there were at least twenty postgraduate translation courses in the UK and several designated 'Centres of Translation'. Caminade and Pym (1995) list at least 250 university-level bodies in over sixty countries offering four-year undergraduate degrees and/or postgraduate courses in translation. These courses, which attract thousands of students, are mainly oriented towards training future professional commercial translators and interpreters and serve as highly valued entry-level qualifications for the translating and interpreting professions.

Other courses, in smaller numbers, focus on the practice of literary translation. In the UK, these include major courses at Middlesex University and the University of East Anglia (Norwich), the latter of which also houses the British Centre for Literary Translation. In Europe, there is now a network of centres where literary translation is studied, practised and promoted. Apart from Norwich, these include Amsterdam (the Netherlands), Arles (France), Bratislava (Slovakia), Dublin (Ireland), Rhodes (Greece), Sineffe (Belgium), Strälen (Germany), Tarazona (Spain) and Visby (Sweden).

The 1990s also saw a proliferation of conferences, books and journals on translation in many languages. Long-standing international translation studies journals such as *Babel* (the Netherlands), *Meta* (Canada), *Parallèles* (Switzerland) and *Traduire* (France) have now been joined by, amongst others, *Across Languages and Cultures* (Hungary), *Cadernos de Tradução* (Brazil), *Literature in Translation* (UK), *Perspectives* (France), *Rivista Internazionale di Tecnica della Traduzione* (Italy), *Target* (Israel/Belgium), *The Translator* (UK), *Turjuman* (Morocco) and the Spanish *Hermeneus*, *Livius* and *Sendebar*, as well as a whole host of other single language, modern languages, applied linguistics, comparative literature and other journals whose primary focus may not be translation but where articles on translation are often published. The lists of European publishers such as John Benjamins, Multilingual Matters, Rodopi, Routledge and St Jerome now contain considerable numbers of books in the field of translation studies. In addition, there are various professional publications dedicated to the practice of translation (in the UK these include *The Linguist* of the Institute of Linguists, *The ITI Bulletin* of the Institute for Translating and Interpreting and *In Other Words*, the literary-oriented publication of the Translators' Association). Other smaller periodicals such as *TRANSST* (Israel) and *BET* (Spain), now disseminated through the internet, give details of forthcoming events, conferences and translation prizes. In the year 1999–2000, for instance, international translation conferences were held in a large number of countries and on a wide variety of key themes, including:

- translation and training translators (Bratislava, Slovakia);
- literary translation (Mons, Belgium);
- research models in translation studies (UMIST, Manchester, UK);
- gender and translation (Norwich, UK);
- translation as/at the crossroads of culture (Lisbon, Portugal);
- translation and globalization (Tangiers, Morocco);
- legal translation (Geneva, Switzerland);
- translation and meaning (Maastricht, the Netherlands and Lodz, Poland);
- the history of translation (Leon, Spain);
- transadaptation and pedagogical challenges (Turku, Finland);
- translation-focused comparative literature (Pretoria, South Africa and Salvador, Brazil).

In addition, various translation events were held in India, and an on-line translation symposium was organized by Anthony Pym from Spain in January 2000. The fact that such events are now attempting to narrow their focus is indicative of the richness and abundance of the activity being undertaken in the field as a whole. From being a little-established field a relatively short time ago, translation studies has now become one of the most active and dynamic new areas of research encompassing an exciting mix of approaches.

This chapter sets out to examine what exactly is understood by this fast-growing field and briefly describes the history of the development and aims of the discipline.

1.3 A brief history of the discipline

Writings on the subject of translating go far back in recorded history. The practice of translation was discussed by, for example, Cicero and Horace (first century BCE) and St Jerome (fourth century CE); as we shall see in chapter 2, their writings were to exert an important influence up until the twentieth century. In St Jerome's case, his approach to translating the Greek Septuagint Bible into Latin would affect later translations of the Scriptures. Indeed, the translation of the Bible was to be – for well over a thousand years and especially during the Reformation in the sixteenth century – the battleground of conflicting ideologies in western Europe.

However, although the practice of translating is long established, the study of the field developed into an academic discipline only in the second half of the twentieth century. Before that, translation had normally been merely an element of language learning in modern language courses. In fact, from the late eighteenth century to the 1960s, language learning in secondary schools in many countries had come to be dominated by what was known as the grammar-translation method. This method, which was applied to classical Latin and Greek and then to modern foreign languages, centred on the rote study of the grammatical rules and structures of the foreign language. These rules were both practised and tested by the translation of a series of usually unconnected and artificially constructed sentences exemplifying the structure(s) being studied, an approach that persists even nowadays in certain countries and contexts. Typical of this is the following rather bizarre and decontextualized collection of sentences to translate into Spanish, for the practice of Spanish tense use. They appear in K. Mason's *Advanced Spanish Course*, still to be found on some secondary school courses in the UK:

1　The castle stood out against the cloudless sky.
2　The peasants enjoyed their weekly visits to the market.
3　She usually dusted the bedrooms after breakfast.
4　Mrs Evans taught French at the local grammar school.

(Mason 1969/74: 92)

The gearing of translation to language teaching and learning may partly explain why academia considered it to be of secondary status. Translation exercises were regarded as a means of learning a new language or of reading a foreign language text until one had the linguistic ability to read the original. Study of a work in translation was generally frowned upon once the student had acquired the necessary skills to read the original. However, the grammar-translation method fell into increasing disrepute, particularly in many English-language countries, with the rise of the direct method or communicative approach to English language teaching in the 1960s and 1970s. This approach places stress on students' natural capacity to learn language and attempts to replicate 'authentic' language learning conditions in the classroom. It often privileges spoken over written forms, at least initially, and tends to shun the use of the students' mother tongue. This focus led to the abandoning of translation in language learning. As far as teaching was concerned, translation then tended to become restricted to higher-level and university language courses and professional translator training, to the extent that present first-year undergraduates in the UK are unlikely to have had any real practice in the skill.

In the USA, translation – specifically literary translation – was promoted in universities in the 1960s by the **translation workshop** concept. Based on I. A. Richards's reading workshops and practical criticism approach that began in the 1920s and in other later creative writing workshops, these translation workshops were first established in the universities of Iowa and Princeton. They were intended as a platform for the introduction of new translations into the target culture and for the discussion of the finer principles of the translation process and of understanding a text (for further discussion of this background, see Gentzler 1993: 7–18). Running parallel to this approach was that of **comparative literature**, where literature is studied and compared transnationally and transculturally, necessitating the reading of some literature in translation. This would later link into the growth of courses of the cultural studies type (these are described below).

Another area in which translation became the subject of research was **contrastive analysis**. This is the study of two languages in contrast in an attempt to identify general and specific differences between them. It developed into a systematic area of research in the USA from the 1930s onwards and came to the fore in the 1960s and 1970s. Translations and translated examples provided much of the data in these studies (e.g. Di Pietro 1971, James 1980). The contrastive approach heavily influenced other studies, such as Vinay and Darbelnet's (1958) and Catford's (1965), which overtly stated their aim of assisting translation research. Although useful, contrastive analysis does not, however, incorporate sociocultural and prag-matic factors, nor the role of translation as a communicative act. Neverthe-less, the continued application of a linguistic approach in general, and specific linguistic models such as generative grammar or functional grammar (see chapters 3, 5 and 6), has demonstrated an inherent and gut link with translation. While, in some universities, translation continues to be studied as a module on applied linguistics courses, the evolving field of translation studies can point to its own systematic models that have incorporated other linguistic models and developed them for its own purposes. At the same time, the construction of the new discipline has involved moving away from considering translation as primarily connected to language teaching and learning. Instead, the new focus is the specific study of what happens in and around translating and translation.

The more systematic, and mostly linguistic-oriented, approach to the study of translation began to emerge in the 1950s and 1960s. There are a number of now classic examples:

- Jean-Paul Vinay and Jean Darbelnet produced their *Stylistique comparée du français et de l'anglais* (1958), a contrastive approach that categorized what they saw happening in the practice of translation between French and English;
- Alfred Malblanc (1963) did the same for translation between French and German;
- Georges Mounin's *Les problèmes théoriques de la traduction* (1963) examined linguistic issues of translation;
- Eugene Nida (1964a) incorporated elements of Chomsky's then fashion-able generative grammar as a theoretical underpinning of his books, which were initially designed to be practical manuals for Bible translators.

This more systematic and 'scientific' approach in many ways began to mark out the territory of the academic investigation of translation. The word 'science' was used by Nida in the title of his 1964 book (*Toward a Science of Translating*, 1964a); the German equivalent, 'Übersetzungswissenschaft', was taken up by Wolfram Wilss in his teaching and research at the Universität des Saarlandes at Saarbrücken, by Koller in Heidelberg and by the Leipzig

school, where scholars such as Kade and Neubert became active. At that
time, even the name of the emerging discipline remained to be determined,
with candidates such as 'translatology' in English – and its counterparts
'translatologie' in French and 'traductología' in Spanish – staking their claim.

1.4 The Holmes/Toury 'map'

A seminal paper in the development of the field as a distinct discipline was
James S. Holmes's 'The name and nature of translation studies' (Holmes
1988b/2000). In his *Contemporary Translation Theories*, Gentzler (1993: 92)
describes Holmes's paper as 'generally accepted as the founding statement
for the field'. Interestingly, in view of our discussion above of how the field
evolved from other disciplines, the published version was an expanded form
of a paper Holmes originally gave in 1972 in the translation section of the
Third International Congress of Applied Linguistics in Copenhagen. Holmes
draws attention to the limitations imposed at the time by the fact that translation research was dispersed across older disciplines. He also stresses the need
to forge 'other communication channels, cutting across the traditional disciplines to reach all scholars working in the field, from whatever background'
(1988b/2000: 173).

Crucially, Holmes puts forward an overall framework, describing what
translation studies covers. This framework has subsequently been presented
by the leading Israeli translation scholar Gideon Toury as in figure 1.1. In

Figure 1.1
Holmes's 'map' of translation studies (from Toury 1995: 10)

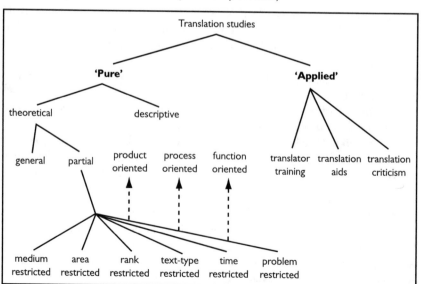

Holmes's explanations of this framework (Holmes 1988b/2000: 176–81), the objectives of the 'pure' areas of research are:

1   the description of the phenomena of translation (**descriptive translation theory**);
2   the establishment of general principles to explain and predict such phenomena (**translation theory**).

The 'theoretical' branch is divided into general and partial theories. By 'general', Holmes is referring to those writings that seek to describe or account for every type of translation and to make generalizations that will be relevant for translation as a whole. 'Partial' theoretical studies are restricted according to the parameters discussed below.

The other branch of 'pure' research in Holmes's map is descriptive. Descriptive translation studies (DTS) has three possible foci: examination of (1) the product, (2) the function and (3) the process:

1   **Product-oriented DTS** examines existing translations. This can involve the description or analysis of a single ST–TT pair or a comparative analysis of several TTs of the same ST (into one or more TLs). These smaller-scale studies can build up into a larger body of translation analysis looking at a specific period, language or text/discourse type. Larger-scale studies can be either diachronic (following development over time) or synchronic (at a single point or period in time) and, as Holmes (p. 177) foresees, 'one of the eventual goals of product-oriented DTS might possibly be a general history of translations – however ambitious such a goal might sound at this time'.

2   By **function-oriented DTS**, Holmes means the description of the 'function [of translations] in the recipient sociocultural situation: it is a study of contexts rather than texts' (p. 177). Issues that may be researched include which books were translated when and where, and what influences they exerted. This area, which Holmes terms 'socio-translation studies' – but which would nowadays probably be called cultural-studies-oriented translation – was less researched at the time of Holmes's paper but is more popular in current work on translation studies (see chapters 8 and 9).

3   **Process-oriented DTS** in Holmes's framework is concerned with the psychology of translation, i.e. it is concerned with trying to find out what happens in the mind of a translator. Despite some later work on think-aloud protocols (where recordings are made of translators' verbalization of the translation process as they translate), this is an area of research which has still not yet been systematically analyzed.

The results of DTS research can be fed into the theoretical branch to evolve either a general theory of translation or, more likely, partial theories of translation 'restricted' according to the subdivisions in figure 1.1 above.

- **Medium-restricted theories** subdivide according to translation by machine and humans, with further subdivisions according to whether the machine/computer is working alone or as an aid to the human translator, to whether the human translation is written or spoken and to whether spoken translation (interpreting) is consecutive or simultaneous.
- **Area-restricted theories** are restricted to specific languages or groups of languages and/or cultures. Holmes notes that language-restricted theories are closely related to work in contrastive linguistics and stylistics.
- **Rank-restricted theories** are linguistic theories that have been restricted to a specific level of (normally) the word or sentence. At the time Holmes was writing, there was already a trend towards text linguistics, i.e. text-rank analysis, which has since become far more popular (see chapters 5 and 6 of this book).
- **Text-type restricted theories** look at specific discourse types or genres; e.g. literary, business and technical translation. Text-type approaches came to prominence with the work of Reiss and Vermeer, amongst others, in the 1970s (see chapter 5).
- The term **time-restricted** is self-explanatory, referring to theories and translations limited according to specific time frames and periods. The history of translation falls into this category.
- **Problem-restricted theories** can refer to specific problems such as equivalence – a key issue of the 1960s and 1970s – or to a wider question of whether universals of translated language exist.

Despite this categorization, Holmes himself is at pains to point out that several different restrictions can apply at any one time. Thus, the study of the translation of novels by the contemporary Colombian novelist Gabriel García Márquez, analyzed in chapter 11, would be area restricted (translation from Colombian Spanish into English and other languages, and between the Colombian culture and the TL cultures), text-type restricted (novels and short stories) and time restricted (1960s to 1990s).

The 'applied' branch of Holmes's framework concerns:

- **translator training**: teaching methods, testing techniques, curriculum design;
- **translation aids**: such as dictionaries, grammars and information technology;
- **translation criticism**: the evaluation of translations, including the marking of student translations and the reviews of published translations.

Another area Holmes mentions is **translation policy**, where he sees the translation scholar advising on the place of translation in society, including what place, if any, it should occupy in the language teaching and learning curriculum.

If these aspects of the applied branch are developed, the right-hand side of figure 1.1 would look something like figure 1.2. The divisions in the 'map' as

Figure 1.2
The applied branch of translation studies

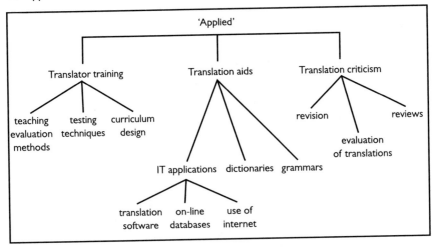

a whole are in many ways artificial, and Holmes himself is concerned to point out (1988b/2000: 78) that the theoretical, descriptive and applied areas do influence one another. The main merit of the divisions, however, is – as Toury states (1991: 180, 1995: 9) – that they allow a clarification and a division of labour between the various areas of translation studies which, in the past, have often been confused. The division is nevertheless flexible enough to incorporate developments such as the technological advances of recent years, although these advances still require considerable further investigation.

The crucial role played by Holmes's paper is the delineation of the potential of translation studies. The map is still often employed as a point of departure, even if subsequent theoretical discussions (e.g. Snell-Hornby 1991, Pym 1998) have attempted to rewrite parts of it; also, present-day research has progressed considerably since 1972. The fact that Holmes devoted two-thirds of his attention to the 'pure' aspects of theory and description surely indicates his research interests rather than a lack of possibilities for the applied side. 'Translation policy' would nowadays far more likely be related to the ideology that determines translation than was the case in Holmes's description. The different restrictions, which Toury identifies as relating to the descriptive as well as the purely theoretical branch (the discontinuous vertical lines in figure 1.1), might well include a discourse-type as well as a text-type restriction. Inclusion of interpreting as a sub-category of human translation would also be disputed by some scholars. In view of the very different requirements and activities associated with interpreting, it would probably be best to consider interpreting as a parallel field, maybe under the title of 'interpreting studies'. Additionally, as Pym points out (1998: 4), Holmes's map omits any mention of the individuality of the style, decision-making processes and working practices of human translators involved in the translation process.

1.5 Developments since the 1970s

The surge in translation studies since the 1970s has seen different areas of Holmes's map come to the fore. Contrastive analysis has fallen by the way-side. The linguistic-oriented 'science' of translation has continued strongly in Germany, but the concept of equivalence associated with it has declined. Germany has seen the rise of theories centred around text types (Reiss; see chapter 5) and text purpose (the skopos theory of Reiss and Vermeer; see chapter 5), while the Hallidayan influence of discourse analysis and systemic functional grammar, which views language as a communicative act in a socio-cultural context, has been prominent over the past decades, especially in Australia and the UK, and has been applied to translation in a series of works by scholars such as Bell (1991), Baker (1992) and Hatim and Mason (1990, 1997). The late 1970s and the 1980s also saw the rise of a descriptive approach that had its origins in comparative literature and Russian Formal-ism. A pioneering centre has been Tel Aviv, where Itamar Even-Zohar and Gideon Toury have pursued the idea of the literary polysystem in which, amongst other things, different literatures and genres, including translated and non-translated works, compete for dominance. The polysystemists have worked with a Belgium-based group including José Lambert and the late André Lefevere (who subsequently moved to the University of Austin, Texas), and with the UK-based scholars Susan Bassnett and Theo Hermans. A key volume was the collection of essays edited by Hermans, *The Manipula-tion of Literature: Studies in Literary Translation* (Hermans 1985a), which gave rise to the name of the 'Manipulation School'. This dynamic, culturally oriented approach held sway for much of the following decade, and linguistics looked very staid.

The 1990s saw the incorporation of new schools and concepts, with Canadian-based translation and gender research led by Sherry Simon, the Brazilian cannibalist school promoted by Else Vieira, postcolonial transla-tion theory, with the prominent figures of the Bengali scholars Tejaswini Niranjana and Gayatri Spivak and, in the USA, the cultural-studies-oriented analysis of Lawrence Venuti, who champions the cause of the translator.

For years, the practice of translation was considered to be derivative and secondary, an attitude that inevitably devalued any academic study of the activity. Now, after much neglect and repression, translation studies has become well established. It is making swift advances worldwide, although not without a hint of trepidation. Translation and translation studies often con-tinue to take place within the context of modern language departments, and the practice of translation is still often denied parity with other academic research. For example, the research assessment exercise in the UK (a formal external audit and evaluation of individuals' and departments' research output) still values academic articles higher than translations, even translations of whole books, notwithstanding the fact that the practice of translation must be an essential experience for the translation theorist and trainer.

It was precisely this split between theory and practice that Holmes, himself both a literary translator and a researcher, sought to overcome. The early manifestations and effects of such a split are clearly expressed by Kitty van Leuven-Zwart (1991: 6). She describes translation teachers' fear that theory would take over from practical training, and literary translators' views that translation was an art that could not be theorized. On the other hand, academic researchers were 'very sceptical' about translation research or felt that translation already had its place in the modern languages curriculum. Van Leuven-Zwart's paper is contained in the proceedings of the First James S. Holmes Symposium on Translation Studies, held at the Department of Translation Studies of the University of Amsterdam in December 1990 in memory of Holmes's contribution to the subject. The breadth of contributions to the proceedings emphasizes the richness of linguistic, literary and historical approaches encompassed by the field.

1.6 Aim of this book and a guide to chapters

Translation studies covers an extremely wide field, in which a considerable number of scholars and practitioners are active. Many translators have entered the area from the starting point of more traditional disciplines. This book covers major areas of the now established discipline of translation studies, with particular reference to systematic translation theories and models of contemporary importance. It aims to bring together and clearly summarize the major strands of translation studies that have previously been dispersed, in order to help readers acquire an understanding of the discipline and the necessary background and tools to begin to carry out their own research on translation. It also aims to provide a theoretical framework into which professional translators and trainee translators can place their own practical experience. The book is organized as follows.

Chapter 2 describes some of the major issues that are discussed in writings about translation up to the middle of the twentieth century. This huge range of over two thousand years, beginning with Cicero in the first century BCE, focuses on the 'literal vs. free' translation debate, an imprecise and circular debate from which theorists have emerged only in the last fifty years. The chapter describes some of the classic writings on translation over the years, making a selection of the most well-known and readily available sources. It aims to initiate discussion on some of the key issues.

Chapter 3 deals with the concepts of meaning, equivalence and 'equivalent effect'. Translation theory in the 1960s under Eugene Nida shifted the emphasis to the receiver of the message. This chapter encompasses Nida's generative-influenced model of translation transfer and his concepts of formal equivalence and dynamic equivalence. Newmark's similarly influential categories of semantic translation and communicative translation are also discussed, as is Koller's analysis of equivalence.

Chapter 4 details attempts that have been made to provide a taxonomy of the linguistic changes or 'shifts' which occur in translation. The main model described here is Vinay and Darbelnet's classic taxonomy, but reference is also made to Catford's linguistic model and van Leuven-Zwart's translation shift approach from the 1980s.

Chapter 5 covers Reiss and Vermeer's text-type and skopos theory of the 1970s and 1980s and Nord's text-linguistic approach. In this chapter, translation is analyzed according to text type and function in the TL culture, and prevailing concepts of text analysis – such as word order, information structure and thematic progression – are employed.

Linked closely to the previous chapter, chapter 6 moves on to consider House's register analysis model and the development of discourse-oriented approaches in the 1990s by Baker and Hatim and Mason, who make use of Hallidayan linguistics to examine translation as communication within a sociocultural context.

Chapter 7 investigates systems theories and the field of target-oriented 'descriptive' translation studies, following Even-Zohar, Toury and the work of the Manipulation School.

Chapter 8 examines varieties of cultural studies approaches in translation studies. These start with Lefevere's work of the 1980s and early 1990s – which itself arose out of a comparative literature and Manipulation School background – and move on to more recent developments in gender studies and translation (in Canada) and to postcolonial translation theories (in India, Brazil and Ireland). The chapter then focuses on a case study of translation from Asia.

Chapter 9 follows Berman and Venuti in examining the foreign element in translation and the 'invisibility' of the translator. The idea is explored that the practice of translation, especially in the English-speaking world, is considered to be a derivative and second-rate activity, and that the prevailing method of translation is 'naturalizing'. The role of literary translators and publishers is also described.

Chapter 10 investigates a selection of philosophical issues of language and translation, ranging from Steiner's 'hermeneutic motion', Pound's use of archaisms, Walter Benjamin's 'pure' language, and Derrida and the deconstruction movement.

Chapter 11 sets out an interdisciplinary approach to translation studies. It discusses Snell-Hornby's 'integrated approach' and looks at recent studies that have combined linguistic and cultural analysis. The future of translation studies and the role of modern technologies, including the internet, are also discussed.

Summary of the present chapter

Translation studies is a relatively new academic research area that has expanded explosively in recent years. While translation was formerly studied as a language-learning methodology or as part of comparative literature, translation 'workshops' and contrastive linguistics courses, the new discipline owes much to the work of James S. Holmes, whose 'The name and nature of translation studies' proposed both a name and a structure for the field. The interrelated branches of theoretical, descriptive and applied translation studies have structured much recent research and have assisted in bridging the gulf that had grown between the theory and practice of translation.

Discussion and research points

1   How is the practice of translation (and interpreting) structured in your own country? How many universities offer first degrees in the subject? How many postgraduate courses are there? How do they differ? Is a postgraduate qualification a prerequisite for working as a professional translator?

2   Find out how research-based translation studies fits into the university system in your country. How many universities offer 'translation studies' (or similar) courses? In what ways do they differ from or resemble each other? In which university departments are they housed? What do you conclude is the status of translation studies in your country?

3   What specific research in translation studies is being carried out in your country? How do you find out? Is the work being carried out by isolated researchers or by larger and co-ordinated groups? How, if at all, would it fit in with Holmes's 'map' of translation studies?

4   Trace the history of translation and translation studies in your own country. Has the focus been mainly on the theory or on the practice of translation? Why do you think this is so?

2 Translation theory before the twentieth century

Key concepts

- The 'word-for-word' ('literal') vs. 'sense-for-sense' ('free') debate.
- The vitalization of the vernacular: Luther and the German Bible.
- Key notions of 'fidelity', 'spirit' and 'truth'.
- The influence of Dryden and the triad of metaphrase, paraphrase, imitation.
- Attempts at a more systematic prescriptive approach from Dolet and Tytler.
- Schleiermacher: a separate language of translation and respect for the foreign.
- The vagueness of the terms used to describe translation.

Key texts

Baker, M. (ed.) (1997a) *The Routledge Encyclopedia of Translation Studies*, Part II: *History and Traditions*, London and New York: Routledge.

Bassnett, S. (1980, revised edition 1991) *Translation Studies*, London and New York: Routledge, chapter 2.

Dryden, J. (1680/1992) 'Metaphrase, paraphrase and imitation', in R. Schulte and J. Biguenet (eds) (1992), pp. 17–31.

Robinson, D. (1997b) *Western Translation Theory from Herodotus to Nietzsche*, Manchester: St Jerome. For extracts from Cicero, St Jerome, Dolet, Luther and Tytler.

Schleiermacher, F. (1813/1992) 'On the different methods of translating', in R. Schulte and J. Biguenet (eds) (1992), pp. 36–54.

Schulte, R. and **J. Biguenet** (eds) (1992) *Theories of Translation*, Chicago, IL and London: University of Chicago Press.

Störig, H.-J. (ed.) (1963) *Das Problem des Übersetzens*, Darmstadt: Wissenschaftliche Buchgesellschaft. For German originals of Luther and Schleiermacher.

2.0 Introduction

The aim of this chapter is not to attempt a comprehensive history of translation or translators through the ages; this would be beyond the scope of the book. Instead, the main focus is the central recurring theme of 'word-for-word' and 'sense-for-sense' translation, a debate that has dominated much of translation theory in what Newmark (1981: 4) calls the 'pre-linguistics period of translation'. It is a theme which Susan Bassnett, in 'The history of translation theory' section of her book *Translation Studies* (1991), sees as 'emerging again and again with different degrees of emphasis in accordance with differing concepts of language and communication' (1991: 42). In this chapter, we focus on a select few of the influential and readily available writings from the history of translation; namely Cicero, St Jerome, Dolet, Luther, Dryden, Tytler and Schleiermacher. The reason for choosing these particular writings is the influence they have exerted on the history of translation theory and research.

Of course, this is a restricted selection and the list of further reading will note others that have a justifiable claim for inclusion. There has also historically been a very strong tendency to concentrate on western European writing on translation, starting with the Roman tradition; the rich traditions of non-Western cultures – such as China, India and the Arab world – have been neglected, although more recent works in English such as Delisle and Woodsworth's *Translators Through History* (1995) and Baker's *The Routledge Encyclopedia of Translation Studies* (1997a) have now begun to address the wider geographic framework. This chapter also includes some of these newer findings, and readers are again encouraged to consider the issues as they relate to the history and translation traditions of their own countries and languages.

2.1 'Word-for-word' or 'sense-for-sense'?

Up until the second half of the twentieth century, translation theory seemed locked in what George Steiner (1998: 319) calls a 'sterile' debate over the 'triad' of **'literal'**, **'free'** and **'faithful'** translation. The distinction between **'word-for-word'** (i.e. 'literal') and **'sense-for-sense'** (i.e. 'free') translation goes back to Cicero (first century BCE) and St Jerome (late fourth century CE) and forms the basis of key writings on translation in centuries nearer to our own.

Cicero outlined his approach to translation in *De optimo genere oratorum* (46 BCE/1960 CE), introducing his own translation of the speeches of the Attic orators Aeschines and Demosthenes:

> And I did not translate them as an interpreter, but as an orator, keeping the same ideas and forms, or as one might say, the 'figures' of thought, but in language which conforms to our usage. And in so doing, I did not hold it necessary to render word for word, but I preserved the general style and force of the language.[1]
>
> (Cicero 46 BCE/1960 CE: 364)

The 'interpreter' of the first line is the literal ('word-for-word') translator, while the 'orator' tried to produce a speech that moved the listeners. In Roman times, 'word-for-word' translation was exactly what it said: the replacement of each individual word of the ST (invariably Greek) with its closest grammatical equivalent in Latin. This was because the Romans would read the TTs side by side with the Greek STs.

The disparagement of word-for-word translation by Cicero, and indeed by

Horace, who, in a short but famous passage from his *Ars Poetica* (20 BCE?),[2] underlines the goal of producing an aesthetically pleasing and creative text in the TL, had great influence on the succeeding centuries. Thus, St Jerome, the most famous of all translators, cites the authority of Cicero's approach to justify his own Latin translation of the Greek Septuagint Old Testament. Jerome's translation strategy is formulated in *De optimo genere interpretandi*, a letter addressed to the senator Pammachius in 395 CE.[3] In perhaps the most famous statement ever on the translation process, St Jerome, defending himself against criticisms of 'incorrect' translation, describes his strategy in the following terms:

> Now I not only admit but freely announce that in translating from the Greek –
> except of course in the case of the Holy Scripture, where even the syntax contains
> a mystery – I render not word-for-word, but sense-for-sense.[4]
>
> (St Jerome 395 CE/1997: 25)

Although some scholars (e.g. Lambert 1991: 7) argue that these terms have been misinterpreted,[5] Jerome's statement is now usually taken to refer to what came to be known as 'literal' (word-for-word') and 'free' (sense-for-sense) translation. Jerome disparaged the word-for-word approach because, by following so closely the form of the ST, it produced an absurd translation, cloaking the sense of the original. The sense-for-sense approach, on the other hand, allowed the sense or content of the ST to be translated. In these poles can be seen the origin of both the 'literal vs. free' and 'form vs. content' debate that has continued until modern times. To illustrate the concept of the TL taking over the sense of the ST, Jerome uses the military image of the original text being marched into the TL like a prisoner by its conqueror (Robinson 1997b: 26). Interestingly, however, as part of his defence St Jerome stresses the special mystery of both the meaning and syntax of the Bible, for to be seen to be altering the sense was liable to bring a charge of heresy.

Although St Jerome's statement is usually taken to be the clearest expression of the 'literal' and 'free' poles in translation, the same type of concern seems to have occurred in other rich and ancient translation traditions such as in China and the Arab world. For instance, Hung and Pollard use similar terms when discussing the history of Chinese translation of Buddhist sutras from Sanskrit (see box 2.1). Although the vocabulary of this description (such as the gloss on '*yiyi*') shows the influence of modern western translation terminology, the general thrust of the argument is still similar to the Cicero/St Jerome poles described above. Aesthetic and stylistic considerations are again noted, and there appear to be the first steps towards a rudimentary differentiation of text types, with non-literary STs being treated differently from literary TTs.

The 'literal' and 'free' poles surface once again in the rich translation tradition of the Arab world, which created the great centre of translation in Baghdad. There was intense translation activity in the Abbasid period

Box 2.1

> Sutra translation provided a fertile ground for the practice and discussion of differ-
> ent translation approaches. Generally speaking, translations produced in the first
> phase [eastern Han Dynasty and the Three Kingdoms Period (c.148–265)] were
> word-for-word renderings adhering closely to source-language syntax. This was
> probably due not only to the lack of bilingual ability amongst the [translation] forum
> participants, but also to a belief that the sacred words of the enlightened should not
> be tampered with. In addition to contorted target-language syntax, transliteration
> was used very liberally, with the result that the translations were fairly incompre-
> hensible to anyone without a theological grounding. The second phase [Jin Dynasty
> and the Northern and Southern Dynasties (c.265–589)] saw an obvious swing
> towards what many contemporary Chinese scholars call *yiyi* (free translation, for
> lack of a better term). Syntactic inversions were smoothed out according to target
> language usage, and the drafts were polished to give them a high literary quality.
> Kumarajiva was credited as a pioneer of this approach. In extreme cases, the polish-
> ing might have gone too far, and there are extant discussions of how this affected the
> original message. During the third phase [Sui Dynasty, Tang Dynasty and Northern
> Song Dynasty (c.589–1100)], the approach to translation was to a great extent
> dominated by Xuan Zang, who had an excellent command of both Sanskrit and
> Chinese, and who advocated that attention should be paid to the style of the original
> text: literary polishing was not to be applied to simple and plain source texts. He
> also set down rules governing the use of transliteration, and these were adopted by
> many of his successors.
>
> (Hung and Pollard 1997: 368)

(750–1250), centred on the translation into Arabic of Greek scientific and philosophical material, often with Syriac as an intermediary language (Delisle and Woodsworth 1995: 112). The Egyptian-born translation scholar Baker (1997a: 320–1), following Rosenthal (1965/94), describes the two trans-lation methods that were adopted during that period:

> The first [method], associated with Yuḥanna Ibn al-Batrīq and Ibn Nāʿima al-Ḥimsi, was highly literal and consisted of translating each Greek word with an equivalent Arabic word and, where none existed, borrowing the Greek word into Arabic.
>
> (Baker 1997a: 320–1)

This word-for-word method proved to be unsuccessful and had to be revised using the second, sense-for-sense method:

> The second method, associated with Ibn Isḥāq and al-Jawahari, consisted of trans-lating sense-for-sense, creating fluent target texts which conveyed the meaning of the original without distorting the target language.
>
> (Baker 1997a: 321)

Once again, the terminology of this description is strongly influenced by the classical western European discourse on translation; yet, this does not negate the visibility in the Arab culture of the two poles of translation which were identified by Cicero and St Jerome. Of course, there are also other ways of considering the question. Salama-Carr (Delisle and Woodsworth 1995: 112–15) concentrates more on the way translation approaches 'helped establish a new system of thought that was to become the foundation of Arabic–Islamic culture – both on the conceptual and terminological levels' with, over the years, the increased use of Arab neologisms rather than transliteration. Arab translators also became very creative in supplying instructive and explanatory commentaries and notes.

2.2 Martin Luther

Within Western society, issues of free and literal translation were for over a thousand years after St Jerome bound up with the translation of the Bible and other religious and philosophical texts. The preoccupation of the Roman Catholic Church was for the 'correct' established meaning of the Bible to be transmitted. Any translation diverging from the accepted interpretation was likely to be deemed heretical and to be censured or banned. An even worse fate lay in store for some of the translators. The most famous example is that of the French humanist Etienne Dolet. He was burned at the stake having been condemned by the theological faculty of Sorbonne University in 1546, apparently for adding, in his translation of one of Plato's dialogues, the phrase *rien du tout* ('nothing at all') in a passage about what existed after death. The addition led to the charge of blasphemy, the assertion being that Dolet did not believe in immortality. For such a translation 'error' he was executed.

Non-literal or non-accepted translation came to be seen and used as a weapon against the Church. The most famous example of this is Martin Luther's crucially influential translation into East Middle German of the New Testament (1522) and later the Old Testament (1534). Luther played a pivotal role in the Reformation while, linguistically, his use of a regional yet socially broad dialect went a long way to reinforcing that form of the German language as standard. In response to accusations that he had altered the Holy Scriptures in his translations, Luther defended himself in his famous *Sendbrief vom Dolmetschen* ('Circular Letter on Translation') of 1530 (Luther 1530/1963).[6] One particularly famous criticism levelled at Luther echoes that of Dolet. It centres around Luther's translation of Paul's words in Romans 3:28:

> Arbitramus hominem iustificari ex fide absque operibus.
> Wir halten, daß der Mensch gerecht werde ohne des Gesetzes Werk, allein durch den Glauben.[7]
> [We hold, that man becomes rectified without the work of the law, only through belief.]

Luther had been heavily criticized by the Church for the addition of the word *allein* ('alone/only'), because there was no equivalent Latin word (e.g. *sola*) in the ST. The charge was that the German implies that the individual's belief is sufficient for a good life, making 'the work of the law' (i.e. religious law) redundant. Luther counters by saying that he was translating into 'pure, clear German',[8] where *allein* would be used for emphasis.

Luther follows St Jerome in rejecting a word-for-word translation strategy since it would be unable to convey the same meaning as the ST and would sometimes be incomprehensible. An example he gives is from Matthew 12:34:

> Ex abundantia cordis os loquitur.

The English King James version translates this literally as:

> Out of the abundance of the heart the mouth speaketh.

Luther translates this with a common German proverb:

> Wes der Herz voll ist, des geht der mund über.[9]

This idiom means 'to speak straight from the heart'.

While Luther's treatment of the free and literal debate does not show any real advance on what St Jerome had written eleven hundred years before, his infusion of the Bible with the language of ordinary people and his consideration of translation in terms focusing on the TL and the TT reader were crucial. Typical of this is his famous quote extolling the language of the people:

> You must ask the mother at home, the children in the street, the ordinary man in the market [sic] and look at their mouths, how they speak, and translate that way; *then* they'll understand and see that you're speaking to them in German.[10]

From that time onwards, the language of the ordinary German speaks clear and strong, thanks to Luther's translation.

2.3 Faithfulness, spirit and truth

Flora Amos, in her *Early Theories of Translation*, sees the history of the theory of translation as 'by no means a record of easily distinguishable, orderly progression' (Amos 1920/73: x). Theory was generally unconnected; it amounted to an albeit broad series of prefaces and comments by practitioners who often ignored, or were ignorant of, most of what had been written before. One explanation for this is the following:

> This lack of consecutiveness in criticism is probably partially accountable for the slowness with which translators attained the power to put into words, clearly and unmistakably, their aims and methods.
>
> (Amos, 1920/73: x)

For instance, Amos notes (p. xi) that early translators often differed considerably in the meaning they gave to terms such as 'faithfulness', 'accuracy' and even the word 'translation' itself.

Such concepts are investigated by Louis Kelly in *The True Interpreter* (1979). Kelly looks in detail at the history of translation theory, starting with the teachings of the writers of Antiquity and tracing the history of what he calls (p. 205) the 'inextricably tangled' terms 'fidelity', 'spirit' and 'truth'. The concept of **fidelity** (or at least the translator who was *fidus interpres*, i.e. the 'faithful interpreter') had initially been dismissed as literal word-for-word translation by Horace. Indeed, it was not until the end of the seventeenth century that fidelity really came to be identified with faithfulness to the meaning rather than the words of the author. Kelly (1979: 206) describes **spirit** as similarly having two meanings: the Latin word *spiritus* denotes creative energy or inspiration, proper to literature, but St Augustine used it to mean the Holy Spirit, and his contemporary St Jerome employed it in both senses. For St Augustine, spirit and **truth** (*veritas*) were intertwined, with truth having the sense of 'content'; for St Jerome, truth meant the authentic Hebrew text to which he returned in his Vulgate translation. Kelly considers that it was not until the twelfth century that truth was fully equated with 'content'.

It is easy to see how, in the translation of sacred texts, where 'the Word of God' is paramount, there has been such an interconnection of fidelity (to both the words and the perceived sense), spirit (the energy of the words and the Holy Spirit) and truth (the 'content'). However, by the seventeenth century, fidelity had come to be generally regarded as more than just fidelity to words, and spirit lost the religious sense it originally possessed and was thenceforth used solely in the sense of the creative energy of a text or language.

2.4 Early attempts at systematic translation theory: Dryden, Dolet and Tytler

For Amos (1920/73: 137), the England of the seventeenth century – with Denham, Cowley and Dryden – marked an important step forward in translation theory with 'deliberate, reasoned statements, unmistakable in their purpose and meaning'. At that time, translation into English was almost exclusively confined to verse renderings of Greek and Latin classics, some of which were extremely free. Cowley, for instance, in his preface to *Pindaric Odes* (1640), attacks poetry that is 'converted faithfully and word for word into French or Italian prose' (Cowley 1640, cited in Amos 1920/73: 149). His approach is also to counter the inevitable loss of beauty in translation by using 'our wit or invention' to create new beauty. In doing this, Cowley admits he has 'taken, left out and added what I please' to the Odes (Amos, p. 150). Cowley even proposes the term *imitation* for this very free method of translating (Amos, p. 151). The idea was not, as in the Roman period, that such a free method would enable the translator to surpass the original; rather that this was the method that permitted the 'spirit' of the ST to be best reproduced (Amos, p. 157).

Such a very free approach to translation produced a reaction, notably from another English poet and translator, John Dryden, whose description of the translation process would have enormous impact on subsequent translation theory and practice. In the preface to his translation of Ovid's *Epistles* in 1680, Dryden (1680/1992: 17) reduces all translation to three categories:

1 **'metaphrase'**: 'word by word and line by line' translation, which corresponds to literal translation;
2 **'paraphrase'**: 'translation with latitude, where the author is kept in view by the translator, so as never to be lost, but his words are not so strictly followed as his sense'; this involves changing whole phrases and more or less corresponds to faithful or sense-for-sense translation;
3 **'imitation'**: 'forsaking' both words and sense; this corresponds to Cowley's very free translation and is more or less adaptation.

Dryden criticizes translators such as Ben Johnson, who adopts metaphrase, as being a 'verbal copier' (Dryden 1680/1992: 18). Such 'servile, literal' translation is dismissed with a now famous simile: ''Tis much like dancing on ropes with fettered legs – a foolish task.' Similarly, Dryden rejects imitation, where the translator uses the ST 'as a pattern to write as he supposes that author would have done, had he lived in our age and in our country' (p. 19). Imitation, in Dryden's view, allows the translator to become more visible, but does 'the greatest wrong . . . to the memory and reputation of the dead' (p. 20). Dryden thus prefers paraphrase, advising that metaphrase and imitation be avoided.

This triadic model proposed by Dryden was to exert considerable influence on later writings on translation. Yet it is also true that Dryden himself changes his stance, with the dedication in his translation of Virgil's *Aeneid* (1697) showing a shift to a point between paraphrase and literal translation:

> I thought fit to steer betwixt the two extremes of paraphrase and literal translation; to keep as near my author as I could, without losing all his graces, the most eminent of which are in the beauty of his words.
>
> (Dryden 1697/1992: 26).

The description of his own translation approach then bears resemblance to his definition of imitation above: 'I may presume to say . . . I have endeavoured to make Virgil speak such English as he would himself have spoken, if he had been born in England, and in this present age' (Dryden 1697/1992: p. 26).

In general, therefore, Dryden and others writing on translation at the time are very prescriptive, setting out what has to be done in order for successful translation to take place. However, despite its importance for translation theory, Dryden's writing remains full of the language of his time: the 'genius' of the ST author, the 'force' and 'spirit' of the original, the need to 'perfectly comprehend' the sense of the original, and the 'art' of translation.

Other writers on translation also began to state their 'principles' in a similarly prescriptive fashion. One of the first had been Etienne Dolet, whose sad fate was noted above, in his 1540 manuscript *La manière de bien traduire d'une langue en aultre* ('The way of translating well from one language into another'; Dolet 1540/1997). Dolet set out five principles in order of importance as follows:[11]

1   The translator must perfectly understand the sense and material of the original author, although he [sic] should feel free to clarify obscurities.
2   The translator should have a perfect knowledge of both SL and TL, so as not to lessen the majesty of the language.
3   The translator should avoid word-for-word renderings.
4   The translator should avoid Latinate and unusual forms.
5   The translator should assemble and liaise words eloquently to avoid clumsiness.

Here again, the concern is to reproduce the sense and to avoid word-for-word translation, but the stress on eloquent and natural TL form was rooted in a desire to reinforce the structure and independence of the new vernacular French language.

In English, perhaps the first systematic study of translation after Dryden is Alexander Fraser Tytler's 'Essay on the principles of translation' (1797). Rather than Dryden's author-oriented description ('write as the original author would have written had he known the target language'), Tytler defines a 'good translation' in TL-reader-oriented terms to be:

> That in which the merit of the original work is so completely transfused into another language as to be as distinctly apprehended, and as strongly felt, by a native of the country to which that language belongs as it is by those who speak the language of the original work.
>
> (Tytler 1797: 14)

And, where Dolet has five 'principles', Tytler (1797: 15) has three general 'laws' or 'rules':

1   The translation should give a complete transcript of the ideas of the original work.
2   The style and manner of writing should be of the same character with that of the original.
3   The translation should have all the ease of the original composition.

Tytler's first law ties in with Dolet's first two principles in that it refers to the translator having a 'perfect knowledge' of the original (Tytler 1797: 17), being competent in the subject and giving 'a faithful transfusion of the sense and meaning' of the author. Tytler's second law, like Dolet's fifth principle, deals with the style of the author and involves the translator both identifying 'the true character' (p. 113) of this style and having the ability and 'correct taste' to recreate it in the TL. The third law (pp. 199–200) talks of having 'all the ease of composition' of the ST. Tytler regards this as the most difficult task and likens it, in a traditional metaphor, to an artist producing a copy of a painting. Thus, 'scrupulous imitation' should be avoided, since it loses the 'ease and spirit of the original'. Tytler's solution (p. 203) is for the translator to 'adopt the very soul of his author'.

Tytler himself recognizes that the first two laws represent the two widely different opinions about translation. They can be seen as the poles of faith-fulness of content and faithfulness of form, or even reformulations of the sense-for-sense and word-for-word diad of Cicero and St Jerome. Import-antly, however, just as Dolet had done with his principles, Tytler ranks his three laws in order of comparative importance. Such hierarchical categor-izing gains in importance in more modern translation theory; for instance, the discussion of translation 'loss' and 'gain' is in some ways presaged by Tytler's suggestion that the rank order of the laws should be a means of determining decisions when a 'sacrifice' has to be made (p. 215). Thus, ease of composition would be sacrificed if necessary for manner, and a departure would be made from manner in the interests of sense.

2.5 Schleiermacher and the valorization of the foreign

While the seventeenth century had been about imitation and the eighteenth century about the translator's duty to recreate the spirit of the ST for the reader of the time, the Romanticism of the early nineteenth century dis-cussed the issues of translatability or untranslatability. In 1813, the German theologian and translator Friedrich Schleiermacher wrote a highly influential treatise on translation, *Über die verschiedenen Methoden des Übersetzens* ('On the different methods of translating').[12] Schleiermacher is recognized as the founder of modern Protestant theology and of modern hermeneutics, a Romantic approach to interpretation based not on absolute truth but on the individual's inner feeling and understanding.

Distinct from other translation theory we have discussed so far in this chapter, Schleiermacher first distinguishes two different types of translator working on two different types of text; these are:

1   the '**Dolmetscher**', who translates commercial texts;
2   the '**Übersetzer**', who works on scholarly and artistic texts.

It is this second type that Schleiermacher sees as being on a higher creative plane, breathing new life into the language (1813/1992: 38). Although it may seem impossible to translate scholarly and artistic texts – since the ST mean-ing is couched in language that is very culture-bound and to which the TL can never fully correspond – the real question, according to Schleiermacher, is how to bring the ST writer and the TT reader together. He moves beyond the issues of word-for-word and sense-for-sense, literal, faithful and free translation, and considers there to be only two paths open for the 'true' translator:

> Either the translator leaves the writer alone as much as possible and moves the reader toward the writer, or he [sic] leaves the reader alone as much as possible and moves the writer toward the reader.[13]

(Schleiermacher 1813/1992: 41–2)

Schleiermacher's preferred strategy is the first, moving the reader towards the writer. This entails not writing as the author would have done had he written in German but rather 'giving the reader the same impression that he as a German would receive reading the work in the original language' (1813/1992: 43).[14] To achieve this, the translator must adopt an 'alienating' (as opposed to 'naturalizing') method of translation, orienting himself or herself by the language and content of the ST. He or she must valorize the foreign and transfer that into the TL.

There are several consequences of this approach, including;

1   if the translator is to seek to communicate the same impression which he or she received from the ST, this impression will also depend on the level of education and understanding among the TT readership, and this is likely to differ from the translator's own understanding;
2   a special language of translation may be necessary, for example compensating in one place with an imaginative word where elsewhere the translator has to make do with a hackneyed expression that cannot convey the impression of the foreign (Schleiermacher 1813/1992: 45).

Schleiermacher's influence has been enormous. Indeed, Kittel and Polterman (1997: 424) claim that 'practically every modern translation theory – at least in the German-language area – responds, in one way or another, to Schleiermacher's hypotheses. There appear to have been no fundamentally new approaches.' Schleiermacher's consideration of different text types becomes more prominent in Reiss's text typology (see chapter 5 of this volume). The 'alienating' and 'naturalizing' opposites are taken up by Venuti as 'foreignization' and 'domestication' (see chapter 9). Additionally, the vision of a 'language of translation' is pursued by Walter Benjamin and the description of the hermeneutics of translation is apparent in George Steiner's 'hermeneutic motion' (see chapter 10).

2.6 Translation theory of the nineteenth and early twentieth centuries in Britain

In Britain, the nineteenth century and the early part of the twentieth century focused on the status of the ST and the form of the TL. Typical of this is the polemic between Francis Newman and Matthew Arnold over the translation of Homer (see Venuti 1995: 118–41; see also Robinson 1997b: 250–8). Newman emphasized the foreignness of the work by a deliberately archaic translation and yet saw himself as reaching out to a wide audience. This was violently opposed by Matthew Arnold in his lecture On Translating Homer (1861/1978), which advocated a transparent translation method. Importantly,

Arnold, whose argument won the day, advises his audience to put their faith in scholars, who, he suggests, are the only ones who are qualified to compare the effect of the TT to the ST. As Bassnett (1991: 69–70) points out, such an élitist attitude led both to the devaluation of translation (because it was felt that a TT could never reach the heights of an ST and it was always preferable to read the work in the original language) and to the marginalization of translation (translations were to be produced for only a select élite). This attitude may even be said to be prevalent in Britain up to the present day. For example:

- Pre-university and even university students of languages are often dissuaded from turning to translations for help.
- Very little popular literature is translated into English.
- Relatively few subtitled foreign films are screened in mainstream cinemas and on the major BBC1 and ITV television channels in the UK.

2.7 Towards contemporary translation theory

George Steiner, in his detailed, idiosyncratic classification of the early history of translation theory, lists a small number of fourteen writers who represent 'very nearly the sum total of those who have said anything fundamental or new about translation' (Steiner 1998: 283). This list includes St Jerome, Luther, Dryden and Schleiermacher and also takes us into the twentieth century with Ezra Pound and Walter Benjamin, amongst others. Steiner (p. 283) in fact describes as 'very small' the range of theoretical ideas covered in this period:

> We have seen how much of the theory of translation – if there is one as distinct from idealized recipes – pivots monotonously around undefined alternatives: 'letter' or 'spirit', 'word' or 'sense'. The dichotomy is assumed to have analysable meaning. This is the central epistemological weakness and sleight of hand.
>
> (Steiner 1998: 290)

Other modern theoreticians concur that the main problem with the writings on translation in this period was that the criteria for judgements were vague and subjective (Bassnett 1991: 134) and the judgements themselves were highly normative (Wilss 1996: 128). As a reaction against such vagueness and contradictions, translation theory in the second half of the twentieth century made various attempts to redefine the concepts 'literal' and 'free' in operational terms, to describe 'meaning' in scientific terms, and to put together systematic taxonomies of translation phenomena. These approaches form the core of the following chapters in this book.

Case studies

The following case studies look briefly at two areas where the vocabulary of the 'literal vs. free' debate continues to be used in contemporary writing on translation. Case study 1 examines two examples of criteria for assessing translations. Case study 2 looks at a modern translator's preface, from the 1981 and 1992 revised English translations of Marcel Proust's *A la recherche du temps perdu*.[15] In both cases the aim is to identify how far the ideas and vocabulary of early theory held sway in later writing on translation.

Case study 1: Assessment criteria

The area of assessment criteria is one where a more expert writer (a marker of a translation examination or a reviser of a professional translation) addresses a less expert reader (usually a candidate for an examination or a junior professional translator). It is interesting to see how far the vocabulary used is the rather vague vocabulary of early translation theory.

The Institute of Linguists' (IoL) Diploma in Translation is the most widely known initial qualification for translators in the UK. In the IoL's *Notes for Candidates*,[16] the criteria for assessing the translations are given:

1   accuracy: the correct transfer of information and evidence of complete comprehension;
2   the appropriate choice of vocabulary, idiom, terminology and register;
3   cohesion, coherence and organization;
4   accuracy in technical aspects of punctuation, etc.[17]

The question of 'accuracy' appears twice (criteria 1 and 4). 'Accuracy' is in some ways the modern linguistic equivalent of 'faithfulness', 'spirit' and 'truth'; in the IoL text, there is an attempt at closer definition of accuracy, comprising 'correct transfer of information' and 'complete comprehension'. As we discuss in chapter 3, these terms are influenced by terminology suggested by Nida in the 1960s. Criterion 2's 'appropriate choice of vocabulary, etc.' suggests a more TL approach, while criterion 3 (cohesion and coherence) leads us into the area of discourse analysis (see chapter 6).

Thus, these criteria make an attempt at formalizing clear rules for translation. However, examiners' reports on the candidates' performances, although containing detailed examples of errors and of good translations, tend to be sprinkled with the vaguer and controversial vocabulary of early translation theory. A typical IoL examiners' report (French into English, paper 1, November 1997) explains many student errors in considerable detail, but still stresses the criterion of TL fluency. Thus, 'awkwardness' is a criticism levelled at four translations, and candidates are praised for altering sentence structure 'to give a more natural result in English'. Perhaps the most interesting point is the use of the term 'literal translation'. 'Literal' is used four times – and always as a criticism – concerning, for example, literal translations of false friends. Interestingly enough, however, 'literal' is used as a relative term. For example, '*too* literal a style of translating' (my emphasis) produced TT expressions such as '*transmitting* the budget to the Chamber' (rather than '*delivering* the budget'), and a '*totally* literal translation' (my emphasis) of *déjeuner-débat* 'produced very unnatural English'; presumably, the 'totally literal' translation was something like 'lunch-debate' rather than 'lunchtime talk'. However, the qualification of the adjective 'literal' by the adverbs 'too' and 'totally' suggests that 'literal' alone is not now being viewed as the extreme. Rather, as was suggested in section 2.1 above, 'literal' is being used to mean a close lexical translation; only when this strategy is taken to an extreme (when it is 'too' or 'totally' literal) is the 'naturalness' of the TL infringed.

Similar criteria are repeated in Unesco's *Guidelines for Translators*.[18] 'Accuracy' is again 'the very first requirement'. The description of the aim of translation is that, after reaching an understanding of what the ST writer 'was trying to say', the translator should put this meaning into (in this case) English 'which will, so far as possible, produce the same impression on the English-language reader as the original would have done on the appropriate foreign-language reader'. This bears quite close resemblance to the wording of Schleiermacher's recipe for moving the reader towards the author. Yet the method Unesco suggests as appropriate for achieving this is not to follow an 'alienating' strategy but to find an intermediate way between something that 'sounds' like a translation and something which is so 'aggressively characteristic' of the translator's idiolect that it strikes the reader as 'unusual'.

There are several additional points of particular interest concerning the Unesco criteria:

- First, the balance between the two poles ('sounding like a translation' and being 'aggressively characteristic') is described using an image ('a perpetual feat of tight-rope walking') which is very close to Dryden's famous simile of the clumsy literal translator as 'dancing on ropes with fettered legs'.
- Second, the Unesco document makes allowance for the TT readers, who are sometimes non-native speakers of the TL.
- Third, the suggested solution varies according to text type: the style of articles translated for periodicals should be 'readable', while politically sensitive speeches require a 'very close translation' to avoid being misinterpreted.

The first of these points indicates the extent to which old metaphors of translation persist even in contemporary writings. The second point touches on a more reader-oriented approach, although the document rejects the existence of a 'special' language of translation. The third point shows an awareness that different approaches may be valid for different texts, a point that Schleiermacher noted in his division of categories into business and philosophical texts but which, as we discuss in chapter 5, has far more to do with the text-type approach of Reiss.

Case study 2 the translator's preface

Translators' prefaces are a source of extensive information on the translation approach adopted in earlier centuries. However, they are far more of a rarity in current publications and are now sometimes restricted to a justification for producing a new translation of a classic work. This is the case with the revised English language translation of Proust's *A la Recherche du Temps Perdu*.[19] Originally translated from French into English by the celebrated C. K. Scott Moncrieff in the 1920s, the English was revised in 1981 by Terence Kilmartin and in 1992 by D. J. Enright.

In the introduction of the 1981 translation (p. x), the reasons given by Kilmartin for the revision were that there had been later publications of revised and corrected editions of the French original, and that there was a need to correct 'mistakes and misinterpretations' in the translation. The 1981 translation also contained a four page 'Note on the translation' by Kilmartin. One of the most interesting points about Kilmartin's comments is the vocabulary he uses to describe the revisions he has carried out:

> I have refrained from officious tinkering [with the translation] for its own sake, but a translator's loyalty is to the original author, and in trying to be faithful to Proust's meaning and tone of voice I have been obliged, here and there, to make extensive alterations.
>
> (p. ix)

The concept of 'loyalty' to the author and being 'faithful' to the meaning could almost have come straight from the writings of the seventeenth century. The division between 'meaning' and 'tone of voice' could also be taken to originate in the debate on form vs. content. The use of general terms such as 'tone' in the commentary also echoes the imprecision of earlier writing.

The perceived 'literal' translation of the ST is criticized. Kilmartin (p. x), referring to the translation of the 1920s, describes Scott Moncrieff's 'tendency to translate French idioms and turns of phrase literally', which makes them 'sound weirder', and his 'sticking too closely' to the original syntax especially in long sentences packed with subordinate clauses which seem 'unEnglish' in the TT: 'a whiff of Gallicism clings to some of the longer periods, obscuring the sense and falsifying the tone', claims Kilmartin (p. x). The negative connotation of 'whiff of Gallicism' seems quite surprising in this context. Kilmartin is criticizing the apparent foreignness of the structure of the translation of one of the great French writers and has a preference for a totally 'naturalizing' (to use Schleiermacher's term) English style in the translation.

Discussion of case studies

These two brief case studies indicate that the vocabulary of early translation theory persists widely to the present day. 'Literal', 'free', 'loyalty', 'faithfulness', 'accuracy', 'meaning', 'style' and 'tone' are words that reappear again and again, even in areas (such as assessment criteria) which draw on a more systematic theoretical background. The tendency in most of the comments noted above is for a privileging of a 'natural' TT, one which reads as if it were originally written in the TL. In this case, one can say that 'literal' translation has lost out, and that the élitist Victorian-style translations proposed by Matthew Arnold are no longer acceptable. The 'alienating' strategy promoted by Schleiermacher has not been followed. What remains is the 'natural', almost 'everyday' speech style proposed by Luther. Yet the pre-modifications of the term 'literal' in the IoL texts indicate the shift in use of this term over the centuries. 'Literal' now means 'sticking very closely to the original'. Translators who go further than this leave themselves open to criticism. The 'imaginative' and 'idiomatic' translation is still preferred. However, the texts examined in the case studies were written mainly for the general reader or novice translator. As we shall see in the next chapter, the direction of translation theory in the second half of the twentieth century was generally towards a systematization of different elements of the translation process.

Summary

Much of translation theory from Cicero to the twentieth century centred on the recurring and sterile debate as to whether translations should be literal (word-for-word) or free (sense-for-sense), a diad that is famously discussed by St Jerome in his translation of the Bible into Latin. Controversy over the translation of the Bible and other religious texts was central to translation theory for over a thousand years. Early theorists tended to be translators who presented a justification for their approach in a preface to the translation, often paying little attention to (or not having access to) what others before them had said. Dryden's proposed triad of the late seventeenth century marked the beginning of a more systematic and precise definition of translation, while Schleiermacher's respect for the foreign text was to have considerable influence over scholars in modern times.

Further reading

There are a considerable number of collections and histories of translation. In addition to those works included in the list of key texts at the beginning of this chapter, the following are of special interest: Amos (1920/73), Delisle and Woodsworth (1995), Kelly (1979), G. Steiner (1975/98), T. Steiner (1975), and the source writings in the collections by Robinson (1997b), Schulte and Biguenet (1992), Lefevere (1992b) and Störig (1963). Readers are recommended to follow their specific interests regarding country, period, cultures and languages. Delisle and Woodsworth (1995) and Baker (ed.) (1997a) are of particular use in giving the background to translation in a wider range of cultures. Kelly (1979) is especially strong on the Latin tradition. Pym (1998) may also be useful as a presentation of investigative methods in translation history.

Discussion and research points

1   Find recent reviews of translations in the press in your own languages. What kinds of comments are made about the translation itself? How far is the vocabulary used similar to that described in this chapter?

2   Modern translation theory tends to criticize the simplicity of the 'literal vs. free' debate. Why, then, do you think that the vocabulary of that earlier period often continues to be used in reviews of translation, in comments by teachers and examiners, and in writings by literary translators themselves?

3   Investigate what writing was produced on translation in your own languages and cultures before the twentieth century. How closely does it resemble the writings discussed in this chapter? Are there significant differences in early translation theory written in different languages?

4   The Italian axiom *traduttore, traditore* ('the translator is a traitor') has become a cliché. What elements discussed in this chapter may help to explain its origin?

5   How useful do you consider Dolet's principles and Tytler's laws to be for guiding a translator?

6   'I have endeavoured to make Virgil speak such English as he would himself have spoken, if he had been born in England, and in this present age', wrote Dryden in 1697 in his preface to his translation of the *Aeneid*. How do you imagine he would have set about doing this? What issues does it raise for the literary translator?

7   Do translators' prefaces frequently appear in translations in your own country? Why do you think this is? If they do, what function do they serve, and what kind of language do they use to describe the translation?

3 Equivalence and equivalent effect

Key texts

Bassnett, S. (1980, revised edition 1991) *Translation Studies*, London and New York: Routledge, chapter 1.

Jakobson, R. (1959/2000) 'On linguistic aspects of translation', in L. Venuti (ed.) (2000) pp. 113–18.

Koller, W. (1979a) *Einführung in die Übersetzungswissenschaft*, Heidelberg-Wiesbaden: Quelle und Meyer.

Koller, W. (1979b/89) 'Equivalence in translation theory', translated by A. Chesterman, in A. Chesterman (ed.) (1989), pp. 99–104.

Newmark, P. (1981) *Approaches to Translation*, Oxford and New York: Pergamon.

Newmark, P. (1988) *A Textbook of Translation*, New York and London: Prentice-Hall.

Nida, E. (1964a) *Toward a Science of Translating*, Leiden: E. J. Brill.

Nida, E. (1964b/2000) 'Principles of Correspondence', in L. Venuti (ed.), pp. 126–40.

Nida, E. and **C. Taber** (1969) *The Theory and Practice of Translation*, Leiden: E. J. Brill.

3.0 Introduction

After the centuries of circular debates around literal and free translation (see chapter 2), theoreticians in the 1950s and 1960s began to attempt more systematic analyzes of translation. The new debate revolved around certain key linguistic issues. The most prominent of these issues were those of meaning and 'equivalence', discussed in Roman Jakobson's 1959 paper (see section 3.1 below). Over the following twenty years many further attempts were made to define the nature of equivalence. In this chapter, we shall look at several major works of the time: Eugene Nida's seminal concepts of formal and dynamic equivalence and the principle of equivalent effect (section 3.2), Peter Newmark's semantic and communicative translation (section 3.3), and Werner Koller's Korrespondenz and Äquivalenz (section 3.4).

3.1 Roman Jakobson: the nature of linguistic meaning and equivalence

In chapter 1 we saw how, in his paper 'On linguistic aspects of translation' (1959/2000), the Russian-born American structuralist Roman Jakobson describes three kinds of translation: intralingual, interlingual and inter-semiotic, with interlingual referring to translation between two different written languages. Jakobson goes on to examine key issues of this type of translation, notably **linguistic meaning** and **equivalence**.

Jakobson follows the relation set out by Saussure between the signifier (the spoken and written signal) and the signified (the concept signified). Together, the signifier and signified form the linguistic sign, but that sign is arbitrary or unmotivated (Saussure 1916/83: 67–9). Thus, the English word *cheese* is the acoustic signifier which 'denotes' the concept 'food made of pressed curds' (the signified), although there is no inherent reason for that to be so. Jakobson stresses that it is possible to understand what is signified by a word even if we have never seen or experienced the concept or thing in real life. Examples he gives are *ambrosia* and *nectar*, words which modern readers will have read in Greek myths even if they have never come across the substances in real life; these contrast with *cheese*, which they almost certainly have encountered first hand.

Jakobson then moves on to consider the thorny problem of **equivalence in meaning** between words in different languages. He points out (1959/2000: 114) that 'there is ordinarily no full equivalence between code-units'. He gives the example of *cheese* in English, which is not identical to the Russian *syr* (or, for that matter, the Spanish *queso*, the German *Käse*, etc.) since the Russian 'code-unit' does not include the concept of *cottage cheese*. That would be *tvarok* and not *syr* in Russian. While one might quibble that the English *cheese* only really covers the realm of cottage cheese by the addition of the term *cottage*, the general principle of interlinguistic difference between terms and semantic fields is established.

In Jakobson's description, interlingual translation involves 'substitut[ing] messages in one language not for separate code-units but for entire messages in some other language':

The translator recodes and transmits a message received from another source. Thus translation involves two equivalent messages in two different codes.

(Jakobson 1959/2000: 114)

For the message to be 'equivalent' in ST and TT, the code-units will be different since they belong to two different sign systems (languages) which partition reality differently (the *cheese/syr* example above). From a linguistic and semiotic angle, Jakobson approaches the problem of equivalence with the following, now-famous, definition: 'Equivalence in difference is the cardinal problem of language and the pivotal concern of linguistics.' In Jakobson's discussion, the problem of meaning and equivalence thus focuses on differences in the structure and terminology of languages rather than on any inability of one language to render a message that has been written in another verbal language. Thus, Russian can still express the full semantic meaning of *cheese* even if it breaks it down into two separate concepts.

For Jakobson, cross-linguistic differences centre around obligatory grammatical and lexical forms: 'Languages differ essentially in what they *must* convey and not in what they *may* convey' (p. 116). Examples of differences are easy to find. They occur at:

- the level of gender: e.g. *house* is feminine in Romance languages, neuter in German and English; *honey* is masculine in French, German and Italian, feminine in Spanish, neuter in English, etc.;
- the level of aspect: in Russian, the verb morphology varies according to whether the action has been completed or not;
- the level of semantic fields: e.g. the German *Geschwister* is normally explicated in English as *brothers and sisters*; and the English *children* in the statement 'I've got two children' is translated as the gender-specific *hijas* in Spanish if both children are female.

Even what for many Western languages is a basic relational concept such as *be* (English), *être* (French) and *sein* (German) is broken down in Spanish to *ser* and *estar*, while Russian does not use such a verb explicitly in the present tense. These examples illustrate differences between languages, but they are still concepts that can be rendered interlingually. Only poetry – where form expresses sense, where 'phonemic similarity is sensed as semantic relationship' – is considered 'untranslatable' by Jakobson and requires 'creative transposition' (p. 118).

The questions of meaning, equivalence and translatability became a constant theme of translation studies in the 1960s and were tackled by a new 'scientific' approach followed by one of the most important figures in translation studies, the American Eugene Nida.

3.2 Nida and 'the science of translating'

Eugene Nida's theory of translation developed from his own practical work from the 1940s onwards when he was translating and organizing the translation of the Bible. His theory took concrete form in two major works in the 1960s: *Toward a Science of Translating* (1964a) and the co-authored *The Theory and Practice of Translation* (Nida and Taber 1969). The title of the first book is significant; Nida attempts to move translation (Bible translation in his case) into a more scientific era by incorporating recent work in linguistics. Nida's more systematic approach borrows theoretical concepts and terminology both from semantics and pragmatics and from Noam Chomsky's work on syntactic structure which formed the theory of generative–transformational grammar (Chomsky 1957, 1965).

3.2.1 The nature of meaning: advances in semantics and pragmatics

Nida (1964a: 33ff) describes various 'scientific approaches to meaning' related to work that had been carried out by theorists in semantics and pragmatics. Central to Nida's work is the move away from the old idea that an orthographic word has a fixed meaning and towards a functional definition of meaning in which a word 'acquires' meaning through its context and can produce varying responses according to culture.

Meaning is broken down into **linguistic meaning** (borrowing elements of Chomsky's model), **referential meaning** (the denotative 'dictionary' meaning) and **emotive** (or connotative) **meaning**. A series of techniques, adapted from work in linguistics, is presented as an aid for the translator in determining the meaning of different linguistic items. Techniques to determine referential and emotive meaning focus on analyzing the structure of words and differentiating similar words in related lexical fields. These include **hierarchical structuring**, which differentiates series of words according to their level (for instance, the superordinate *animal* and its hyponyms *goat, dog, cow,* etc.) and techniques of **componential analysis**. The latter seek to identify and discriminate specific features of a range of related words. The results can be plotted visually to assist in making an overall comparison. One example (Nida 1964a: 84–5) is the plotting of relationship terms (*grandmother, mother, cousin,* etc.) according to the values of sex (male, female), generation (the same, one, two or more apart) and lineality (direct ancestor/descendant or not). Such results are useful for a translator working with languages that have very different kinship terms.

Another technique is **semantic structure analysis** in which Nida (1964a: 107) separates out visually the different meanings of *spirit* ('demons', 'angels', 'gods', 'ghost', 'ethos', 'alcohol', etc.) according to their characteristics (human vs. non-human, good vs. bad, etc.). The central idea of this analysis is to encourage the trainee translator to realize that the sense of a complex semantic term such as *spirit* (or, to take another example, *bachelor*) varies and most particularly is 'conditioned' by its context. *Spirit* thus does not always have a religious significance. Even (or perhaps especially) when it does, as in the term *Holy Spirit*, its emotive or connotative value varies according to the target culture (Nida 1964a: 36). The associations 'attached' to the word are its connotative value, and these are considered to belong to the realm of pragmatics or 'language in use'. Above all, Nida (p. 51) stresses the importance of context for communication when dealing with meta-phorical meaning and with complex cultural idioms, for example, where the sense of the phrase often diverges from the sum of the individual elements. Thus, the Hebrew idiom *bene Chuppah* [lit. 'children of the bridechamber'] refers to the wedding guests, especially the friends of the bridegroom (Nida 1964a: 95).

In general, techniques of componential analysis are proposed as a means of clarifying ambiguities, elucidating obscure passages and identifying cultural differences. They may serve as a point of comparison between different languages and cultures.

3.2.2 The influence of Chomsky

Chomsky's generative–transformational model analyzes sentences into a series of related levels governed by rules. In very simplified form, the key features of this model can be summarized as follows:

1   Phrase-structure rules generate an underlying or **deep structure** which is
2   transformed by transformational rules relating one underlying structure to another (e.g. active to passive), to produce
3   a final **surface structure**, which itself is subject to phonological and morphemic rules.

The structure relations described in this model are held by Chomsky to be a universal feature of human language. The most basic of such structures are **kernel sentences**, which are simple, active, declarative sentences that require the minimum of transformation.

Nida incorporates key features of Chomsky's model into his 'science' of translation. In particular, Nida sees that it provides the translator with a technique for decoding the ST and a procedure for encoding the TT (Nida 1964a: 60), although he reverses Chomsky's model when analyzing the ST. Thus, the surface structure of the ST is analyzed into the basic elements of the deep structure; these are 'transferred' in the translation process and then restructured semantically and stylistically into the surface structure of the TT. This three-stage system of translation (analysis, transfer and restructuring) is presented in figure 3.1:

Nida and Taber's own description of the process (p. 68) emphasizes the 'scientific and practical' advantages of this method compared to any attempt to draw up a fully comprehensive list of equivalences between specific pairs of SL and TL systems. 'Kernel' is a key term in this model. Just as kernel sentences were the most basic structures of Chomsky's initial model, so, for Nida, kernels 'are the basic structural elements out of which language builds its elaborate surface structures' (Nida and Taber 1969: 39). Kernels are to be obtained from the ST surface structure by a reductive process of

Figure 3.1
Nida's three-stage system of translation (from Nida and Taber 1969: 33)

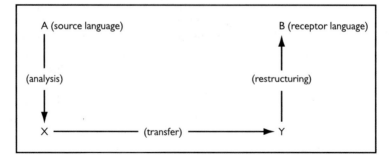

back-transformation (Nida 1964a: 63–9). This involves analysis using generative–transformational grammar's four types of functional class:

- events (often but not always performed by verbs);
- objects (often but not always performed by nouns);
- abstracts (quantities and qualities, including adjectives);
- relationals (including gender, prepositions and conjunctions).

Examples of analysis (Nida 1964a: 64), designed to illustrate the different constructions with the preposition *of*, are:

surface structure: *will of God*
back transform: B (object, *God*) performs A (event, *wills*)

[and]

surface structure: *creation of the world*
back transform: B (object, *the world*) is the goal of A (event, *creates*).

Nida and Taber (1969: 39) claim that *all* languages have between six and a dozen basic kernel structures and 'agree far more on the level of kernels than on the level of more elaborate structures'. Kernels are the level at which the message is transferred into the receptor language before being transformed into the surface structure in three stages: 'literal transfer', 'minimal transfer' and 'literary transfer'. An example of this transfer process is the verse from John 1:6 in box 3.1 (cited in Nida 1964a: 185–7). The two examples of literary transfer are different stylistically, notably in syntax, the first being more formal and archaic. The reason for this may be the kind of equivalence and effect that is intended, a crucial element of Nida's model, which is discussed in the next section.

Box 3.1

- Greek ST:

  | 1 | 2 | 3 | 4 | 5 | 6 | 7 | 8 |

  egeneto anthrōpos, apestalmenos para theou, onoma autō Iōannēs

- Literal transfer (stage 1):

  | 1 | 2 | 3 | 4 | 5 | 6 | 7 | 8 |

  became/happened man, sent from God, name to-him John

- Minimal transfer (stage 2):

  | 1 | 2 | 3 | 4 | 5 | 6 | 7 | 8 |

  There CAME/WAS *a* man, sent from God, WHOSE name *was* John

- Literary transfer (stage 3, example taken from the *American Standard Version*, 1901):

  | 1 | 2 | 3 | 4 | 5 | 6 | 7 | 8 |

  There CAME *a* man, sent from God, WHOSE name *was* John

  or (example taken from *Phillips New Testament in Modern English*, 1958[1]):

  | 2 | 6 | 7 8 | 3 | 4 |

  A man, NAMED * John WAS sent BY God

Notes: Adjustments from the ST are indicated as follows: changes in order are indicated by the numeral order, omissions by an *, structural alterations by SMALL CAPITALS and additions by *italics*.

3.2.3 Formal and dynamic equivalence and the principle of equivalent effect

The old terms such as 'literal', 'free' and 'faithful' translation, which were examined in chapter 2, are discarded by Nida in favour of 'two basic orientations' or 'types of equivalence' (Nida 1964a: 159): (1) formal equivalence and (2) dynamic equivalence. These are defined by Nida as follows:

1   **Formal equivalence**:

> Formal equivalence focuses attention on the message itself, in both form and content ... One is concerned that the message in the receptor language should match as closely as possible the different elements in the source language.
>
> (Nida 1964a: 159)

Formal equivalence is thus keenly oriented towards the ST structure, which exerts strong influence in determining accuracy and correctness. Most typical of this kind of translation are 'gloss translations', with a close approximation to ST structure, often with scholarly footnotes, allowing the student (since this type of translation will often be used in an academic environment) to gain close access to the language and customs of the source culture.

2   **Dynamic equivalence**: Dynamic equivalence is based on what Nida
     calls 'the principle of equivalent effect', where 'the relationship between
     receptor and message should be substantially the same as that which
     existed between the original receptors and the message' (Nida 1964: 159).
     The message has to be tailored to the receptor's linguistic needs and
     cultural expectation and 'aims at complete naturalness of expression'.
     'Naturalness' is a key requirement for Nida. Indeed, he defines the goal
     of dynamic equivalence as seeking 'the closest natural equivalent to the
     source-language message' (Nida 1964a: 166, Nida and Taber 1969: 12).
     This receptor-oriented approach considers adaptations of grammar, of
     lexicon and of cultural references to be essential in order to achieve
     naturalness; the TT language should not show interference from the SL,
     and the 'foreignness' of the ST setting is minimized (Nida 1964a: 167–8)
     in a way that would now be criticized by later culturally oriented transla-
     tion theorists (see chapters 8 and 9).

For Nida, the success of the translation depends above all on achieving
equivalent response. It is one of the 'four basic requirements of a
translation', which are (p. 164):

1   making sense;
2   conveying the spirit and manner of the original;
3   having a natural and easy form of expression;
4   producing a similar response.

It is interesting to note the similarity with Tytler's principles of translation in
one of the early attempts at systematizing translation theory at the end of the
eighteenth century (see chapter 2).

Although dynamic equivalence is aimed at, it is also a graded concept since
Nida accepts that the 'conflict' between the traditional notions of content
and form cannot always be easily resolved. As a general rule for such con-
flicts, Nida underlines that 'correspondence in meaning must have priority
over correspondence in style' if equivalent effect is to be achieved.

3.2.4 Discussion of the importance of Nida's work

The key role played by Nida is to point the road away from strict word-for-
word equivalence. His introduction of the concepts of formal and dynamic
equivalence were crucial in introducing a receptor-based (or reader-based)
orientation to translation theory. However, both the principle of equivalent
effect and the concept of equivalence have come to be heavily criticized for a
number of reasons: Lefevere (1993: 7) feels that equivalence is still overly
concerned with the word level, while van den Broeck (1978: 40) and Larose
(1989: 78) consider equivalent effect or response to be impossible (how is the
'effect' to be measured and on whom? how can a text possibly have the same
effect and elicit the same response in two different cultures and times?).

Indeed, the whole question of equivalence inevitably entails subjective judgement from the translator or analyst.

It is interesting that the debate continued into the 1990s in leading translation journals. In 1992 and 1993, for example, *Meta*, the international journal of translation studies, published a series of papers by Qian Hu whose express aim was to demonstrate the 'implausibility' of equivalent response. The focus in these papers is notably on the impossibility of achieving equivalent effect when meaning is bound up in form, for example the effect of word order in Chinese and English, especially in literary works (Qian Hu 1993: 455–6). Also, that 'the closest natural equivalent may stand in a contradictory relation with dynamic equivalents', for example in Chinese 'over-translations' of English words *animal*, *vegetable* and *mineral*. Qian Hu also discusses cultural references, and the argument which recalls the kind of criticism that has surrounded a notorious example where Nida (1964a: 160) considers that *give one another a hearty handshake all round* 'quite naturally translates' *greet one another with a holy kiss.*

The criticism that Nida's work is subjective raises the question of whether Nida's theory of translation really is 'scientific'. While the techniques for the analysis of meaning and for transforming kernels into TT surface structures are carried out in a systematic fashion, it remains debatable whether a translator follows these procedures in practice. However, Nida's detailed description of real translation phenomena and situations is an important rejoinder to the vague writings on translation that had preceded it. Additionally, Nida is aware of what he terms (1964a: 3) 'the artistic sensitivity which is an indispensable ingredient in any first-rate translation of a literary work'.

One of Nida's fiercest critics is Edwin Gentzler, whose *Contemporary Translation Theories* (1993) contains a chapter on 'the "science" of translation' (Genztler's quotation marks). Gentzler, working from within a deconstructionist perspective (see chapter 10), denigrates Nida's work for its theological and proselytizing standpoint with the concept that dynamic equivalence serves the purpose of converting the receptors, no matter what their culture, to the dominant discourse and ideas of Protestant Christianity. Ironically, Nida is also taken to task by certain religious groups who maintain that the word of God is sacred and unalterable, the changes necessary to achieve dynamic equivalence thus verging on the sacrilegious.

However, Nida – working 'in the field' in the 1960s, dealing daily with real and practical translation problems and attempting to train translators for work in very different cultures – achieved what few of his predecessors attempted: he went a long way to producing a systematic analytical procedure for translators working with all kinds of text and he factored into the translation equation the receivers of the TT and their cultural expectations. Despite the heated debate it has provoked, Nida's systematic linguistic approach to translation has been influential on many subsequent and prominent translation scholars, among them Peter Newmark in the UK and Werner Koller in Germany.

3.3 Newmark: semantic and communicative translation

Newmark's *Approaches to Translation* (1981) and *A Textbook of Translation* (1988) have been widely used on translator training courses[2] and combine a wealth of practical examples of linguistic theories of meaning with practical applications for translation. Yet Newmark departs from Nida's receptor-oriented line, feeling that the success of equivalent effect is 'illusory' and that 'the conflict of loyalties, the gap between emphasis on source and target language will always remain as the overriding problem in translation theory and practice' (Newmark 1981: 38). Newmark suggests narrowing the gap by replacing the old terms with those of 'semantic' and 'communicative' translation:

> Communicative translation attempts to produce on its readers an effect as close as possible to that obtained on the readers of the original. Semantic translation attempts to render, as closely as the semantic and syntactic structures of the second language allow, the exact contextual meaning of the original.
>
> (Newmark 1981: 39)

This description of **communicative translation** resembles Nida's dynamic equivalence in the effect it is trying to create on the TT reader, while **semantic translation** has similarities to Nida's formal equivalence. However, Newmark distances himself from the full principle of equivalent effect, since that effect 'is inoperant if the text is out of TL space and time' (1981: 69). An example would be a modern British English translation of Homer. The translator (indeed any modern translator, no matter what the TL) cannot possibly hope or expect to produce the same effect on the TT reader as the ST had on listeners in ancient Greece. Newmark (p. 51) also raises further questions concerning the readers to whom Nida directs his dynamic equivalence, asking if they are 'to be handed everything on a plate', with everything explained for them.

Newmark's definitions (1981: 39–69) of his own terms reveal other differences; table 3.1 summarizes these definitions. Newmark (p. 63) indicates that semantic translation differs from literal translation in that it 'respects context', interprets and even explains (metaphors, for instance). Literal translation, on the other hand, as we saw in chapter 2, means word-for-word in its extreme version and, even in its weaker form, sticks very closely to ST lexis and syntax.

Importantly, literal translation is held to be the best approach in both semantic and communicative translation:

> In communicative as in semantic translation, provided that equivalent effect is secured, the literal word-for-word translation is not only the best, it is the only valid method of translation.
>
> (Newmark 1981: 39)

This assertion can be related to what other theorists (e.g. Levý 1967/2000,

Table 3.1
Comparison of Newmark's semantic and communicative translation

Parameter	Semantic translation	Communicative translation
Transmitter/addressee focus	Focus on the thought processes of the transmitter as an individual; should only help TT reader with connotations if they are a crucial part of message	Subjective, TT reader focused, oriented towards a specific language and culture
Culture	Remains within the SL culture	Transfers foreign elements into the TL culture
Time and origin	Not fixed in any time or local space; translation needs to be done anew with every generation	Ephemeral and rooted in its own contemporary context
Relation to ST	Always 'inferior' to ST; 'loss' of meaning	May be 'better' than the ST; 'gain' of force and clarity even if loss of semantic content
Use of form of SL	If ST language norms deviate, then this must be replicated in TT; 'loyalty' to ST author	Respect for the form of the SL, but overriding 'loyalty' to TL norms
Form of TL	More complex, awkward, detailed, concentrated; tendency to overtranslate	Smoother, simpler, clearer, more direct, more conventional; tendency to undertranslate
Appropriateness	For serious literature, autobiography, 'personal effusion', any important political (or other) statement	For the vast majority of texts, e.g. non-literary writing, technical and informative texts, publicity, standardized types, popular fiction
Criterion for evaluation	Accuracy of reproduction of the significance of ST	Accuracy of communication of ST message in TT

Toury 1995) have said about the translator's work, where the constraints of time and working conditions often mean that the translator has to maximize the efficiency of the cognitive processes by concentrating energy on especially difficult problems, devoting less effort to those parts of the text which produce a reasonable translation by the 'literal' procedure. However, if there is a conflict between the two forms of translation (namely if semantic translation would result in an 'abnormal' TT or would not secure equivalent effect in the TL) then communicative translation should win out. An example of this, provided by Newmark (1981: 39), is the common sign *bissiger Hund* and *chien méchant*, translated communicatively as *beware the dog!* in order to communicate the message, not semantically as *dog that bites!* and *bad dog!*

3.3.1 Discussion of Newmark

Newmark's terms semantic translation and communicative translation have often been quoted in the literature of translation theory, but they have generally received far less discussion than Nida's formal and dynamic equivalence. This may be because, despite Newmark's relevant criticisms of equivalent effect, they raise some of the same points concerning the translation process and the importance of the TT reader. One of the difficulties encountered by translation studies in systematically following up advances in theory may indeed be partly attributable to the overabundance of terminology. Newmark himself, for instance (1981: 52), defines Juliane House's pair of 'overt' and 'covert' translation (see chapter 6) in terms of his own semantic and communicative translation.

Newmark has been criticized for his strong prescriptivism, and the language of his evaluations still bears traces of what he himself calls the 'pre-linguistics era' of translation studies: translations are 'smooth' or 'awkward', while translation itself is an 'art' (if semantic) or a 'craft' (if communicative). Nonetheless, the large number of examples in Newmark's work provide ample guidance and advice for the trainee and many of the questions he tackles are of important practical relevance to translation.

3.4 Koller: Korrespondenz and Äquivalenz

Nida's move towards a science of translation has proved to be especially influential in Germany, where the common term for translation studies is *Übersetzungswissenschaft*. Among the most prominent German scholars in the translation science field during the 1970s and 1980s were Wolfram Wilss, of the Universität des Saarlandes, and, from the then German Democratic Republic, the Leipzig School, including Otto Kade and Albert Neuber.[3]

Important work on equivalence was also carried out by Werner Koller in Heidelberg and Bergen. Koller's *Einführung in die Übersetzungswissenschaft* (1979a; see also Koller 1979b/89: 'Research into the science of translation') examines more closely the concept of equivalence and its linked term correspondence (Koller 1979a: 176–91). The two terms can be differentiated as shown in table 3.2.

Thus, **correspondence** falls within the field of contrastive linguistics, which compares two language systems and describes contrastively

Table 3.2
Differentiation of equivalence and correspondence (following description in Koller 1979: 183–5)

Field	Contrastive Linguistics	Science of Translation
Research area	**Correspondence** phenomena and conditions, describing corresponding structures and sentences in the TL and SL systems	**Equivalence** phenomena, describing hierarchy of utterances and texts in SL and TL according to equivalence criterion
Knowledge	Langue	Parole
Competence	Foreign language competence	Translation competence

differences and similarities. Its parameters are those of Saussure's *langue* (Saussure 1916/83). Examples given by Koller are the identification of false friends and of signs of lexical, morphological and syntactic interference. **Equivalence**, on the other hand, relates to equivalent items in specific ST–TT pairs and contexts. The parameter is that of Saussure's *parole*. Importantly, Koller (p. 185) points out that, while knowledge of correspondences is indicative of competence in the foreign language, it is knowledge and ability in equivalences that are indicative of competence in translation. However, the question still remains as to what exactly has to be equivalent.

In an attempt to answer this question, Koller (1979a: 186–91; see also 1976/89: 99–104) goes on to describe five different types of equivalence:

1   **Denotative equivalence** is related to equivalence of the extralinguistic content of a text. Other literature, says Koller, calls this 'content invariance'.
2   **Connotative equivalence** is related to the lexical choices, especially between near-synonyms. Koller sees this type of equivalence as elsewhere being referred to as 'stylistic equivalence'.
3   **Text-normative equivalence** is related to text types, with different kinds of texts behaving in different ways. This is closely linked to work by Katharina Reiss (see chapter 5).
4   **Pragmatic equivalence**, or 'communicative equivalence', is oriented towards the receiver of the text or message. This is Nida's 'dynamic equivalence'.
5   **Formal equivalence**, which is related to the form and aesthetics of the text, includes word plays and the individual stylistic features of the ST. It is elsewhere referred to as 'expressive equivalence' and is not to be confused with Nida's term.

Table 3.3

Characteristics of research foci for different equivalence types (following Koller 1979: 187–91)

Type of equivalence	How attainable	Research focus
Denotative	By analysis of correspondences and their interaction with textual factors	Lexis
Connotative	'One of the most difficult problems of translation, and in practice is often only approximate' (Keller 1979b/89: 189); theory needs to identify the connotative dimensions in different languages	Additional dimensions: formality (poetic, slang, etc.), social usage, geographical origin, stylistic effect (archaic, 'plain', etc.), frequency, range (general, technical, etc.), evaluation, emotion
Text-normative	Description and correlation of patterns of usage between languages using functional text analysis	Look at usage in different communicative situations
Pragmatic	Translating the text for a particular readership, overriding the requirements of other equivalences	Analyze the communicative conditions valid for different receiver groups in different language pairs and texts
Formal	An analogy of form in the TL, using the possibilities of the TL and even creating new ones	Analyze the potential of equivalence in rhyme, metaphor and other stylistic forms

Koller goes on to identify different types of equivalence in terms of their research foci. These are summarized in table 3.3. Having identified different equivalence types and the phenomena related to them, Koller then importantly highlights how this can aid the translator and what the role of translation theory is:

With every text as a whole, and also with every segment of text, the translator who consciously makes such a choice must set up a *hierarchy of values to be preserved in translation*; from this he [sic] can derive a *hierarchy of equivalence requirements* for the text or segment in question. This in turn must be preceded by a *translationally relevant text analysis*. It is an urgent task of translation theory – and one on which no more than some preliminary work has so far been done – to develop a methodology and conceptual apparatus for this kind of text analysis, and to bring together and system-atize such analyzes in terms of translationally relevant typologies of textual features.

(Koller 1979b/89: 104; emphasis is Koller's)

The crucial point again is that the equivalences need to be hierarchically ordered according to the communicative situation. Yet how this is to be done is open to debate. Koller himself (1979b: 211–16) proposes a checklist for translationally relevant text analysis under the headings of:

- language function;
- content characteristics;
- language-stylistic characteristics;
- formal–aesthetic characteristics;
- pragmatic characteristics.

Other text analysis typologies and lists, some of which are related to Koller's, are discussed in chapters 4 to 6.

3.5 Later developments in equivalence

The notion of equivalence held sway as a key issue in translation throughout the 1970s and beyond. Thus, for instance, in their general books on transla-tion studies, Chesterman (1989: 99) notes that 'equivalence is obviously a central concept in translation theory' while Bassnett (1991) devotes a section to 'problems of equivalence' in the chapter entitled 'central issues' of trans-lation studies. Mona Baker, in *In Other Words*, her influential 'coursebook' for translators that continues to be popular at the time of writing, structures her chapters around different kinds of equivalence – at the levels of the word, phrase, grammar, text, pragmatics, etc. (see chapter 6), but with the proviso that equivalence 'is influenced by a variety of linguistic and cultural factors and is therefore always relative' (Baker 1992: 6).

Therefore, equivalence continues to be a central, if criticized, concept. Kenny (1997: 77) summarizes criticism that has targeted the 'circularity' of the definitions of equivalence: 'equivalence is supposed to define translation, and translation, in turn, defines equivalence'.

As might be imagined, scholars working in non-linguistic translation studies have been especially critical of the notion of equivalence. Bassnett summarizes the major problem as she sees it:

> Translation involves far more than replacement of lexical and grammatical items between languages ... Once the translator moves away from close linguistic equivalence, the problems of determining the exact nature of the level of equiva-lence aimed for begin to emerge.
>
> (Bassnett 1980/91: 25)

Perhaps the biggest bone of contention in the comparison of an ST and a TT is the so-called *tertium comparationis*, an invariant against which two text segments can be measured to gauge variation. The problem of the inevitable subjectivity that the invariant entails has been tackled by many scholars from a range of theoretical backgrounds. In chapter 4, we discuss taxonomic lin-guistic approaches that have attempted to produce a comprehensive model of translation shift analysis. Chapter 7 considers modern descriptive translation studies; its leading proponent, Gideon Toury, has moved away from a prescriptive definition of equivalence and, accepting as given that a TT is 'equivalent' to its ST, instead seeks to identify the web of relations between the two. Yet, there is still a great deal of practically oriented writing on translation that continues a prescriptive discussion of equivalence. Translator training courses also, perhaps inevitably, have this focus: errors by the trainee translators are often corrected prescriptively according to a notion of equivalence held by the trainer. For this reason, equivalence is an issue that will remain central to the practice of translation, even if translation studies and translation theory has, for the time being at least, marginalized it.

Case study

The following case study considers two series of translations from the point of view of Nida's formal and dynamic equivalence. The first three extracts in box 3.2 are from English translations from the Hebrew of the opening of Genesis, the first book of the Old Testament of the Christian Bible.

Much theological debate has centred on the relation of verse two to verse one, namely whether 'in the beginning' refers to the act of creation of the earth on the first day, or whether the first verse is a summary of the chapter, meaning that a formless and empty earth existed before the creation of light in verse three. Both the NEB and NAB texts are also published with an extensive exegesis to guide the reader's understanding.

Box 3.2

---

1   King James version (KJV, originally published 1611)
    1:1 In the beginning God created the heaven and the earth.
    1:2 And the earth was without form, and void; and darkness was upon the face of the deep. And the Spirit of God moved upon the face of the waters.
    1:3 And God said, 'Let there be light': And there was light.

2   New English Bible (NEB, originally published 1970)
    1:1 In the beginning God created the heavens and the earth.
    1:2 Now the earth was without shape and empty, and darkness was over the surface of the watery deep, but the Spirit of God was moving over the surface of the water.
    1:3 And God said, 'Let there be light': And there was light.

3   New American Bible (NAB, originally published 1970)
    1:1 In the beginning, when God created the heavens and the earth,
    1:2 the earth was a formless wasteland, and darkness covered the abyss, while a mighty wind swept over the waters.
    1:3 And God said, 'Let there be light': And there was light.

Of equal interest linguistically, especially as it may serve to demonstrate the usefulness of Nida's form of analysis of meaning and equivalence, is verse two, where there are a number of differences between the translations. The translations *deep* (KJV), *watery deep* (NEB) and *abyss* (NAB) refer to what is traditionally understood to be the lifeless salt ocean (*thwm* in Hebrew). In this case, it is the NEB which goes furthest to explaining the concept in terms the modern reader would immediately understand. Similarly, the NEB uses the term *surface* in place of the metaphorical *face* of KJV, a metaphor to be found in the original Hebrew (*)(-pny)*. The NAB omits *face/surface* altogether, incorporating the sense instead into the verbs *covered* and *swept over*. Finally, the translation *Spirit of God* (KJV, NEB) is *a mighty wind* in NAB. The Hebrew original (*rwh*) refers to wind or breath, and metaphorically to spirit. The NAB retains the element of wind, but sees God as simply representing a superlative, hence the interpretation *mighty*. Other possible translations are *wind from God* or *breath of God*, preserving both elements. The KJV's *Spirit of God* is firmly entrenched as the traditional rendering. On some occasions, for example in John 3, the ST (in that case Greek) makes a play on the word *pneuma*, translated by KJV first as *spirit* and then *wind*.

It is with such words that Nida's techniques of semantic structure analysis (see figure 3.1 above) can help the translator decide on the appropriate TL term. Yet the brief analysis in this case study suggests that the translation will vary according both to the interpretation of the translator (e.g. what does 'in the beginning' actually refer to?) and the degree to which the translator feels that the message requires adaptation in order to be understood by the TT reader (e.g. 'deep/abyss/watery deep', 'face/surface', 'Spirit of God/mighty wind'). While all the translations quoted seek dynamic equivalence in the sense of creating a response in the audience similar to that of the original text, the 'naturalness' of expression inevitably alters across time: today the KJV has come to be considered a canonized and formal archaic form in English, while the NEB is modern British English and the NAB's more narrative version is modern American English.

The means by which the translations attempt to achieve equivalent effect also differ: the NEB spells out the links, including the choice of *now* at the start of verse two, and explicates *surface*, *watery deep*, and *Spirit of God*; the NAB maintains a focus on the desolate wilderness, with *formless wasteland* and *mighty wind*, even if links are added with the conjunctions *when* and *while*. The KJV maintains the imagery of the ST closely with '*face* of the deep', '*face* of the waters'. It also retains the threefold literal repetition of the conjunction *and* in verse two, a formal syntactic device used throughout the Hebrew and Greek of the Bible and which Nida (1964a: 224) views as requiring 'certain adjustments' to avoid 'babyish' English. This suggests that the KJV is most concerned with formal equivalence with the original, whereas the NEB and NAB are more oriented towards dynamic equivalence, making important adjustments for the receivers.

There is no room for such adjustments or interpretation in legal documents, where the translation technique is invariably one of formal equivalence. An example taken from versions of the Treaty on European Union common provisions Article 1 in English and Portuguese is given in box 3.3. In law, all versions of the Treaty stand as equally valid. As a legal document, they have a high degree of formal equivalence, for example:

By this   Treaty,   the HIGH   CONTRACTING PARTIES
Pelo presente Tratado, as ATLAS PARTES CONTRATANTES

establish among themselves a EUROPEAN UNION,   hereinafter
instituem entre   si   uma UNIÃO EUROPEIA, adiante

called   'the Union'.
designada por «União».

Adjustments are minimal and systemic, such as the Portuguese cohesive *presente* for the English demonstrative pronoun *this*, the addition of the preposition 'designada *por*' in Portuguese and the English definite article '*the* Union'. Although the formal structures are very close in these examples, they still follow Nida's recipe of choosing the 'closest natural equivalent': in both cases the language used is typical legal terminology and the syntax is 'natural'.

The goal of equivalent effect is also crucial in a legal text such as this. In order to function correctly, each text must stand for the same idea in each language and produce the same response. Otherwise, varied interpretations would give rise to legal confusion and potential loopholes. In this respect it is perhaps surprising that the French version of the Treaty should contain a slightly different perspective. While, in the English, the Treaty 'marks a new stage in the process of creating an ever closer union' (suggesting an ongoing process, which tallies with the Portuguese), the relevant passage in the French is 'Le présent traité marque une nouvelle étape créant une union sans cesse plus étroite.' Here, the present participle *créant* ('creating') suggests that,

Box 3.3

I English

By this Treaty, the HIGH CONTRACTING PARTIES establish among themselves a EUROPEAN UNION, hereinafter called 'the Union'.

This Treaty marks a new stage in the process of creating an ever closer union among the peoples of Europe, in which decisions are taken as openly as possible and as closely as possible to the citizen.

2 Portuguese

Pelo presente Tratado, as ALTAS PARTES CONTRATANTES instituem entre si uma UNIÃO EUROPEIA, adiante designada por «União».

O presente Tratado assinala uma nova etapa no processo de criaçao de uma união cada vez mais estrita entre os povos da Europa, em que as decisões serão tomadas de uma forma tão aberta quanto possível e ao nível mais próximo possível dos cidadãos.

---

rather than a continuing process, the goal of closer union is in fact being achieved by the Treaty. It would be interesting to compare longer stretches of the different texts to see whether, despite careful translation, any further segments present a different focus in meaning.

Discussion of case study

The two series of texts given in boxes 3.2 and 3.3 above are markedly different in genre. Nida's model enables a more detailed analysis of meaning than was possible with earlier theories and points to the kind of effect the texts may have on their receivers. However, it is still not possible to measure that effect 'scientifically' and questions persist as to the precise identity of the receiver. With the Treaty on European Union, it may be a legal expert within the TT culture. How does the translator ensure, however, that the effect will be the same on a Portuguese or British legal expert as it is on a French expert? When it comes to the translation of religious text, such as the Bible, these questions multiply.

Finally, it is well to remember that Nida's work is aimed above all at training translators who do not have expertise in linguistics but who have to deal with very different cultures. It may, therefore, be helpful now to attempt to adopt his model not for the analysis of existing translations (where the focus is on identifying what the translator has done and what the effect is on the known audience) but for the analysis of an ST that is to be translated.

Summary

This chapter has examined important questions of translation raised by linguistics in the 1950s and 1960s. The key terms are meaning and equivalence, discussed by Roman Jakobson in 1959 and crucially developed by Nida, whose books analyze meaning systematically and propose that a translation should aim for equivalent effect. Despite subsequent questioning of the feasibility of that goal, Nida's great achievement is to have drawn translation theory away from the stagnant 'literal vs. free' debate and into the modern era. His concepts of formal and dynamic equivalence place the receiver in the centre of the equation and have exerted huge influence over subsequent theoreticians, especially in Germany. In the next chapter, we look at other scholars who have incorporated linguistics into the study of translation.

Further reading

Nida's work has been discussed in a large range of publications. Extensive criticism is to be found in Larose (1989) and Qian Hu (1993). For analyzes of meaning, see Osgood et al. (1957), Lyons (1977), Leech (1983), Carter (1987), and, on translation, Larson (1984). For equivalence and correspondence, see

Catford (1965; see also chapter 4), Kade (1968) and Ivir (1981). For German *Übersetzungswissenschaft*, see Wilss (1977, 1982, 1996).

Discussion and research points

1   Follow up the forms of analysis of meaning in Nida and the further reading section. Try out some of these techniques on STs that you yourself have to translate. What are their advantages and disadvantages?

2   Equivalence and the principle of equivalence are keystones of Nida's theory of translation. In this chapter there has been space to summarize only a few of the main questions. Research more deeply the arguments around the issues and how the concepts have developed over the years (see further reading section for initial references). Why do you consider there has been such heated debate? How can the concepts be used in translator training today?

3   'Nida provides an excellent model for translation which involves a manipulation of a text to serve the interests of a religious belief, but he fails to provide the groundwork for what the West in general conceives of as a science' (Gentzler 1993: 60). Do you agree with Gentzler? Is this model tied to religious texts? How well does it work for other genres (e.g. advertising, scientific texts, literature, etc.)?

4   Look more closely at the descriptions supplied by Nida and Newmark. What differences are there between dynamic/formal equivalence and semantic/ communicative translation?

5   Examine more closely different versions of the Treaty on European Union (http:// www.europarl.eu.int/). If possible, look at longer and more varied passages. Can it be said that the versions have achieved dynamic or formal equivalence? What *tertium comparationis* are you using in making your judgements?

6   Nida's ideas have had an important influence on German *Übersetzungswissenschaft* (see further reading section above). Examine how German scholars other than Koller have employed Nida's concepts. What lines have they followed and what additions have they made to Nida's 'science of translating'?

7   Investigate what Qian Hu and other academics in non-European cultures and languages say about the issue of equivalence. Has the Western concept influenced other areas?

8   'A successful translation is probably more dependent on the translator's empathy with the writer's thought than on affinity of language and culture' (Newmark 1981: 54). What examples of translations can you find that seem to support or disprove this claim?

4   The translation shift approach

Key concepts

- Translation shifts = small linguistic changes occurring in translation of ST to TT.
- Vinay and Darbelnet (1958): classical taxonomy of linguistic changes in translation.
- Catford's (1965) term translation 'shift' in his linguistic approach to translation.
- Theoretical work by Czech scholars Levý, Popovič and Miko (1960s–1970s) who adopt stylistic and aesthetic parameters of language.
- Most detailed model of translation shifts: van Leuven-Zwart's, an attempt to match shifts to discourse and narratological function.
- The problem of the subjectivity of the invariant that is used to compare ST and TT.

Key texts

Catford, J. (1965/2000) *A Linguistic Theory of Translation*, London: Oxford University Press (1965). See also extract ('Translation shifts') in L. Venuti (ed.) (2000), pp. 141–7.

Fawcett, P. (1997) *Translation and Language: Linguistic Approaches Explained*, Manchester: St Jerome, chapters 4 and 5.

Leuven-Zwart, K. van (1989 and 1990) 'Translation and original: similarities and dissimilarities, I and II', *Target* 1.2: 151–81 and *Target* 2.1: 69–95.

Levý, J. (1967/2000) 'Translation as a decision process', in L. Venuti (ed.) (2000), pp. 148–59.

Vinay, J. P. and J. Darbelnet (1958, 2nd edition 1977) *Stylistique comparée du français et de l'anglais: Méthode de traduction*, Paris: Didier, translated and edited by J. Sager, and M.-J. Hamel (1995) as *Comparative Stylistics of French and English: A Methodology for Translation*, Amsterdam and Philadelphia, PA: John Benjamins. (See also the extract 'A methodology for translation', in L. Venuti (ed.) (2000), pp. 84–93.)

4.0 Introduction

Since the 1950s, there has been a variety of linguistic approaches to the analysis of translation that have proposed detailed lists or taxonomies in an effort to categorize the translation process. The scope of this book necessarily restricts us to describing a small number of the best-known and most representative models. Thus, the focus in this chapter is on the following three models:

1   Vinay and Darbelnet's taxonomy in *Stylistique comparée du français et de l'anglais* (1958/95), which is the classical model and one which has had a very wide impact;
2   Catford's (1965) linguistic approach, which included the introduction of the term 'shift' of translation;
3   van Leuven-Zwart's (1989, 1990) very detailed model, designed for the analysis of the key concept of small 'microlevel' translation shifts and the gauging of their effect on the more general 'macrolevel'.

4.1 Vinay and Darbelnet's model

Vinay and Darbelnet carried out a comparative stylistic analysis of French and English. They looked at texts in both languages, noting differences between the languages and identifying different translation strategies and 'procedures'. Although their *Stylistique comparée du français et de l'anglais* (1958) is based solely on French and English, its influence has been much wider. Amongst others it has formed the basis for a work in the same series on French–German translation (Malblanc's *Stylistique comparée du français et de l'allemand*, 1963) and two similar books on English–Spanish translation: Vázquez-Ayora's *Introducción a la traductología* (1977) and García Yebra's *Teoría y práctica de la traducción* (1982). Ironically, at the time of writing the present volume, Vinay and Darbelnet's work is difficult to obtain in French but is available in revised form in its English translation, first published in 1995, thirty-seven years after the original. Because of the theoretical revisions that were incorporated into the later English version, references are made to that edition unless otherwise stated. Where appropriate, the original French terminology is also given.

The two general translation strategies identified by Vinay and Darbelnet (2000: 84–93) are **direct translation** and **oblique translation**, which hark back to the 'literal vs. free' division discussed in chapter 2. Indeed, 'literal' is given by the authors as a synonym for direct translation (p. 84). The two strategies comprise seven procedures, of which **direct translation** covers three:

1   **Borrowing**: The SL word is transferred directly to the TL. This grouping (p. 85) covers words such as the Russian *rouble*, *datcha* or, more recently, *glasnost* and *perestroika*, that are used in English and other languages to fill a semantic gap in the TL. Sometimes borrowings are employed to add local colour (*pétanque*, *armagnac* and *bastide* in a tourist brochure about south west France, for instance).
2   **Calque**: This is 'a special kind of borrowing' (p. 85) where the SL expression or structure is transferred in a literal translation. For example, the French calque 'Compliments de la Saison' for the English 'Compliments of the Season'. Vinay and Darbelnet note that both borrowings and calques often become fully integrated into the TL, although sometimes with some semantic change, which can turn them into false friends.

3   **Literal translation** (pp. 86–8): This is 'word-for-word' translation, which Vinay and Darbelnet describe as being most common between languages of the same family and culture. Their example is 'I left my spectacles on the table downstairs' which becomes 'J'ai laissé mes lunettes sur la table en bas.'

Literal translation is the authors' prescription for good translation: 'literalness should only be sacrificed because of structural and metalinguistic requirements and only after checking that the meaning is fully preserved' (1995: 288).[1] But, say Vinay and Darbelnet (pp. 34–5), the translator may judge literal translation to be 'unacceptable' because it:

(a)   gives a different meaning;
(b)   has no meaning;
(c)   is impossible for structural reasons;
(d)   'does not have a corresponding expression within the metalinguistic experience of the TL';
(e)   corresponds to something at a different level of language.

In those cases where literal translation is not possible, Vinay and Darbelnet say that the strategy of **oblique translation** must be used. This covers a further four procedures:

4   **Transposition** (2000: 88 and 1995: 94–9): This is a change of one part of speech for another without changing the sense. Transposition can be:

- obligatory: 'dès son lever' in a particular past context would be translated as 'as soon as she got up';
- optional: in the reverse direction 'as soon as she got up' could be translated literally as 'dès qu'elle s'est levée' or as a transposition in 'dès son lever'.

Vinay and Darbelnet (1995: 94) see transposition as 'probably the most common structural change undertaken by translators'. They list at least ten different categories, such as:

- verb → noun: 'as soon as she *got up*' → 'dès son *lever*';
- adverb → verb: 'He will *soon* be back' → 'Il *ne tardera pas* à rentrer' [lit. 'He will not tarry in returning'].

5   **Modulation**: This changes the semantics and point of view of the SL. It can be:

- obligatory: e.g. 'the time *when*' translates as 'le moment *où*' [lit. 'the moment *where*'];
- optional, though linked to preferred structures of the two languages: e.g. the reversal of point of view in 'it is not difficult to show' → 'il est facile de démontrer' [lit. 'it is easy to show'].

Modulation is a procedure that is justified, in the words of the English edition, 'when, although a literal, or even transposed, translation results in a grammatically correct utterance, it is considered unsuitable, unidiomatic or awkward in the TL' (2000: 89).

Vinay and Darbelnet place much store by modulation as 'the touch-stone of a good translator', whereas transposition 'simply shows a very good command of the target language' (1995: 246). Modulation at the level of message is subdivided (pp. 246–55) along the following lines:

> abstract for concrete
> cause–effect
> part–whole
> part–another part
> reversal of terms
> negation of opposite
> active to passive (and vice versa)
> space for time
> rethinking of intervals and limits (in space and time)
> change of symbol (including fixed and new metaphors).

This category therefore covers a wide range of phenomena. There is also often a process of originally free modulations becoming fixed expressions. One example given by the authors (p. 254) is 'Vous l'avez échappé belle' [lit. 'You have escaped beautifully']→'You've had a narrow escape'.

6   **Equivalence**: Vinay and Darbelnet use this term (2000: 90) to refer to cases where languages describe the same situation by different stylistic or structural means. Equivalence is particularly useful in translating idioms and proverbs (the sense, though not the image, of 'comme un chien dans un jeu de quilles' [lit. 'like a dog in a set of skittles'] can be rendered as 'like a bull in a china shop'). The use of equivalence in this restricted sense should not be confused with the more common theoretical use discussed in chapter 3 of this book.

7   **Adaptation** (pp. 90–2): This involves changing the cultural reference when a situation in the source culture does not exist in the target culture. For example, Vinay and Darbelnet suggest that the cultural connotation of a reference in an English text to the game of cricket might be best translated into French by a reference to the Tour de France. The authors claim that a refusal to use such adaptation in an otherwise 'perfectly correct' TT 'may still be noticeable by an undefinable tone, something that does not sound quite right' (p. 53). However, whereas their solution may work for some restricted metaphorical uses, it would make little sense to change cricket to cycling in phrases such as 'that isn't cricket' or 'a sleepy Wednesday morning county match at Lords'.

The seven main translation categories are described (pp. 27–30) as operating on three levels; these three levels reflect the main structural elements of the book. They are:

1   the lexicon;
2   syntactic structures;
3   the message.

In this case, 'message' is used to mean approximately the utterance and its metalinguistic situation or context. Two further terms are introduced which look above word level; these are:

1   word order and thematic structure (2000: 211–31, called *démarche* in the French original);
2   connectors (pp. 231–46, called *charnières* in the original), which are cohesive links, discourse markers (*however*, *first*, etc.), deixis (pronouns and demonstrative pronouns such as *this*, *that*) and punctuation.

This level of analysis presages to some extent the higher level text and discourse-based analysis considered in chapters 5 and 6 of this book.
   A further important parameter taken into account by Vinay and Darbelnet is that of servitude and option:

• **servitude** refers to obligatory transpositions and modulations due to a difference between the two language systems;
• **option** refers to non-obligatory changes that are due to the translator's own style and preferences.

Clearly, this is a crucial difference. Vinay and Darbelnet stress (p. 16) that it is option, the realm of stylistics, that should be the translator's main concern. The role of the translator is then 'to choose from among the available options to express the nuances of the message'. The authors continue by giving (pp. 30–1) a list of five steps for the translator to follow in moving from ST to TT; these are:

1   Identify the units of translation.
2   Examine the SL text, evaluating the descriptive, affective and intellectual content of the units.
3   Reconstruct the metalinguistic context of the message.
4   Evaluate the stylistic effects.
5   Produce and revise the TT.

The first four steps are also followed by Vinay and Darbelnet in their analysis of published translations. As far as the key question the 'unit of translation' is concerned, the authors reject the individual word. They consider the unit of translation to be a combination of a 'lexicological unit' and a 'unit of thought' and define it (1995: 21) as: 'the smallest segment of the utterance whose signs are linked in such a way that they should not be translated individually'. In the original French version (1958: 275–7), an example is given of the division, or *découpage*, of a short ST and TT into the units of translation. The divisions proposed include examples of individual words (e.g. *he*, *but*), grammatically linked groups (e.g. *the watch*, *to look*), fixed expressions (e.g. *from time to time*) and semantically linked groups (e.g. *to glance away*). In new analysis in the later, English, version of the book, the units are rather longer: for example, both the groupings 'si nous songeons'/ 'if we speak of' and 'en Grande Bretagne, au Japon'/ 'in Great Britain, Japan' are each given as a single unit (p. 321).

To facilitate analysis where oblique translation is used, Vinay and Darbelnet suggest numbering the translation units in both the ST and TT (for an example, see table 4.2 in the case study section below). The units which have the same number in each text can then be compared to see which translation procedure has been adopted.

4.2 Catford and translation 'shifts'

Although Vinay and Darbelnet do not use the word 'shift', in discussing translation shift, that is in effect what they are describing. The term itself seems to originate in Catford's *A Linguistic Theory of Translation* (1965), where he devotes a chapter to the subject. Catford (1965: 20) follows the Firthian and Hallidayan linguistic model, which analyzes language as communication, operating functionally in context and on a range of different levels (e.g. phonology, graphology, grammar, lexis) and ranks (sentence, clause, group, word, morpheme, etc.).[2]

As far as translation is concerned, Catford makes an important distinction between formal correspondence and textual equivalence, which was later to be developed by Koller (see chapter 3):

- A **formal correspondent** is 'any TL category (unit, class, element of structure, etc.) which can be said to occupy, as nearly as possible, the "same" place in the "economy" of the TL as the given SL category occupies in the SL' (Catford 1965: 27).
- A **textual equivalent** is 'any TL text or portion of text which is observed on a particular occasion . . . to be the equivalent of a given SL text or portion of text'.

Textual equivalence is thus tied to a particular ST–TT pair, while formal equivalence is a more general system-based concept between a pair of languages. When the two concepts diverge, a translation shift is deemed to have occurred. In Catford's own words (2000: 141), translation shifts are thus 'departures from formal correspondence in the process of going from the SL to the TL'.

Catford considers two kinds of shift: (1) shift of level and (2) shift of category:

1   A **level shift** (2000: 141–3) would be something which is expressed by grammar in one language and lexis in another; this could, for example, be:

- by aspect in Russian being translated by a lexical verb in English: e.g. *igrat'* (*to play*) and *sigrat'* (*to finish playing*);

- or cases where the French conditional corresponds to a lexical item in English: e.g. 'trois touristes *auraient été* tués' [lit. 'three tourists would have been killed'] = 'three tourists *have been reported* killed'.

2   Most of Catford's analysis is given over to **category shifts** (2000: 143–7). These are subdivided into four kinds:

   (a) **Structural shifts**: These are said by Catford to be the most common form of shift and to involve mostly a shift in grammatical structure. For example, the subject pronoun + verb + direct object structures of *I like jazz* and *j'aime le jazz* in English and French are translated by an indirect object pronoun + verb + subject noun structure in Spanish (*me gusta el jazz*) and in Italian (*mi piace il jazz*).

   (b) **Class shifts**: These comprise shifts from one part of speech to another. An example given by Catford is the English *a medical student* and the French *un étudiant en médecine*, where the English premodifying adjective *medical* is translated by the adverbial qualifying phrase *en médecine*.

   (c) **Unit shifts** or **rank shifts**: These are shifts where the translation equivalent in the TL is at a different rank to the SL. 'Rank' here refers to the hierarchical linguistic units of sentence, clause, group, word and morpheme.

   (d) **Intra-system shifts**: These are shifts that take place when the SL and TL possess approximately corresponding systems but where 'the translation involves selection of a non-corresponding term in the TL system' (2000: 146). Examples given between French and English are number and article systems, where, although similar systems operate in the two languages, they do not always correspond. Thus, *advice* (singular) in *English* becomes *des conseils* (plural) in French, and the French definite article *la* in 'Il a la jambe cassée' corresponds to the English indefinite article *a* in 'He has *a* broken leg'.

Catford's book is an important attempt to apply to translation advances in linguistics in a systematic fashion. However, his analysis of intra-system shifts betrays some of the weaknesses of his approach. From his comparison of the use of French and English article systems in short parallel texts, Catford concludes (1965: 81–2) that French *le/la/les* 'will have English *the* as its translation equivalent with probability .65', supporting his statement that 'translation equivalence does not entirely match formal correspondence'. This kind of scientific-like statement of probability, which characterizes Catford's whole approach and was linked to the growing interest in machine translation at the time, was later heavily criticized by, amongst others, Delisle (1982) for its static comparative linguistic approach. Henry (1984), revisiting Catford's book twenty years after publication, considers the work to be 'by and large of historical academic interest' only (p. 157). He does, however, (p. 155) point out the usefulness of Catford's final chapter, on the limits of translatability. Of particular interest is Catford's assertion that translation equivalence depends on communicative features such as function, relevance, situation and culture rather than just on formal linguistic criteria. However, as Catford himself notes (p. 94), deciding what is 'functionally relevant' in a given situation is inevitably 'a matter of opinion'.

Despite the steps taken by Catford to consider the communicative function of the SL item and despite the basis of his terminology being founded on a functional approach to language, the main criticism of Catford's book is that his examples are almost all idealized (i.e. invented and not taken from actual translations) and decontextualized. He never looks at whole texts, nor even above the level of the sentence.

4.3 Czech writing on translation shifts

Other writing on translation shifts in the 1960s and 1970s from the then Czechoslovakia introduces a literary aspect, that of the 'expressive function' or style of a text. Jiří Levý's ground-breaking work on literary translation (*Umění překladu*, 1963) – translated into German as *Die literarische Übersetzung: Theorie einer Kunstgattung* (Levý 1969) – links into the tradition of the Prague school of structural linguistics. In this book, Levý looks closely at the translation of the surface structure of the ST and TT, with particular attention to poetry translation, and sees literary translation as both a reproductive and a creative labour with the goal of equivalent aesthetic effect (pp. 65–9). He, too, gives a categorization of features of texts where equivalence may need to be achieved. These are (p. 19): denotative meaning, connotation, stylistic arrangement, syntax, sound repetition (rhythm, etc.), vowel length and articulation. Their importance in a translation depends on the type of text. Thus, vowel length and articulation must not vary in dubbing, while, in a technical text, denotative meaning is of prime importance and must not vary. Levý's work was crucial for the development of translation theory in Czechoslovakia before his early death, and it has subsequently influenced scholars internationally. Another of his papers, 'Translation as a decision process' (1967/2000), has also had an important impact, relating the 'gradual semantic shifting' of translators' linguistic choices to game theory. Hence, Levý sees real-world translation work as being 'pragmatic':

> The translator resolves for that one of the possible solutions which promises a maximum of effect with a minimum of effort. That is to say, he intuitively resolves for the so-called MINIMAX STRATEGY.
>
> (Levý 1967/2000: 156)

Two other papers on translation shifts by Czech writers were published in the influential volume *The Nature of Translation: Essays on the Theory and Practice of Literary Translation* (Holmes 1970). František Miko concentrates on discussing different theoretical aspects of what he terms 'shifts of expression' or style in translation. He maintains (Miko 1970: 66) that retaining the expressive character or style of the ST is the main and perhaps only goal of the translator. Miko suggests an analysis of style under categories such as operativity, iconicity, subjectivity, affectation, prominence and contrast. In the same volume, Anton Popovič (1970: 85) emphasizes the importance of the shift of expression concept:

> An analysis of the shifts of expression, applied to all levels of the text, will bring to light the general system of the translation, with its dominant and subordinate elements.

This is an important development. Shift analysis can be seen as a way of influencing the system of norms which govern the translation process, a concept which is discussed in more detail in chapter 7. Popovič (p. 80), in terms very similar to Levý's, relates shifts to the 'literal vs. free' debate, considering them to arise from the tension between the original text and the translation ideal, and to be the result of the translator's conscious efforts faithfully to reproduce the aesthetic totality of the original. A clarification of these principles is to be seen in Popovič's short *Dictionary for the Analysis of Literary Translation* (1976), where the entry 'adequacy of translation' is defined as synonymous with both 'faithfulness to the original' and 'stylistic equivalence in translation'. Stylistic equivalence is itself defined (p. 6) as 'functional equivalence of elements in both original and translation aiming at an expressive identity with an invariant of identical meaning'. However, in their articles neither Popovič nor Miko applies the ideas in detail to the analysis of translated texts.

4.4 Van Leuven-Zwart's comparative–descriptive model of translation shifts

The most detailed attempt to produce and apply a model of shift analysis has been carried out by Kitty van Leuven-Zwart of Amsterdam. Van Leuven-Zwart's model takes as its point of departure some of the categories proposed by Vinay and Darbelnet and Levý and applies them to the descriptive analysis of a translation, attempting both to systematize comparison and to build in a discourse framework above the sentence level. Originally published in Dutch in 1984 as a doctoral thesis it is more widely known in its abbreviated English version which consists of two articles in *Target* (van Leuven-Zwart 1989, 1990). The model is 'intended for the description of integral translations of fictional texts' (1989: 154) and comprises (1) **a comparative model** and (2) **a descriptive model**. Like Popovič, van Leuven-Zwart considers that trends identified by these complementary models provide indications of the translational norms adopted by the translator. The characteristics of each model are as follows:

1   The **comparative model** (1989: 155–70) involves a detailed comparison of ST and TT and a classification of all the microstructural shifts (within sentences, clauses and phrases). Van Leuven-Zwart's method (1989: 155–7) is as follows:

- Van Leuven-Zwart first divides selected passages into 'comprehensible textual unit[s]' called 'transemes'; 'she sat up quickly' is classed as a transeme, as is its corresponding Spanish TT phrase 'se enderezó'.
- Next, she defines the 'Architranseme', which is the invariant core sense of the ST transeme. This serves as an interlingual comparison or *tertium comparationis* (see chapter 3). In the above example, the Architranseme is 'to sit up'.
- A comparison is then made of each separate transeme with the Architranseme and the relationship between the two transemes is established.

If both transemes have a synonymic relationship with the Architranseme, no shift is deemed to have occurred. The absence of a synonymic relationship indicates a shift in translation, and shifts are divided into three main categories with numerous subcategories. The three main categories are **modulation, modification** and **mutation**; these are explained in table 4.1. An illustrative example of the application of the analysis is the following quotation from a short story by Katherine Mansfield and its Spanish translation:

> As to the boy – well, thank heaven, mother had taken him; he was mother's, or Beryl's, or anybody's who wanted him.
> En cuanto al pequeño . . . menos mal, por fortuna su madre se había encargado de él; era suyo, o de Beryll, o de cualquiera que lo quisiere.

> (in van Leuven-Zwart 1990: 85)

Table 4.1

Main categories of van Leuven-Zwart's comparative model (from van Leuven-Zwart 1989)

Category of shift	Definition
Modulation (pp. 159–64)	One of the transemes tallies with the Architranseme, but the other differs either semantically or stylistically: the *sit up* example would be classed as modulation because the English phrase has an extra element (*quickly*)
Modification (pp. 165–8)	Both transemes show some form of disjunction (semantically, stylistically, syntactically, pragmatically, or some combination of these) compared to the Architranseme; for example, *you had to cry* and *hacía llorar* ('it caused you to cry')
Mutation (pp. 168–9)	It is impossible to establish an Architranseme either because of addition, deletion or 'some radical change in meaning' in the TT

Focusing on the ST transeme *mother's* and the TT transeme *suyo* [lit. 'hers'], van Leuven-Zwart's identifies two microshifts:

- syntactic–semantic modification: the noun + Saxon genitive *mother's* becomes the possessive pronoun *suyo*;
- syntactic–pragmatic modification: the selection of *mother's* rather than *hers* meaning that more pragmatic information is supplied to the reader in the English ST than in the Spanish TT, where the reader has to understand the link to *madre*.

Once all the shifts are identified and categorized on this low 'microstructural' level, the number of occurrences in each category is totalled and their cumulative effect is then calculated by using a descriptive model, as follows:

2 The **descriptive model** (van Leuven-Zwart 1989: 171–9) is a macrostructural model, designed for the analysis of translated literature. It is based on concepts borrowed from narratology (Bal 1985) and stylistics (Leech and Short 1981). It attempts to interweave the concepts of 'discourse level' (the linguistic expression of the fictional world) and 'story level' (the narration of the text, including narratorial point of view) with three linguistic 'metafunctions' (interpersonal, ideational and textual[3]). Van Leuven-Zwart illustrates the perceived interaction of these elements by means of a complex chart (1990: 87) that matches specific micro- and macro-structural shifts to the three functions on the discourse and story levels. For instance, each case of syntactic–pragmatic modulation is said to affect the interpersonal function on the story level. Thus, in the *mother's/suyo* example above, the extra pragmatic information provided by *mother's* in the ST is not necessary; however, its presence emphasizes the relationship, which might serve to stress the mother's disinterest in looking after the baby (van Leuven-Zwart 1990: 85). This disappears in the TT, shifting the interpersonal nature of the narrative.

The analytical model involves totalling the number of instances of each kind of shift in five thousand word extracts and examining the patterns that emerge. The model has been applied by around seventy of van Leuven-Zwart's postgraduate students to Dutch translations of mainly Spanish and Latin American literary texts. The results show a preponderance of semantic shifts, while specification and explanation are also frequent. Van Leuven-Zwart (1990: 92–3) considers the translation strategy of the works that she analyzes to be TT-oriented, with a consequent emphasis on acceptability in the target culture. This extra step of relating the results to higher-level discourse considerations and attempting to identify the norms in operation means that van Leuven-Zwart's model goes further than the mainly linguistic comparisons which characterize Vinay and Darbelnet's and Catford's work. This is an important development and ties in with Toury's work on norms and acceptability which is discussed in chapter 7.

There are, however, drawbacks to this model, and these drawbacks relate to taxonomies in general. First, as van Leuven-Zwart herself partly recognizes (1989: 153–4), the comparative model is extremely complex. There are practical implications in allocating the different kinds of shift since there are eight different categories and thirty-seven subcategories, not all clearly differentiated. Second, keeping track of all the shifts throughout a long text is also difficult. It may be that this second problem can be overcome to some extent by computer-assisted analysis of electronic texts (see chapter 11). Third, the use of the Architranseme as an equivalence measure encounters the same kind of problem concerning its subjectivity as we saw with the *tertium comparationis* in chapter 3.

Finally, the statistical matching of category of shift with metafunction and story/discourse level does not appear to discriminate between the relative importance of different examples of each category. It exposes itself to some of the criticisms made about the 'number-crunching' applications of stylistics.[4] What needs to be developed is a detailed *critical* analysis of the effect of the microshifts on the realization of the communicative situation and the narrative structure.

Case study

Over the years Vinay and Darbelnet's model has exerted considerable influence on translation theorists. We use it as the basis for this case study, applying it to a short illustrative text. This text is a brief extract about the area of Greenwich in London, taken from a tourist brochure for boat tours on the river Thames. Boxes 4.1 and 4.2 are extracts from the English ST and the French TT respectively.[5]

Following the model outlined in section 4.2 above, we first divide the ST into units of translation and match those units with the TT segments. Table 4.2 shows this division. The first problems to arise are the boundaries of segmentation, what Vinay and Darbelnet had defined as the 'smallest' segment that can be translated in isolation. Often there are simultaneous lexical correspondences of both small and longer segments. For instance, ST translation unit 13 (*built by the Romans*) could be considered as three separate,

Box 4.1

Greenwich

The ancient town of Greenwich has been a gateway to London for over a thousand years. Invaders from the continent passed either by ship or the Old Dover Road, built by the Romans, on their way to the capital.

In 1012, the Danes moored their longships at Greenwich and raided Canterbury, returning with Archbishop Alfege as hostage and later murdering him on the spot where the church named after him now stands.

Box 4.2

Greenwich

Les envahisseurs venant du continent passaient par cette ancienne ville, par bateau ou par la Old Dover Road (construite par les Romans) pour se rendre à la capitale.

En 1012, les Danois amarrèrent leurs drakkars à Greenwich avant de razzier Canterbury et de revenir avec l'archevêque Alphège, pris en otage puis assassiné là où se trouve désormais l'église portant son nom.

Table 4.2
Segmentation of text into units of translation

ST (English)		TT (French)
Greenwich	1	Greenwich
The ancient town of Greenwich	2	
has been	3	
a gateway	4	
to London	5	
for over a thousand years.	6	
Invaders from the continent	7	Les envahisseurs venant du continent
passed	8	passaient
	4	par
	2	cette ancienne ville
either	9	
by ship	10	par bateau
or	11	ou
the Old Dover Road,	12	par la Old Dover Road
built by the Romans,	13	(construite par les Romans)
on their way	14	pour se rendre
to the capital.	15	à la capitale.
In 1012,	16	En 1012,
the Danes	17	les Danois
moored their longships	18	amarrèrent leurs drakkars
at Greenwich	19	à Greenwich
and	20	avant de
raided Canterbury,	21	razzier Canterbury
returning	22	et de revenir
with Archbishop Alfege	23	avec l'archevêque Alphège,
as hostage	24	pris en otage
and later	25	puis
murdering him	26	assassiné
on the spot where	27	là où
the church named after him	28	
now stands.	29	se trouve désormais
	28	l'église portant son nom.

Box 4.3

1 The title is originally a borrowing from English to French of the name *Greenwich*, which has now become a standard literal translation.

2 The corresponding unit in the TT is *cette ancienne ville*, located after unit 7 in the TT. There is thus word order shift. In addition, the change from ST repetition *of Greenwich* to the TT connector *cette* (*ancienne ville*) is an example of economy and of transposition (proper noun → demonstrative pronoun).

3 Omission.

4 *a gateway* is only hinted at in the French by the preposition *par* after unit 7. Again this is economy and transposition (noun → preposition).

5 Omission.

6 Omission.

7 Transposition (preposition *from* → verb + preposition + article *venant du*). This is also amplification.

8 Literal translation.

9 Omission.

10 Literal translation.

11 Literal translation.

12 Supplementation (a specific kind of amplification) involving the addition of *par*. Borrowing of *Old Dover Road*, although with addition of article *la*.

13 Literal translation, although there is a change in punctuation.

14 Transposition, adverbial adjunct (*on their way*) → verbal phrase (*pour se rendre*). There is also modulation of the message here (effect → cause).

15 Literal translation.

16 Literal translation.

17 Literal translation.

18 Literal translation. This could also be classed as fixed modulation (whole → part) in that the origin of *drakkar* is the dragon sculpture on the prow of the longboats.

19 Literal translation.

20 Change of connector, *and* → *avant de*.

21 Literal translation.

22 Amplification, addition of connector *et* indicating logical relationship.

23 Literal translation, including borrowing of name *Alfege* with change of graphology (*Alphège*).

24 Amplification (addition of *pris*).

25 Economy with omission of connector (*and later* → *puis*).

26 Change of point of view (cause → effect, *murdering him* → *assassiné*).

27 Economy, deictic transposition of noun by demonstrative (*on the spot where* → *là où*).

28 Units 28 and 29 show word order shift in TT. In addition, ST unit 28 shows cause → effect modulation (*named after him* → *portant son nom*) and transposition (prepositional phrase → noun phrase).

29 Word order shift and modulation, change of point of view involving different limit of time (*now* → *désormais*).

Chapter 4

clearly understandable segments: *built*, *by* and *the Romans*. Similarly, ST units 23 (*with Archbishop Alfege*) and 24 (*as hostage*) could be considered as a single unit of thought. The *par* of TT unit 12 (*par la Old Dover Road*) could also be a separate unit, being an addition to the equivalent ST unit. This type of segmentation problem recurs constantly. Categorization of the translations of ST units from table 4.2 is shown in box 4.3.

Discussion of case study

Analysis of this box shows around thirteen direct translations out of twenty-nine translation units. In other words, a little under half the translations might be termed direct, and more complex 'cultural' procedures such as equivalence and adaptation are absent. Most of the oblique translation procedures revealed affect the lexical or syntactic level, although there is some shift in prosody and structure. The figures can only be approximate because there is a crucial problem of determining the translation unit and the boundaries between the categories are vague. Some units (e.g. units 2 and 14) show more than one shift; others (e.g. units 4 and 18) pose particular problems of evaluation. Most importantly, although Vinay and Darbelnet purport to describe the translation *process*, their model in fact focuses on the translation *product*. Unlike van Leuven-Zwart's later model, there is no incorporation of higher-level discourse considerations nor a means of discussing the effect the changes might have on the reader.

Summary

The 1950s and 1960s saw the emergence of attempts at detailed taxonomies of small linguistic changes ('shifts') in ST–TT pairs. Vinay and Darbelnet's classical taxonomy continues to exert influence today and was useful in bringing to light a wide range of different translation techniques. However, like Catford, who in the 1960s applied a systematic contrastive linguistic approach to translation, theirs is a static linguistic model. Fuzziness of category boundaries and the automatic counting of shifts are problems that have continued to affect later attempts, such as van Leuven-Zwart's, whose model tries to systematize the evaluation of an ST–TT pair and relate shifts to higher-level discourse levels. Another approach to the analysis of shifts came from Czechoslovakia in the 1960s and 1970s, where Levý, Popovič and Miko paid greater attention to the translation of style.

Further reading

See Larose (1989) and Hermans (1999) for further discussion of models described here. As noted above, Vinay and Darbelnet's model has been adapted for other language pairs; note especially Malblanc (1963) and Vázquez-Ayora (1977). The Czech school's approach is worthy of further

attention, especially Levý (1969) who has many fine insights into the translation of literature. Mounin (1963) is an early linguistic model from France,
while the strong Russian tradition can be followed up in Fyodorov (1968) and
Švecjer (1987). From the USA, Malone (1988) presents another detailed
theoretical model.

Discussion and research points

1   Look at the analysis in the case study. Are there points where you disagree with the
    analysis? What does this tell us about the use of this kind of model?
2   Boxes 4.4–4.6 are extracts from the German, Italian and Spanish TTs of the case study
    extract. Analyze these TTs into units of translation and the translation procedures that
    have been followed, using Vinay and Darbelnet's model. How does the analysis differ
    from that of the French translation?
3   Read Vinay and Darbelnet's own description of their model and try applying it to ST–
    TT pairs in your own languages. Make a list of phenomena that are easy and difficult to
    categorize using their model. Are there any language combinations for which their
    taxonomy is problematic?
4   Follow up the description of van Leuven-Zwart's model in *Target*. Try to apply it to an
    ST–TT pair of your choice and summarize the results obtained. How far do you
    consider the criticisms of the model (see section 4.4 above) to be justified?
5   Beaugrande (1978: 11) gives the following dismissal of Catford's book: 'Catford's
    "theory of translation" stands as an allegory of the limitations of linguistics at that
    time.' However, read Catford's theory in full and list its strengths and possible
    applications.
6   The Czech school of Levý, Popovič and Miko was influential in its time but is little
    mentioned in current theory. Look at what they wrote. How different are they from
    other writers on translation shifts? How practical do you think it is to analyze
    stylistic shifts? Look, too, at more recent work on the translation of style by Parks
    (1998).
7   Imagine you have been asked to draw up a taxonomy specifically for the analysis of
    translations produced by trainee translators. Try putting together a classification, using
    and adapting whatever elements you see as useful from the models set out in this
    chapter. If possible, ask others to test out and evaluate your model according to how
    systematic, practical and useful it is.

Box 4.4

Greenwich
Seit über 1000 Jahren ist die historische Stadt Greenwich ein Tor zu London. Vom
Kontinent kommende Invasoren passierten sie auf ihrem Weg nach London
entweder per Schiff oder über Strasse Old Dover Road.

1012 legten die Dänen mit ihren Wikingerbooten in Greenwich an und überfielen
Canterbury. Sie kehrten mit dem Erzbischof Alfege als Geisel zurück und ermore-
deten ihn später an der Stelle, an der heute die nach ihm benannte Kirche steht.

Box 4.5

Greenwich

L'antica città di Greenwich è una via di ingresso per Londra da più di mille anni. Gli invasori provenienti dal continente passavano sulle navi o lungo la Old Dover Road, costruita dai Romani, mentre si dirigevano verso la capitale.

Nel 2010 i Danesi attraccarono le loro navi a Greenwich e fecero razzia a Canterbury, tornando con l'arcivescovo Alfege, come ostaggio e più tardi assassinandolo sul luogo dove sorge ora la chiesa che porta il suo nome.

Box 4.6

Greenwich

El antiguo pueblo de Greenwich ha sido la entrada a Londres durante miles de años.

Los invasores del continente pasaban por barco o a través de la Vieja Carretera de Dover, construida por los romanos, en su camino hacia la capital.

En el año 1012, los daneses amarraron sus grandes barcos en Greenwich, regresando con el arzobispo Alfege como rehén y posteriormente le mataron en el lugar donde ahora se encuentra la iglesia con su nombre.

---

5 Functional theories of translation

Key concepts

- Functional theories from Germany in the 1970s–1980s mark a move away from static linguistic typologies.
- Reiss stresses equivalence at text level, linking language functions to text types and translation strategy.
- Holz-Mänttäri's theory of translational action: a communicative process involving a series of players.
- Vermeer's skopos theory of translation strategy depending on purpose of TT is expanded in Reiss and Vermeer.
- Nord's translation-oriented text analysis: a functional approach with more attention to ST.

Key texts

Holz-Mänttäri, J. (1984) *Translatorisches Handeln: Theorie und Methode*, Helsinki: Suomalainen Tiedeakatemia.

Nord, C. (1988/91) *Text Analysis in Translation: Theory, Methodology and Didactic Application of a Model for Translation-Oriented Text Analysis*, Amsterdam: Rodopi.

Nord, C. (1997) *Translating as a Purposeful Activity: Functionalist Approaches Explained*, Manchester: St Jerome.

Reiss, K. (1971/2000) *Möglichkeiten und Grenzen der Übersetzungskritik*, Munich: Max Hueber, translated by E. Rhodes (2000) as *Translation Criticism: Potential and Limitations*, Manchester: St Jerome and American Bible Society.

Reiss, K. (1977/89) 'Text types, translation types and translation assessment', translated by A. Chesterman, in A. Chesterman (ed.) (1989), pp. 105–15.

Reiss, K. (1981/2000) 'Type, kind and individuality of text: decision making in translation', translated by S. Kitron, in L. Venuti (ed.) (2000), pp. 160–71.

Reiss, K. and **H. Vermeer** (1984) *Grundlegung einer allgemeinen Translationstheorie*, Tübingen: Niemeyer.

Vermeer, H. (1989/2000) 'Skopos and commission in translational action', in L. Venuti (ed.) (2000), pp. 221–32.

5.0 Introduction

The 1970s and 1980s saw a move away from the static linguistic typologies of translation shifts and the emergence and flourishing in Germany of a functionalist and communicative approach to the analysis of translation. In this chapter, we look at:

1   Katharina Reiss's early work on text type and language function;
2   Justa Holz-Mänttäri's theory of translational action;
3   Hans J. Vermeer's skopos theory which centred on the purpose of the TT;
4   Christiane Nord's more detailed text-analysis model which continued the functionalist tradition in the 1990s.

5.1 Text type

Katharina Reiss's work in the 1970s builds on the concept of equivalence (see chapter 3) but views the text, rather than the word or sentence, as the level at which communication is achieved and at which equivalence must be sought (Reiss 1977/89: 113–14). Her functional approach aims initially at systematizing the assessment of translations. It borrows Karl Bühler's three-way categorization of the functions of language.[1] Reiss links the three functions to their corresponding language 'dimensions' and to the text types or communicative situations in which they are used. These links can be seen in table 5.1. The main characteristics of each text type are summarized by Reiss (1977/89: 108–9) as follows:

1   'Plain communication of facts': information, knowledge, opinions, etc. The language dimension used to transmit the information is logical or referential, the content or 'topic' is the main focus of the communication, and the text type is **informative**.
2   'Creative composition': the author uses the aesthetic dimension of language. The author or 'sender' is foregrounded, as well as the form of the message, and the text type is **expressive**.
3   'Inducing behavioural responses': the aim of the appellative function is to appeal to or persuade the reader or 'receiver' of the text to act in a certain way. The form of language is dialogic, the focus is appellative and Reiss calls this text type **operative**.
4   **Audiomedial** texts, such as films and visual and spoken advertisements which supplement the other three functions with visual images, music, etc. This is Reiss's fourth type, which is not represented in table 5.1.

Examples of text varieties or genres (*Textsorte*) associated with each of the three text types are given by Reiss (1976: 20) and presented visually by Chesterman (see figure 5.1). Following this diagram, the reference work is the text

Table 5.1
Functional characteristics of text types and links to translation methods (adapted from Reiss 1971)

Text type	Informative	Expressive	Operative
Language function	Informative (representing objects and facts)	Expressive (expressing sender's attitude)	Appellative (making an appeal to text receiver)
Language dimension	Logical	Aesthetic	Dialogic
Text focus	Content-focused	Form-focused	Appellative-focused
TT should	Transmit referential content	Transmit aesthetic form	Elicit desired response
Translation method	'Plain prose', explicitation as required	'Identifying' method, adopt perspective of ST author	'Adaptive', equivalent effect

Figure 5.1
Reiss's text types and text varieties (Chesterman 1989: 105, based on a handout prepared by Roland Freihoff)

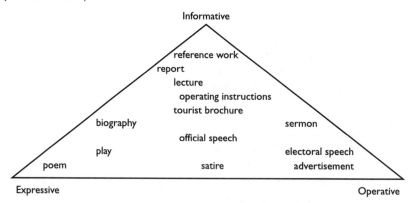

variety which is the most fully informative text type; the poem is a highly expressive, form-focused type, and an advertisement is the clearest operative text type (attempting to persuade someone to buy or do something). Between these poles are positioned a host of hybrid of types. Thus, a biography might be somewhere between the informative and expressive types, since it provides information about the subject while also partly performing the expressive function of a piece of literature. Similarly, a sermon gives information (about the religion) while fulfilling the operative function by attempting to persuade the congregation to a certain way of behaving.

Despite the existence of such hybrid types, Reiss (1977/89: 109) states that 'the transmission of the predominant function of the ST is the determining factor by which the TT is judged'. She suggests 'specific translation methods according to text type' (Reiss 1976: 20). These methods occupy the last two rows of table 5.1 and can be described as follows:

1   The TT of an informative text should transmit the full referential or conceptual content of the ST. The translation should be in 'plain prose', without redundancy and with the use of explicitation when required.
2   The TT of an expressive text should transmit the aesthetic and artistic form of the ST. The translation should use the 'identifying' method, with the translator adopting the standpoint of the ST author.
3   The TT of an operative text should produce the desired response in the TT receiver. The translation should employ the 'adaptive' method, creating an equivalent effect among TT readers.
4   Audio-medial texts require the 'supplementary' method, supplementing written words with visual images and music.

Reiss (1971: 54–88) also lists a series of intralinguistic and extralinguistic instruction criteria (*Instruktionen*) by which the adequacy of a TT may be assessed. These are:

1   **intralinguistic criteria**: semantic, lexical, grammatical and stylistic features;
2   **extralinguistic criteria**: situation, subject field, time, place, receiver, sender and 'affective implications' (humour, irony, emotion, etc.).

Although interrelated, the importance of these criteria vary according to text type (Reiss 1971: 69). For example, the translation of any content-focused text should first aim at preserving semantic equivalence. However, while a news item TT would probably place grammatical criteria in second place, a popular science book would pay more attention to the individual style of the ST. Similarly, Reiss (p. 62) feels that it is more important for a metaphor to be retained in the translation of an expressive text than in an informative TT, where translation of its semantic value alone will be sufficient.

There are, of course, occasions, as Reiss allows (1977/89: 114), when the function of the TT may differ from that of the ST. An example she gives is Jonathan Swift's *Gulliver's Travels*. Originally written as a satirical novel to attack the government of the day (i.e. a mainly operative text), it is nowadays normally read and translated as 'ordinary entertaining fiction' (i.e. an expressive text). Alternatively, a TT may have a different communicative function from the ST: an operative election address in one language may be translated for analysts in another country interested in finding out what policies have been presented and how (i.e. as an informative and expressive text).

5.1.1 Discussion of the text type approach

Reiss's work is important because it moves translation theory beyond a consideration of lower linguistic levels, the mere words on the page, beyond even the effect they create, towards a consideration of the communicative purpose of translation. However, over the years there have been a number of criticisms of Reiss's work; these are summarized by Fawcett (1997: 106–8). One of the criticisms is why there should only be three types of language function. Nord, although working in the same functionalist tradition as Reiss, perhaps implicitly accepts this criticism by feeling the need to add a fourth 'phatic' function, covering language that establishes or maintains contact between the parties involved in the communication (Nord 1997: 40; see also section 5.4 below).[2] A simple example would be a greeting or phrase such as 'Ladies and gentlemen' that is used to signal the start of a formal speech or an announcement made by a company employee to clients.

There are also question marks as to how Reiss's proposed translation methods are to be applied in the case of a specific text. Even the apparently logical 'plain-prose' method for the informative text can be called into question. Business and financial texts in English contain a large number of simple and complex metaphors: markets are *bullish* and *bearish*, profits *soar, peak, dive* and *plummet*, while *carpetbaggers besiege* building societies and banks employ a *scorched-earth policy* in the face of *hostile take-over bids*. Some of these have a fixed translation in another language, but the more complex and individualistic metaphors do not. Similarly, the translation of business texts *into* English requires more than just attention to the informative value of the ST, since such a method could create an English TT that is lacking in the expressive function of language.

The above example contains an important criticism for Reiss's whole theory. Namely, whether text types can really be differentiated. A business report, classed by Reiss as a strongly informative text, can also show a strongly expressive side. It may also have several functions in the source culture: as an informative text for the company's directors and as an operative text to persuade the shareholders and market analysts that the company is being run efficiently. In figure 5.1, the biography could also easily have an appellative function, endeavouring to persuade the reader to adopt a particular stance towards the subject; and an advertisement, while normally appellative, can have an artistic/expressive or informative function. Co-existence of functions within the same ST and the use of the same ST for a variety of purposes are evidence of the fuzziness that fits uneasily into Reiss's clear divisions. Finally, the translation method employed depends on far more than just text type. The translator's own role and purpose, as well as sociocultural pressures, also affect the kind of translation strategy that is adopted. This is a key question in the rest of this chapter and also in chapter 6.

5.2 *Translational action*

The translational action model proposed by Holz-Mänttäri (*Translatorisches Handeln: Theorie und Methode*)[3] takes up concepts from communication theory and action theory with the aim, amongst others, of providing a model and guidelines applicable to a wide range of professional translation situations. Translational action views translation as purpose-driven, outcome-oriented human interaction and focuses on the process of translation as message-transmitter compounds (*Botschaftsträger im Verbund*) involving intercultural transfer:

> [It] is not about translating words, sentences or texts but is in every case about guiding the intended co-operation over cultural barriers enabling functionally oriented communication.
>
> (Holz-Mänttäri 1984: 7–8; translated)

Interlingual translation is described as 'translational action from a source text' and as a communicative process involving a series of roles and players (pp. 109–11):

- **the initiator**: the company or individual who needs the translation;
- **the commissioner**: the individual who contacts the translator;
- **the ST producer**: the individual within the company who writes the ST, not necessarily always involved in the TT production;
- **the TT producer**: the translator;
- **the TT user**: the person who uses the TT; for example as teaching material or sales literature;
- **the TT receiver**: the final recipient of the TT; for example the students in a TT user's class or clients reading the translated sales literature.

These players each have their own specific primary and secondary goals. The text selected by Holz-Mänttäri for her detailed case study (pp. 129–48) are the instructions for installing a compost toilet. The roles of the different participants in the translational action are analyzed. In the case of the professional translator faced with such a text, the likely goals are primarily to earn money, and secondarily to fulfil the contract and to process the text message (p. 138). According to the analysis given, the translator may be a non-expert both in the text type and specific subject area. Extra input of subject-area knowledge would need to come from the ST writer within the company.

Translatorial action focuses very much on producing a TT that is functionally communicative for the receiver. This means, for example, that the form and genre of the TT must be guided by what is functionally suitable in the TT culture, rather than by merely copying the ST profile. What is functionally suitable has to be determined by the translator, who is the expert in translational action and whose role is to make sure that the intercultural transfer takes place satisfactorily. In the 'translational text operations' (the term Holz-Mänttäri uses for the production of the TT), the ST is analyzed solely for its 'construction and function profile' (pp. 139–48). Relevant features are described according to the age-old split of 'content' and 'form' (p. 126):

1   **Content**, structured by what are called 'tectonics', is divided into (a) factual information and (b) overall communicative strategy.
2   **Form**, structured by 'texture', is divided into (a) terminology and (b) cohesive elements.

The needs of the receiver are the determining factors for the TT. Thus, as far as terminology is concerned, a technical term in an ST manual may require clarification for a non-technical TT user. Additionally, in order to maintain cohesion for the TT reader, a single term will need to be translated consistently (p. 144).

5.2.1 Discussion of the model of translational action

The value of Holz-Mänttäri's work is the placing of translation (or at least the professional non-literary translation which she describes) within its sociocultural context, including the interplay between the translator and the initiating institution. She later also describes the 'professional profile' of the translator (Holz-Mänttäri 1986). Some scholars offer fulsome praise:

> Holz-Mänttäri's concept of translatorial action is considered relevant for all types of translation and the theory is held to provide guidelines for every decision to be taken by the translator.
>
> (Schäffner 1997: 5)

The inclusion of real-world commercial translation constraints is welcome in addressing some of the decisions faced by translators. However, the model could be criticized, not least for the complexity of its jargon (for example *message-transmitter compounds*), which does little to explain practical translation situations for the individual translator. Also, since one of the aims of the model is to offer guidelines for intercultural transfer, it is disappointing that it fails to consider cultural difference in more detail or in the kinds of terms proposed by the culturally oriented models discussed in chapters 8 and 9.

Nord (1991: 28) also takes issue with Holz-Mänttäri's disregard of the ST. She stresses that, while 'functionality is the most important criterion for a translation', this does not allow the translator absolute licence. There needs to be a relationship between ST and TT, and the nature of this relationship is determined by the purpose or skopos.

5.3 Skopos theory

Skopos is the Greek word for 'aim' or 'purpose' and was introduced into translation theory in the 1970s by Hans J. Vermeer as a technical term for the purpose of a translation and of the action of translating. The major work on skopos theory (*Skopostheorie*) is *Grundlegung einer allgemeine Translationstheorie* ('Groundwork for a General Theory of Translation'), a book Vermeer co-authored with Katharina Reiss (Reiss and Vermeer 1984). Although skopos theory predates Holz-Mänttäri's theory of translational action, it can be considered to be part of that same theory, as it deals with a translational action which is ST-based, which has to be negotiated and performed, and which has a purpose and a result (Vermeer 1989/2000: 221). Skopos theory focuses above all on the purpose of the translation, which determines the translation methods and strategies that are to be employed in order to produce a functionally adequate result. This result is the TT, which Vermeer calls the *translatum*. Therefore, in skopos theory, knowing why an ST is to be translated and what the function of the TT will be are crucial for the translator.[4]

As the title of their 1984 book suggests, Reiss and Vermeer aim at a general translation theory for all texts. The first part sets out a detailed explanation of Vermeer's skopos theory; the second part, 'special theories', adapts Reiss's functional text-type model to the general theory. In this chapter, for reasons of space, we concentrate on the basic underlying 'rules' of the theory (Reiss and Vermeer 1984: 119). These are:

1   A *translatum* (or TT) is determined by its skopos.
2   A TT is an offer of information (*Informationsangebot*) in a target culture and TL concerning an offer of information in a source culture and SL.
3   A TT does not initiate an offer of information in a clearly reversible way.
4   A TT must be internally coherent.
5   A TT must be coherent with the ST.
6   The five rules above stand in hierarchical order, with the skopos rule predominating.

Some explanation is required here. Rule 2 is important in that it relates the ST and TT to their function in their respective linguistic and cultural contexts. The translator is once again (as was the case in Holz-Mänttäri's theory) the key player in a process of intercultural communication and production of the *translatum*. The irreversibility in point 3 indicates that the function of a *translatum* in its target culture is not necessarily the same as in the source culture. Rules 4 and 5 touch on general skopos 'rules' concerning how the success of the action and information transfer is to be judged: the coherence rule, linked to internal textual coherence, and the fidelity rule, linked to intertextual coherence with the ST.

The **coherence rule** states that the TT 'must be interpretable as coherent with the TT receiver's situation' (Reiss and Vermeer 1984: 113). In other words, the TT must be translated in such a way that it is coherent for the TT receivers, given their circumstances and knowledge.

The **fidelity rule** merely states (p. 114) that there must be coherence between the *translatum* and the ST or, more specifically, between:

- the ST information received by the translator;
- the interpretation the translator makes of this information;
- the information that is encoded for the TT receivers.

However, the hierarchical order of the rules means that intertextual coherence (rule 5) is of less importance than intratextual coherence (rule 4), which, in turn, is subordinate to the skopos (rule 1). This down-playing (or 'dethroning', as Vermeer terms it) of the status of the ST is a general fact of both skopos and translational action theory.

An important advantage of skopos theory is that it allows the possibility of the same text being translated in different ways according to the purpose of the TT and the commission which is given to the translator. In Vermeer's words:

> What the skopos states is that one must translate, consciously and consistently, in accordance with some principle respecting the target text. The theory does not state what the principle is: this must be decided separately in each specific case.
>
> (Vermeer 1989/2000: 228)

So, using Vermeer's own example, an ambiguity in a will written in French would need to be translated literally, with a footnote or comment, for a foreign lawyer dealing with the case. On the other hand, if the will appeared in a novel, the translator might prefer to find a slightly different ambiguity that works in the TL without the need of a formal footnote, so as not to interrupt the reading process.

In order for the translational action to be appropriate for the specific case, the skopos needs to be stated explicitly or implicitly in the commission (p. 228). Vermeer describes the commission as comprising (1) a goal and (2) the conditions under which that goal should be achieved (including deadline and fee), both of which should be negotiated between the commissioner and the translator. In this way, the translator should, as the expert, be able to advise the commissioner/client on the feasibility of the goal. The nature of the TT 'is primarily determined by its skopos or commission' (Vermeer 1989/2000: 230) and adequacy (*Adäquatheit*) comes to override equivalence as the measure of the translational action. In Reiss and Vermeer (1984: 139), adequacy describes the relations between ST and TT as a consequence of observing a skopos during the translation process. In other words, if the TT fulfils the skopos outlined by the commission, it is functionally and communicatively adequate. Equivalence is reduced to functional constancy between ST and TT (those cases where the function is the same for both ST and TT). However, functional constancy is seen to be the exception.

5.3.1 Discussion of skopos theory

Nord (1997: 109–22) and Schäffner (1997: 237–8) discuss some of the criticisms that have been made of skopos theory by other scholars. These include the following:

1   What purports to be a 'general' theory is in fact is only valid for non-literary texts. Literary texts are considered either to have no specific purpose and/or to be far more complex stylistically.
2   Reiss's text type approach and Vermeer's skopos theory are in fact considering different functional phenomena and cannot be lumped together.
3   Skopos theory does not pay sufficient attention to the linguistic nature of the ST nor to the reproduction of microlevel features in the TT. Even if the skopos is adequately fulfilled, it may be inadequate at the stylistic or semantic levels of individual segments.

Other possible criticisms are similar to those made of Holz-Mänttäri, namely that jargon such as *translatum* does little to further translation theory, where workable terms already exist, and that consideration of cultural issues and differences must surely be essential when deciding on how, if at all, the skopos can be achieved.

Vermeer (1989/2000: 224) answers the first point above by stressing that goals, purposes, functions and intentions are 'attributed to' actions. Thus, a writer of a poem may have goals of having the resultant *translatum* (poem) published and of keeping copyright over it so as to make money from its reproduction. He or she may also have the intention of creating something that exists for itself ('art for art's sake').

Two points are at issue in the second criticism: to what extent does ST type determine translation method and what is the logic of the link between ST type and translation skopos (compare section 5.1 above). The third criticism in particular is tackled by another functionalist, Christiane Nord, with her model of translation-oriented text analysis.

5.4 Translation-oriented text analysis

Christiane Nord's *Text Analysis in Translation* (1988/91) presents a more detailed functional model incorporating elements of text analysis, which examines text organization at or above sentence level. Nord first makes a distinction between two basic types of translation product (and process), which are documentary translation and instrumental translation:[5]

*   **Documentary translation** 'serves as a document of a source culture communication between the author and the ST recipient' (Nord 1991: 72). Such is the case, for example, in literary translation, where the TT allows the TT receiver access to the ideas of the ST but where the reader is well aware that it is a translation. Other examples of documentary translation given by Nord are word-for-word and literal translation and 'exoticizing translation' (p. 73). In the latter, certain culture-specific lexical items in the ST are retained in the TT in order to maintain the local colour of the ST; for example, food items such as *Quark*, *Roggenbrot* and *Wurst* from a German ST.

- **An instrumental translation** 'serves as an independent message-transmitting instrument in a new communicative action in the target culture, and is intended to fulfil its communicative purpose without the recipient being conscious of reading or hearing a text which, in a different form, was used before in a different communicative situation' (p. 73). In other words, the TT receivers read the TT as though it were an ST written in their own language. The function may be the same for both ST and TT. For instance, a translated computer manual or software should fulfil the function of instructing the TT receiver in the same way as the ST does for the ST reader. Nord calls these 'function-preserving translations'. However, she also gives examples of other kinds of translations where it is not possible to preserve the same function in translation. Such is the case with the translation of Swift's *Gulliver's Travels* for children, and with the translation of Homer into a novel for contemporary audiences.

Nord's *Text Analysis in Translation* is aimed primarily at providing translation students with a model of ST analysis which is applicable to all text types and translation situations. The model is based on a functional concept, enabling understanding of the function of ST features and the selection of translation strategies appropriate to the intended purpose of the translation (Nord 1991: 1). She thus shares many of the premisses of Reiss and Vermeer's work (as well as Holz-Mänttäri's consideration of the other players in the translation action), but pays more attention to features of the ST.[6] Nord's model involves analyzing a complex series of interlinked extratextual factors (1991: 35–78) and intratextual features (pp. 79–129) in the ST. However, in her 1997 book, *Translating as a Purposeful Activity*, Nord proposes a more flexible version of the model. This new version synthesizes many of the elements described in this chapter and highlights 'three aspects of functionalist approaches that are particularly useful in translator training' (1997: 59). These are:

1   the importance of the translation commission (or 'translation brief', as Nord terms it);
2   the role of ST analysis;
3   the functional hierarchy of translation problems.

1   **The importance of the translation commission** (Nord 1997: 59–62): The translator needs to compare ST and TT profiles defined in the commission to see where the two texts may diverge. The translation commission should give the following information for both texts:

- the intended text functions;
- the addressees (sender and recipient);
- the time and place of text reception;
- the medium (speech and writing);
- the motive (why the ST was written and why it is being translated).

This information enables the translator to prioritize what information to include in the TT. In the example given by Nord, a brochure for Heidelberg University, the motive is the celebration of the 600th anniversary of its founding and so clearly events surrounding the anniversary are most important.

2   **The role of ST analysis** (pp. 62–7): Once the above ST–TT profiles have been compared, the ST can be analyzed to decide on functional priorities of the translation strategy. Nord's list of intratextual factors (1991: 79–129) is one possible model for the ST analysis. These factors are:

- subject matter;
- content: including connotation and cohesion;
- presuppositions: real-world factors of the communicative situation presumed to be known to the participants;
- composition: including microstructure and macrostructure;
- non-verbal elements: illustrations, italics, etc.;
- lexic: including dialect, register and specific terminology;
- sentence structure;
- suprasegmental features: including stress, rhythm and 'stylistic punctuation'.

However, Nord stresses that it does not matter which text-linguistic model is used:

> What is important, though, is that [it] include[s] a pragmatic analysis of the communicative situations involved and that the same model be used for both source text and translation brief, thus making the results comparable.
>
> (Nord 1997: 62)

This provides some flexibility, although clearly the form of the analysis is crucial in determining which features are prioritized in the translation.

3   **The functional hierarchy of translation problems**: Nord establishes a functional hierarchy when undertaking a translation:

(a) The intended function of the translation should be decided (documentary or instrumental).

(b) Those functional elements that will need to be adapted to the TT addressees' situation have to be determined (after analysis of the translation commission as in 1 above).

(c) The translation type decides the translation style (source-culture or target-culture oriented).

(d) The problems of the text can then be tackled at a lower linguistic level (as in the ST analysis in 2 above).

In many ways, this synthesized approach brings together strengths of the various functional and action theories:

- The translation commission analysis follows up Holz-Mänttäri's work on the players within the translational action.
- The intended text functions pursue Reiss and Vermeer's skopos. but without giving overall dominance to the skopos.

- The ST analysis, influenced by Reiss's work, gives due attention to the communicative function and genre features of the ST type and language, but without the rigidity of other taxonomies.

In our case study, we therefore try out this synthesized approach on an ST.

Case study

This case study is taken from a real-life translation commission. The ST in question is Usborne Cookery School's *Cooking for Beginners*,[7] an illustrated book of varied recipes to help British children aged 10 and over learn to cook. TTs were to be produced in a range of European languages for sale abroad; however, in order to keep costs down, the many illustrations were to be retained from the ST.

Following Nord's terms above, it is clear that the kind of translation involved here is instrumental: the resulting TT is to function in the target culture as an independent message-transmitting text, with the TT receivers using it to learn how to cook.

The ST–TT profiles in the translation commission would be as follows:

- **The intended text functions**: The ST has an informative function, transmitting information about cookery and specific recipes. It also has an appellative function, since it is appealing to children to act on what they read (to make the recipes and become interested in cooking and food). The TT will be function-preserving as far as is possible.
- **The addressees**: The ST addressees are probably both the British children aged 10 and over mentioned above and their parents (or other older relatives, carers or friends), who are likely to be the purchasers of the book. Many of the recipes also presuppose some assistance from an adult. The TT addressees are the TL children aged 10 and over and their parents (or other adults).
- **The time and place of text reception**: The ST was published in the UK in 1998; the TTs were to appear in Dutch, French, Italian and Spanish over the period 2000–01. The time difference is, therefore, of little importance.
- **The medium**: The ST is a printed paperback book of forty-eight pages with many photographs and illustrations on each page. The TTs are to follow the same format, i.e. the words of the TL simply replace the SL words but the illustrations remain the same.
- **The motive**: The ST has the purpose of teaching British children the basics of cooking in an entertaining way using tools and ingredients that are readily available. The TT has the purpose of doing the same for the TT children.

The divergences in ST–TT profile therefore amount to the difference between the ST addressees and the TT addressees. However, this is a case not only of a difference in language. Were that the only criterion, then the words on the page could simply be transferred into the TL. There are also important differences of culture, especially regarding customs, experience and presuppositions. These become evident during ST analysis.

ST analysis

As noted in section 5.4 above, any pragmatic-oriented analysis is acceptable as long as it allows comparability between ST and TT. For reasons of space, we do not undertake a detailed analysis here, but shall pick out three elements from Nord's list of intralinguistic factors that are of particular relevance in the analysis of the present ST:

1   non-verbal elements;
2   the register of the lexis;
3   presuppositions.

1   **Non-verbal elements**: The features of medium noted above are crucial for the translation process and product. The illustrations cannot be altered and the length of each TT caption/instruction must not exceed the length of the corresponding ST caption/instruction. Clearly these are severe limitations on the translator.
2   **The register of the lexis**: This is a factor that is difficult for the translator to decide. There are two main relevant factors. One, as noted in the intended text functions, is that we are dealing with a recipe book and, as is well known, recipes are a strictly organized text variety or genre with conventions that vary interlingually. Thus, English tends to use imperative forms ('*cut* the tomatoes', '*add* the onion', etc.) whereas some languages use infinitive forms. The other factor is related to the appellative function and the fact that the addressees are children. The lexis in the ST is consequently slightly simplified and rather more interpersonal than in most cookery books. For example, the warning 'Take care that you don't touch anything hot' is unlikely to be given to an adult, while the caption 'Bring the milk to the boil, then turn the heat down low so that it is bubbling very gently' uses the explicitation *bubbling very gently* instead of the more complex and condensed word *simmer*.

The translator must aim to produce a similarly simplified TT that fulfils the same appellative function (as well as the informative function). Depending on the language, this may even mean going against the conventions of the recipe and not using infinitive forms, since they tend to distance the addressee.
3   **Presuppositions**: The real problem for the translator of this text results from the divergence in cultural background between the TT and ST addressees. This becomes evident in analyzing the presuppositions implicit in the ST. A few examples are given in box 5.1.

Box 5.1

> **The selection of dishes**: *Vegetable stir fry, prawn and pepper pilaff, fudgey fruit crumble* and others may not exist in the TT culture. The presupposition in the ST is that the child will have seen these dishes, perhaps made by an adult, and understand what the final product is to look like. In target cultures where these dishes are unknown, the children and the adults may be unsure whether the recipe is turning out correctly. Changing the names of some of the recipes (for example to *Chinese vegetables, exotic rice* and *hot fruit dessert*) may make them more accessible to the TT receivers, although not necessarily easier to cook.
>
> **Ingredients**: Some ingredients, such as fresh ginger, pitta bread, ovenbake chips and mini-croutons are very difficult to obtain in some countries. This means that either the whole recipe would be impossible to make, or the preparation of it would be different. In the TT some of these ingredients can be altered to ones that are more readily available in the target culture.
>
> **Cooking utensils**: Utensils such as kettles, garlic presses and potato mashers are not used in all cultures. In a recipe for creamy fish pie (p. 12), a drawing of a potato masher is followed by the caption: 'Crush the potato by pressing a potato masher down, again and again, on the chunks. Do it until there are no lumps left.'
>
> The translator has to find a translation for *potato masher* that matches the picture, the recipe instructions and the caption space. The Dutch and Italian translations give a single word: *puree-stamper* and *schiacciapatate* respectively. However, in the French and Spanish TTs, the translators tried to overcome the problem that potato-mashers do not exist in their cultures by suggesting a different utensil, in each case orienting the translation towards the target culture. The French caption tells the reader to crush the potatoes (*écrase-les*) or to use a blender (*passe-les à la moulinette*); in the Spanish, a fork is suggested or 'an instrument like the one in the picture' (*con un tenedor o con un utensilio como el de la ilustración*). Both translations are functionally adequate because they describe the picture, fit into the caption space and enable the TT readers to produce the mashed potatoes.

Discussion of case study

The kind of approach followed in the case study allows important elements of the translation process to be identified. Nord's model focuses more on the ST than do other functionalists. This focus enables individual, and groups of, problematic features to be identified. However, as we saw in chapter 4, it would be wrong to think that all phenomena can be categorized easily. In the case of the recipe book, it is the difference in culture and experience of the ST and TT addressees which requires most attention. While functional theories may assist in translating *potato masher*, the link between culture and language is far more complex. The following chapter begins to explore this, and the concept of discourse, in more depth.

Summary

Functionalist and communicative translation theories advanced in Germany in the 1970s and 1980s moved translation from a static linguistic phenomenon to being considered as an act of intercultural communication. Reiss's initial work links language function, text type, genre and translation strategy. Reiss's approach was later coupled to Vermeer's highly influential skopos theory, where the translation strategy is decided by the function of the TT in the target culture. The skopos theory is part of the model of translational action also proposed by Holz-Mänttäri, who places professional commercial translation within a sociocultural context, using the jargon of business and management. Translation is viewed as a communicative transaction involving initiator, commissioner, and the producers, users and receivers of the ST and TT. In this model, the ST is 'dethroned' and the translation is judged not by equivalence of meaning but by its adequacy to the functional goal of the TT situation as defined by the commission. Nord's model, designed for training translators, retains the functional context but includes a more detailed text-analysis model for the ST.

Further reading

The theoretical works discussed in this chapter are all detailed and complex. Readers are strongly recommended to follow up the summaries given here by turning to the original works themselves in order to see these theories in full. Reiss (1971) also appears in English (2000); Nord's two major books (1991 and 1997) are also readily available and provide a solid grounding in the ideas of the functionalists. Baker (ed.) (1997a) includes fine short summaries of translational action, functional approaches and skopos theory (written by Schäffner and Mason), with suggestions for further reading.

Discussion and research points

1   Look at translations that you yourself have done (either in a language class or in professional translation situations). How would you fit them in to Katharina Reiss's text typology? Are there any texts that do not easily fit in?
2   The question of the translation of metaphors in business texts was discussed in section 5.1.1. Look at a variety of text types in your own language pairs to see how metaphors are used. How would you translate them? Does the translation vary according to text type? Are other factors involved?
3   Imagine a situation in which you are working as a freelance translator. You contact a translation agency inquiring for work and are offered a 20,000 word translation from German into your first language. It is a user manual for a lawnmower. You are asked to do a sample translation of 500 words to prove your suitability for the task. How far would the models considered in this chapter assist you? Are they sufficient to analyze the roles that are being played and the decisions the translator needs to make?
4   In the theory of translational action, the translator is considered to be the expert of

intercultural transfer, although not always a trained expert in the subject-specific area of the TT. How far do you agree with this assessment and what does it imply for the role of the translator in modern-day communications?

5   According to skopos theory, a translation commission must give details of the purpose and function of the TT in order for adequate translational action to take place. Try to find examples of translation skopoi to see how detailed they are and to see what this reveals about the translation initiator. For instance, what kind of translation skopos is explicitly and implicitly stated in university examination papers? If you have access to professional translators, investigate how they are informed of and negotiate the skopos of a specific text.

6   The main assessment criterion in skopos theory is functional adequacy (rather than equivalence). Follow up this concept in Reiss and Vermeer (1984: 124–70) and Nord (1997: 34–7) and consider how 'adequacy' is to be judged, and by whom.

7   Read up the detailed description of Nord's ST analysis model (Nord 1991). Do you consider that it works for all texts? Try applying it to other STs: how practical does it seem to be for translator training?

6 Discourse and register analysis approaches

Key concepts

- The 1970s–1990s saw the growth of discourse analysis in applied linguistics. Building on Halliday's systemic functional grammar, it has come to be used in translation analysis.
- House's model for the assessment of translation quality is based on Hallidayan-influenced register analysis.
- Baker's influential coursebook presents discourse and pragmatic analysis for practising translators.
- Hatim and Mason add pragmatic and semiotic levels to register analysis.

Key texts

Baker, M. (1992) *In Other Words: A Coursebook on Translation*, London and New York: Routledge.

Blum-Kulka, S. (1986/2000) 'Shifts of cohesion and coherence in translation', in L. Venuti (ed.) (2000), pp. 298–313.

Fawcett, P. (1997) *Translation and Language: Linguistic Approaches Explained*, Manchester: St Jerome, chapters 7–11.

Hatim, B. and I. Mason (1990) *Discourse and the Translator*, London and New York: Longman.

Hatim, B. and I. Mason (1997) *The Translator as Communicator*, London and New York: Routledge.

House, J. (1997) *Translation Quality Assessment: A Model Revisited*, Tübingen: Niemeyer.

6.0 Introduction

In the 1990s discourse analysis came to prominence in translation studies. There is a link with the text analysis model of Christiane Nord examined in the last chapter in that the organization of the text above sentence level is investigated. However, while text analysis normally concentrates on describing the way in which texts are organized (sentence structure, cohesion, etc.), discourse analysis looks at the way language communicates meaning and social and power relations. The model of discourse analysis that has had the greatest influence is Halliday's systemic functional model, which is described in section 6.1. In the following sections we look at several key works on translation that have employed his model: Juliane House's (1997) *Translation Quality Assessment: A Model Revisited* (section 6.2); Mona Baker's (1992) *In Other Words* (section 6.3); and two works by Basil Hatim and Ian Mason: *Discourse and the Translator* (1990) and *The Translator as Communicator* (1997) (section 6.4). Hatim and Mason go beyond register analysis to consider the pragmatic and semiotic dimensions of translation and the sociolinguistic and semiotic implications of discourses and discourse communities.

6.1 The Hallidayan model of language and discourse

Halliday's model of discourse analysis, based on what he terms **systemic functional grammar**, is geared to the study of language as communication, seeing meaning in the writer's linguistic choices and systematically relating these choices to a wider sociocultural framework.[1] It borrows Bühler's tripartite division of language functions which we discussed in chapter 5. In Halliday's model, there is a strong interrelation between the surface-level realizations of the linguistic functions and the sociocultural framework (for a clear explanation of these, see Eggins 1994). This can be seen in figure 6.1. The arrows in the figure indicate the direction of influence. Thus, the **genre** (the conventional text type that is associated with a specific communicative

Figure 6.1
Relation of genre and register to language

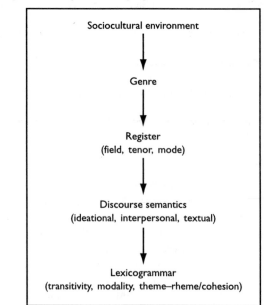

function, for example a business letter) is conditioned by the sociocultural environment and itself determines other elements in the systemic framework. The first of these is **register**, which comprises three variable elements:

1   **field**: what is being written about, e.g. a delivery;
2   **tenor**: who is communicating and to whom, e.g. a sales representative to a customer;
3   **mode**: the form of communication, e.g. written.

Each of the variables of register is associated with a strand of meaning. These strands, which together form the **discourse semantics** of a text, are the three **metafunctions: ideational, interpersonal** and **textual**. The metafunctions are constructed or realized by the **lexicogrammar**, that is the choices of wording and syntactic structure. The links are broadly as follows (see Eggins 1994: 78):

- The **field** of a text is associated with **ideational** meaning, which is realized through **transitivity** patterns (verb types, active/passive structures, participants in the process, etc.).
- The **tenor** of a text is associated with **interpersonal** meaning, which is realized through the patterns of **modality** (modal verbs and adverbs such as *hopefully, should, possibly,* and any evaluative lexis such as *beautiful, dreadful*).
- The **mode** of a text is associated with **textual** meaning, which is realized through the **thematic and information structures** (mainly the order and structuring of elements in a clause) and **cohesion** (the way the text hangs together lexically, including the use of pronouns, ellipsis, collocation, repetition, etc.).

Analysis of the metafunctions has prime place in this model. The close links between the lexicogrammatical patterns and the metafunctions mean that the analysis of patterns of transitivity, modality, thematic structure and cohesion in a text reveals how the metafunctions are working and how the text 'means' (Eggins 1994: 84). For instance, passages from novels by Ernest Hemingway have often been subjected to a transitivity analysis: Fowler (1996: 227–32) analyzes an extract from Hemingway's *Big Two-Hearted River* and finds that the dominant transitivity structure is composed of transitive material processes which emphasize the active character of the protagonist, Nick.

However, Halliday's grammar is extremely complex, and that is why, in common with the works described in the following sections, the present study has chosen to select and simplify those elements which are of particular relevance for translation. In the case of the first model, Juliane House's, the central concept is register analysis.

6.2 House's model of translation quality assessment

Although there are some similarities between, on the one hand, the categories and text analysis of House's model and, on the other hand, the functional analyzes we discussed in the previous chapter, there are key developments. House herself rejects the 'more target-audience oriented notion of translation appropriateness' as 'fundamentally misguided' and for this reason bases her model on comparative ST–TT analysis leading to the assessment of the quality of the translation, highlighting 'mismatches' or 'errors'. House's original model (1977) attracted criticisms that she tackles in her later revision (1997: 101–4). Some of these criticisms echo discussions from the previous two chapters; these concern the nature, complexity and terminology of the analytical categories used, and the absence of poetic–aesthetic texts in House's case studies.

In this section, we concentrate on House's later, 'revisited' model (1997), which incorporates some of her earlier categories into an openly Hallidayan register analysis of field, tenor and mode. The model involves a systematic comparison of the textual 'profile' of the ST and TT (1997: 43). The schema for this comparison is shown in figure 6.2. The comparative model draws on various and sometimes complex taxonomies, but this can be reduced to a register analysis of both ST and TT according to their realization through **lexical**, **syntactic** and **textual** means. **Textual means** refers (1997: 44–5) to:

Figure 6.2

Scheme for analyzing and comparing original and translation texts (House 1997: 108)

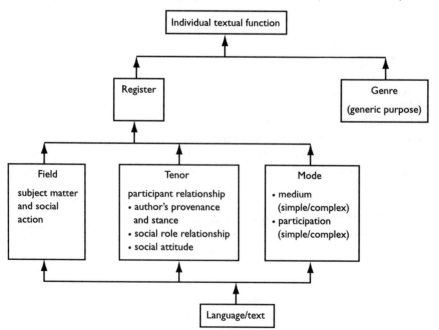

1 **theme-dynamics**: thematic structure and cohesion;
2 **clausal linkage**: additive (*and, in addition*), adversative (*but, however*), etc.;
3 **iconic linkage**: parallelism of structures.

In House's model, as is suggested in figure 6.2, **register** covers a variety of elements, some of which are additional to those expressly stated by Halliday. **Field** refers to the subject matter and social action and covers the specificity of lexical items. **Tenor** includes 'the addresser's temporal, geographical and social provenance as well as his [or her] intellectual, emotional or affective stance (his [or her] "personal viewpoint")' (p. 109). 'Social attitude' refers to formal, consultative or informal style. There is an element of **individuality** to this, as there is to stance. Finally, **mode** relates to 'channel' (spoken/written, etc.) and the degree of participation between addresser and addressee (monologue, dialogue, etc.; p. 109).

House's model operates as follows:

1 A profile is produced of the ST register.
2 To this is added a description of the ST genre realized by the register (pp. 105–7).
3 Together, this allows a 'statement of function' to be made for the ST, including the ideational and interpersonal component of that function (in other words, what information is being conveyed and what the relationship is between sender and receiver).
4 The same descriptive process is then carried out for the TT.
5 The TT profile is compared to the ST profile and a statement of 'mismatches' or errors is produced, categorized according to genre and to the situational dimensions of register and genre; these dimensional errors are referred to as 'covertly erroneous errors' (p. 45), to distinguish them from 'overtly erroneous errors', which are denotative mismatches or target system errors.
6 A 'statement of quality' is then made of the translation.
7 Finally, the translation can be categorized into one of two types: overt translation or covert translation.

An **overt translation** is a TT that does not purport to be an original. In House's rather confusing definition (1997: 66), 'an overt translation is one in which the addressees of the translation text are quite "overtly" not being directly addressed'. Such is the case with the translation after the event of a Second World War political speech by Winston Churchill, which is tied to a particular source culture, time and historical context, and with the translation of works of literature, which are tied to their source culture. With such translations, House believes (p. 112) that equivalence has to be sought at the level of language/text, register and genre. The individual text function cannot, however, be the same for TT and ST since the discourse worlds in which they operate are different. For this reason, House suggests a 'second-level functional equivalence' should be sought, with the TT enabling access to the function of the ST, allowing the TT receivers to 'eavesdrop' on the ST. For example, British readers of Thomas Mann can use an English TT of *The Magic Mountain* to gain access to the ST *Die Zauberberg*, but they know they are reading a translation and the individual function of the two texts cannot be the same.

A **covert translation** is a translation which enjoys the status of an original source text in the target culture' (p. 69). The ST is not linked particularly to the ST culture or audience; both ST and TT address their respective receivers directly. Examples given by House are a tourist information book-let, a letter from a company chairman to the shareholders and an article in the *Unesco Courier*. The function of a covert translation is 'to recreate, reproduce or represent in the translated text the function the original has in its linguacultural framework and discourse world' (p. 114). It does this with-out taking the TT reader into the discourse world of the ST. Hence, equiva-lence is necessary at the level of genre and the individual text function, but what House (p. 114) calls a 'cultural filter' needs to be applied by the transla-tor, modifying cultural elements and thus giving the impression that the TT is an original. This may involve changes at the levels of language/text and register. House (pp. 115–17) discusses the meaning of cultural filter in the context of German–English comparative pragmatic studies which she has conducted and gives examples of different practices in the two cultures that need to be reflected in translation. For instance, she finds that German tends to prefer a more direct content focus, whereas English is more interpersonal. This would need to be reflected in covert translation, the letter from the company chairman being more interpersonal in English, for instance.

House is at pains to point out the fact that the 'overt'–'covert' translation distinction is a cline rather than a pair of binary opposites. Furthermore, in cases where covertly functional equivalence is desired but where the ST genre does not exist in the target culture, the aim should be to produce a covert *version* rather than a covert *translation*. Version is also the term used to describe apparently unforced changes in genre (p. 161).

House applies the model to a number of texts, including (pp. 147–57) an extract from a polemical history text about civilian Germans' involvement in the holocaust (ST English, TT German). A pattern of differences is identified in the dimensions of field and tenor. In field, the repetition of the word *German* in the ST, which serves to highlight German civilian responsibility in the events, is less frequent in the TT. In tenor, there is a reduction in intensi-fiers, superlatives and other emotive lexis. This makes the author's stance less obvious in the TT, and House even suggests (p. 155) that it has an effect on the realization of genre. Whereas the ST is a controversial popular history book (albeit based on the author's doctoral thesis), the TT is a more formal academic treatise. House goes on to posit possible reasons for these changes, notably pressure from the German publishers for political and marketing reasons. The linking of the linguistic analysis to real-world translation conditions is a move that owes something to the theory of translational action which was discussed in chapter 5.

6.3 Baker's text and pragmatic level analysis: a coursebook for translators

House's 1977 book was perhaps the first major translation studies work to use Halliday's now popular model. Another that in recent years has had considerable influence on translation training and consequently on translation studies is Mona Baker's *In Other Words: A Coursebook on Translation* (1992). Baker looks at equivalence at a series of levels: at word, above-word, grammar, thematic structure, cohesion and pragmatic levels. Of particular interest in the present chapter is her application of the systemic approach to thematic structure and cohesion and the incorporation of the pragmatic level, 'the way utterances are used in communicative situations' (Baker 1992: 217).

6.3.1 Thematic and information structures

Baker is typical of many translation scholars who make detailed use of the terminology of functional grammar and discourse analysis in that she devotes by far the most attention to the textual function. Explicit analysis of the ideational and interpersonal functions are few, although Baker does incorporate a comparison of nominalization and verbal forms in theme position in a scientific report in Brazilian Portuguese and English (Baker 1992: 169–71). Thus, for example, the ST begins with a pronominal verbal form (my emphasis):

> *Analisou-se* as relações da dopamina cerebral com as funções motoras.
> [Analysed-were the relations of dopamine with the motor functions.]

The published English translation below presents a normalized word order with the passive verbal form in final position (my emphasis):

> The relations between dopamine and motor functions *were analyzed*.

However, Baker recommends a different thematic structure in order to meet the genre conventions of English abstracts. This involves the use of the nominalized form *analysis*, which is retained in thematic position (my emphasis), and the addition of a different passive verbal form (*is carried out*):

> An *analysis* is carried out of the relations between dopamine and motor functions.

An inherent problem in this kind of study is that thematic structure is realized differently in different languages. Baker gives a number of examples from languages such as Portuguese, Spanish and Arabic. These are verb-inflected languages which often place the verb in first or 'theme' position, as in the Brazilian Portuguese example above. The consequent omission of the subject pronoun also inevitably creates a different thematic pattern. Thus, the following sentence from a speech to the European Parliament (see discussion point 3 at the end of this chapter) produces a different thematic structure in different languages. The structure of the English ST is:

I | discussed this matter in Washington.
theme | rheme.

while thematic analysis of the Portuguese version gives:

Discuti | este assunto em Washington.
theme | rheme.

Using Hallidayan analysis, the inflected verb form *discuti* is thematic rather than a subject pronoun, whereas in the English the verb *discussed* is part of the rheme.

The fact that the Hallidayan model of thematic analysis is English-oriented must cast some doubt on its validity for translation. Baker (pp. 160–7) accepts this, and also outlines the alternative **functional sentence perspective** model of thematic structure, which, because it takes into account 'communicative dynamism' as well as word order, may be more suitable for languages with a frequent VS order.[2] Despite this, Baker (p. 140) concludes that an important advantage of the systemic functional approach is that it is much more straightforward to implement: theme is in first position, come what may.

The most important point for ST thematic analysis is that the translator should be aware of the **relative markedness** of the thematic and information structures. Baker points out (p. 129) that this 'can help to heighten our awareness of meaningful choices made by speakers and writers in the course of communication' and, therefore, help decide whether it is appropriate to translate using a marked form. Again, what is marked varies across languages. Problems in copying the ST pattern into the TT are given by Vázquez-Ayora (1977: 217) and Gerzymisch-Arbogast (1986). The former emphasizes that calquing a rigid English word order when translating into a VS language such as Spanish would produce a monotonous translation. The latter, in her detailed study of German and English (Gerzymisch-Arbogast 1986), considers the German calquing of English cleft sentences (e.g. *What pleases the public is . . .* , *What I meant to say was . . .*) to be clumsy. This illustrates the dilemma, pointed out by Enkvist (1978), of balancing concern for information dynamics with the sometimes incompatible concern for other areas such as basic syntactic patterns.

That it is the textual function, and most especially the thematic structure, which has most frequently been discussed in works on translation theory is perhaps because of the attention paid to this function by influential monolingual works in text linguistics, notably Enkvist (1978) and Beaugrande and Dressler (1981), who have exerted considerable influence on translation theorists. Cohesion, the other element of the textual metafunction, has also been the subject of a number of studies.

6.3.2 Cohesion

Blum-Kulka's well-known study 'Shifts of cohesion and coherence in translation' hypothesizes that increased explicitation of cohesive ties may be a general strategy adopted by all translators. She shows how changes in cohesion in translation may bring about functional shifts in texts, giving the example of a Hebrew translation of a scene from Pinter's *Old Times* (Blum-Kulka 1986/2000: 302–3). Inevitably, because of the inflection of the adjectives, the Hebrew TT has to make explicit the gender referent of the enigmatic opening ST statement, 'Fat or thin?' Hebrew and other languages would need to state whether the character referred to was a man or woman. Similarly, literary translations from verb-inflected languages into English need to make explicit what are sometimes deliberately ambiguous grammatical subjects. The first line of Julio Cortázar's classic novel *Rayuela* begins with the question '¿Encontraría a la Maga?' In English this could be 'Would I/he/she/you find the (female) Magus?'

As with the thematic structure, it is in many ways the density and progression of cohesive ties throughout a text that are important. This web of relationships may have to differ between ST and TT, since the networks of lexical cohesion will not be identical across languages (Baker 1992: 206). As an illustration, Baker (pp. 185–6) puts forward the idea, backed by short extracts and their translations, that Portuguese prefers lexical repetition to pronoun use and (p. 207) that Arabic prefers lexical repetition to variation. The TT must also be coherent, in other words it must hang together logically in the mind of the TT receiver. This has to do with pragmatics, the subject of the last of Baker's chapters.

6.3.3 Pragmatics and translation

Baker considers various aspects of pragmatic equivalence in translation, applying relevant linguistic concepts to interlinguistic transfer. Baker's definition of **pragmatics** is as follows:

> Pragmatics is the study of language in use. It is the study of meaning, not as generated by the linguistics system but as conveyed and manipulated by participants in a communicative situation.
>
> (Baker 1992: 217)

In this section, we briefly consider three major pragmatic concepts: **coherence, presupposition** and **implicature**.

The **coherence** of a text, related to cohesion, 'depends on the hearer's or receiver's expectations and experience of the world' (Baker 1992: 219). Clearly this may not be the same for the ST and TT reader. Baker gives the example (p. 220) of a passage about the London department store Harrods. In order to make sense of the passage, the reader needs to know that *the flagship Harrods* and the description *the splendid Knightsbridge store* are synonyms. TT readers in other cultures may not know this. The Arabic translation therefore makes the link explicit with the addition to the name of a gloss incorporating the repetition of the word *store* (*the main store Harrods*).

The area of **presupposition** is closely related to coherence. It is defined by Baker (p. 259) as 'pragmatic inference', although, perhaps surprisingly, she only discusses it briefly. Presupposition relates to the linguistic and extra-linguistic knowledge the sender assumes the receiver to have or which are necessary in order to retrieve the sender's message. Thus, in the European Parliament in 1999, Commissioner Sir Leon Brittan's phrase *let me now turn to bananas* would presuppose that the receiver knows about the trade dispute between the European Union and the United States over banana imports, or at least can access this information from the linguistic and extralinguistic contexts. This is not unlikely for the immediate receivers, since they are Members of the European Parliament and are aware of the issue. Similarly, the phrase *I discussed this issue in Washington* presupposes knowledge that Washington in this context refers to the seat of government of the United States and the venue for Brittan's talks. The problem for the translator occurs, of course, when the TT receivers cannot be assumed to possess the same background knowledge as the ST receivers, either because of cultural differences and/or because the text is being translated after a time gap when the original information is no longer activated by the reference.[3]

More emphasis is placed on presupposition by Fawcett (1997: 123–34), whose chapter on the subject contains many perceptive and interesting examples; typical (p. 124) is the metaphorical use of the place name *Mohács* in a Hungarian text. The name would mean little to most receivers in other cultures, so a translator would need to replace it with an explicitation such as *crushing defeat*.

Baker gives more attention to **implicature**, another form of pragmatic inference, which she defines (p. 223) as 'what the speaker means or implies rather than what s/he says'. The concept of implicature was developed by Paul Grice (1975), who described a set of 'rules' or 'maxims' that operate in normal co-operative conversation; these are:

1   **Quantity**: Give the amount of information that is necessary; do not give too much or too little.
2   **Quality**: Say only which you know to be true or what you can support.
3   **Relevance**: What you say should be relevant to the conversation.
4   **Manner**: Say what you need to say in a way that is appropriate to the message you wish to convey and which (normally) will be understood by the receiver.

In addition, some theorists add the maxim of **politeness**: Be polite in your comments (see Brown and Levinson 1987).

Participants in conversations assume the person to whom they are speaking is (subconsciously) following these maxims and they themselves co-operate by trying to make sense of what is being said. In turn, they also tend to be co-operative in what they say and the way they say it. Clearly, the linguistic and cultural contexts are also crucial in limiting the range of implicatures.

The maxims may also be deliberately flouted, sometimes for a humorous effect. Such a flouting of the relevance maxim might have occurred, for instance, had Sir Leon Brittan, above, begun to discuss the value of eating bananas for breakfast. Particular problems are posed for the translator when the TL works by different maxims. An example given by Baker (p. 235) is the translation from English to Arabic of a book on Arab political humour, where a vulgar joke about God is omitted in the Arabic TT so as not to upset local sensibilities. This shows a difference in the operation of the maxims of manner and politeness in the two cultures. This is also the case in an example (Gibney and Loveday, quoted in Baker 1992: 233–4) that occurred during negotiations between the USA and Japan in 1970. The Japanese Premier replies to American concerns on textile exports by saying *zensho shimasu* ('I'll handle it as well as I can'). This is understood by the US President as a literal promise to sort out a problem (i.e. it obeys the US-cultural quality and relevance maxims), whereas the Japanese phrase is really a polite formula for ending the conversation (i.e. it obeys the Japanese-cultural maxim of politeness). This clearly shows, as Baker notes (p. 236), that translators need to be fully aware of the different co-operative principles in operation in the respective languages and cultures.

6.4 Hatim and Mason: the semiotic level of context and discourse

Two other works that develop out of the Hallidayan model of language were especially influential for translation studies in the 1990s: Basil Hatim and Ian Mason's *Discourse and the Translator* (1990) and *The Translator as Communicator* (1997). Both authors are based at the Centre for Translation and Interpreting Studies at Heriot-Watt University, Edinburgh. They pay extra attention to the realization in translation of ideational and interpersonal functions (rather than just the textual function) and incorporate into their model a semiotic level of discourse.

An example of Hatim and Mason's analysis of functions is their examination (1997: 7–10) of a key passage from Albert Camus' novel *L'étranger* in which the main character, Meursault, kills an Arab on the beach. Changes in the **transitivity structure** in the English translation are seen to cause a shift in the **ideational function** of the text. The passage in the French ST contains eight material process verbs, of which four are intention action processes. These are: '*j'ai crispé* ma main', '*j'ai touché* le ventre poli de la crosse', '*j'ai tiré*', '*je frappais* sur la porte du malheur' [lit. '*I clenched* my hand', '*I touched* the polished belly of the butt', '*I fired*' and '*I was striking* on the door of misfortune']. In translation, these become 'my grip *closed*', 'the smooth underbelly of the butt *jogged* in my palm', '*I fired*' and 'another loud, fateful *rap* on the door of my undoing' (all my emphasis). In other words, the translations become three event processes and only one real action process (*I fired*). Hatim and Mason's conclusion (p. 10) is that the pattern of shifts in the TT has made Meursault more passive than in the ST, although they also make the point that the reason for these shifts may be the translator's overall reading of the novel, in which Meursault's passivity is a key feature of his character.

Hatim and Mason also consider shifts in **modality** (the **interpersonal** function) with an example (pp. 73–6) of trainee interpreters' problems with the recognition and translation of a French conditional of allegation or rumour in a European Parliament debate. The phrase in question – 'un plan de restructuration qui *aurait* été préparé par les administrateurs judiciaires' – calls for an indication of modality of possibility in English, such as 'a rescue plan which was *probably* prepared by the receivers' or 'a rescue plan which *it is rumoured* was prepared by the receivers'. The majority of the trainee interpreters in Hatim and Mason's sample incorrectly rendered the phrase by a factual statement such as '*had been* prepared', giving the wrong message in the TT.

Hatim and Mason's 'foundations of a model for analyzing texts' (1997: 14–35) incorporate and go beyond House's register analysis and Baker's pragmatic analysis. They combine the kind of bottom–up analysis discussed in the Camus example with some top–down consideration of the semiotic level of the text.[4] Language and texts are considered to be realizations of sociocultural messages and power relations. They represent **discourse** in its wider sense, defined as:

> modes of speaking and writing which involve social groups in adopting a particular attitude towards areas of sociocultural activity (e.g. racist discourse, bureaucratese, etc.).
>
> (Hatim and Mason 1997: 216)

One example they give of the influence of the translator's discourse is the English TT of a Spanish ST about the history of the indigenous American peoples before the arrival of the Spaniards in Mexico. Hatim and Mason show (pp. 153–9) how lexical choices such as *pre-Colombian* and *Indian* in the TT impose a Eurocentric view on an ST that had been written from an indigenous perspective. The European translator is imposing a pro-Western ideology and discourse on the recounting of the history of the Americas.

A semiotic function is also performed by idiolect and dialect. Hatim and Mason (pp. 97–110) consider idiolect within the analysis of tenor and register, examining the Cockney dialect of characters in George Bernard Shaw's play *Pygmalion*. The syntactic, lexical and phonetic features of the dialect are recognized by a British audience and associated with the way of speaking and the values of the uneducated London characters in the play. The systematic recurrence of this purposely functional feature of the speech of certain characters is identified by Hatim and Mason (p. 103) as 'a noteworthy object of the translator's attention'. The peculiarities and connotations of the dialect are unlikely to be replicated easily in any TT culture. Furthermore, literary genre conventions may intervene. A translator into Arabic, for example, might be encouraged to adopt a formal classical style throughout since that is the only style felt to be appropriate for literature in Arab cultures (p. 99).

Although Hatim and Mason propose foundations for a model of analyzing texts, they deal with a large number of concepts. It is not clear that their approach constitutes a model that can be 'applied' in the conventional sense of the term. Alternatively, the authors' proposals can be taken as a list of elements to be considered when examining translation. In particular, they concentrate (pp. 27–35) on identifying '**dynamic**' and '**stable**' elements in a text. These are presented as a continuum and linked to translation strategy: more 'stable' STs may require a 'fairly literal approach', while, with more dynamic STs, 'the translator is faced with more interesting challenges and literal translation may no longer be an option' (pp. 30–1).

6.5 Criticisms of discourse and register analysis approaches to translation

Discourse analysis models have become extremely popular among many linguistics-oriented translation theorists and serve as a useful way of tackling the linguistic structure and meaning of a text. However, the Hallidayan model has been attacked by, amongst others, Fish (1981: 59–64) for being over-complicated in its categorization of grammar and for its apparently inflexible one-to-one matching of structure and meaning. This may cause it to struggle to cope with the variety of possible interpretations of literature, especially experimental literature. Some applications to literature (e.g. Fowler 1986/96 and Simpson 1993) have therefore adopted a more flexible 'toolkit' approach, employing those elements that appear most useful while also incorporating issues from literary criticism.

As far as House's model is concerned, Gutt (1991: 46–9) raises the question as to whether it is possible to recover authorial intention and ST function from register analysis. Even if it is possible, the basis of House's model is to discover 'mismatches' between ST and TT. Yet, while mismatches may indicate translation errors, they may also be caused by other translation strategies such as explicitation or compensation. It is less clear how House's model can interpret these.

The analytical frameworks of the translation theorists discussed in this chapter are English-language oriented. This becomes problematic with other languages, especially in the analysis of thematic and information structures. European languages with a more flexible word order and subject-inflected verb forms, such as Portuguese and Spanish, need to be analyzed differently.

This type of problem becomes even more serious if attempts are made to impose such contrastive discourse analysis on non-European languages whose conceptual structure may differ crucially.

Linguistic differences are of course indicative of cultural differences, and Venuti (1998: 21) is one critic who sees linguistics-oriented approaches as projecting 'a conservative model of translation that would unduly restrict [translation's] role in cultural innovation and change'. As an example, Venuti discusses Grice's maxims (see section 6.3.3 above) and criticizes them for the way in which they support the fluent and 'domesticating' translation strategy that they support. Venuti considers the maxims suitable only for translation in closely defined fields, such as technical or legal documents. Baker herself is aware of the cultural bias of the maxims:

> Grice's maxims seem to reflect directly notions which are known to be valued in the English-speaking world, for instance sincerity, brevity, and relevance.
>
> (Baker 1992: 237)

It is Hatim and Mason who make a greater effort to incorporate a Hallidayan notion of culture and ideology into their analysis of translation, and they devote a chapter to ideology in *The Translator as Communicator* (Hatim and Mason 1997: 143–63). Their findings are illuminating, but, although they analyze a range of text types (written and spoken), their focus often remains linguistics-centred, both in its terminology and in the phenomena investigated ('lexical choice', 'cohesion', transitivity', 'style shifting', 'translator mediation', etc.). The case studies below follow this line by using the discourse analysis approaches presented in this chapter to examine two different films.

Case studies

Case study 1

This case study examines Werner Herzog's German film *The Enigma of Kaspar Hauser* (1974).[5] The film begins with a written introduction that scrolls down the screen (box 6.1). A possible back-translation in English is given in box 6.2. The actual English translation, which appeared two lines at a time, occupies the bottom of the screen; this is given in box 6.3.

House's model of quality assessment would show that, for ST and TT, the **field** is similar: both relate the story of a poor boy found in the town of N. Nevertheless, there are mismatches in the amount of information that is given: in the English, we are not told the boy's name, that he learnt to speak, that food used to be shoved into the cellar while he slept, nor, precisely, that 'the enigma of his origin' remains unsolved.

There is a similar story as far as **mode** is concerned: in both cases the text is written to be read, but the mode of presentation is different. The English is superimposed over part of the German, two lines at a time. To accommodate

Box 6.1

1	Am Pflugstsonntag des Jahres 1828 wurde in der Stadt N. ein verwahrloster Findling aufgegriffen, den man später Kaspar Hauser nannte.
2	Er konnte kaum gehen und sprach nur einen einzigen Satz.
3	Später, als er sprechen lernte, berichtete er, er sei zeit seines Lebens in einem dunklen Kellerloch eingesperrt gewesen, er habe keinerlei Begriff von der Welt gehabt und nicht gewußt, daß es außer ihm noch andere Menschen gäbe, weil man ihm das Essen hereinschob, während er schlief.
4	Er habe nicht gewußt, was ein Haus, ein Baum, was Sprache sei.
5	Erst ganz zuletzt sei ein Mann zu ihm heriengekommen.
6	Das Rätsel seiner Herkunft ist bis heute nicht gelöst.

Box 6.2

1	On Whit Sunday in the year 1828 in the town of N. a ragged foundling was picked up who was later called Kasper Hauser.
2	He could scarcely walk and spoke only one sentence.
3	Later, when he learnt to speak, he reported he had been locked up for his whole life in a dark cellar, he had not had any contact at all with the world and had not known that outside there were other people, because he had food slung in to him, while he slept.
4	He did not know what a house, a tree, what language was.
5	Only right at the end did a man visit him.
6	The enigma of his origin has to this day not been solved.

Box 6.3

1	One Sunday in 1828 a ragged boy was found abandoned in the town of N.
2	He could hardly walk and spoke but one sentence.
3	Later he told of being locked in a dark cellar from birth.
4	He had never seen another human being, a tree, a house before.
5	To this day no one knows where he came from – or who set him free.

this crucial visual constraint, the sentences have been shortened. Sentence 3 in the German contains a complex of reported-speech subordinate clauses, and its length gives a sense of formality befitting the early nineteenth century subject matter and speech patterns of the film. This sentence is mostly omitted in the TT. The English sentences are therefore less varied syntactically, although the thematic profile of the German sentences 1, 3 and 5, where a time adjunct or adverbial is in first position, is effectively mirrored in the English. Some higher-level cohesion is also lost in the immediate translation: the omission of the name *Kaspar Hauser* is unlikely to be crucial, since one would imagine that the TT reader would be able to retrieve it easily from the title of the film or the early scenes. Also, the use of *Rätsel* ('enigma') in German sentence 6 is lost in the translation; however, the word *enigma* appears in the English title of the film. TT sentence 5 is, moreover, far more informal.

There are mismatches of **tenor** arising from the non-translation of the German subjunctive in the reported speech after *berichtete er* ('he told of . . .'). The German *sei, habe, gäbe* and so on are either omitted or translated by a declarative sentence ('He had never seen another human being'). On the other hand, there are stronger interpersonal features in the final sentence in the English TT, with the two interrogatives (*where* and *who*) and the negative *no one*. Yet, from another perspective, this might be an example on the part of the translator of the well-known strategy of compensation, with TT sentence 5 adding to the text an element of modality that was provided by the subjunctive in the German. The concept of mismatches does not really allow for compensation.

The result of the analysis points to the TT being what House calls an 'overt' translation. Subtitling is in fact an evident example of overt translation, since at all times during the film the TT reader is reminded visually of the translated words. However, because of the way the short written ST above has been reworked, it may be more correct to say that it is a summary translation or version.

Case study 2

This case study examines the English translation of the award-winning Mathieu Kassovitz French film *La haine* ('Hate') (1995). It is the stark story of three youths living in a poor area of Paris and of the violence and aggression that characterizes and permeates their environment. Their idiolect (or sociolect, as it is mainly a class-based speech) is indicative of the identity they have constructed for themselves: it is aggressive, full of slang and obscenities, and often with little cohesion. This mirrors the poverty of their surroundings and their youth. It is thus a sociolect that has a purposeful semiotic function in the film. Its systematic recurrence amongst all three friends also fulfils the criteria presented by Hatim and Mason (1997: 103) for discourse that requires careful attention in translation.

The extra formality of the written subtitle tends to dictate against the reproduction of very informal speech patterns. Nevertheless, the translators make an effort to reproduce some of the effect of the lexicogrammatical features, including the evaluative nominal forms *pigs* and *bastards* (for *police*) and *dickhead* and *wanker* (for *idiot*). However, there is a tendency for the TT to normalize the grammatical patterns in the TT, which produces increased cohesion and conventional thematic patterns. Thus, the ST *je lui aurais mis une balle . . . BAAAAAAP!* ['I'd have put a bullet in him . . . ZAAAAAAP!'] becomes the formal and grammatically complex 'If Hubert hadn't been there, I'd have shot him'. It is also difficult to imagine English-speaking youths using the polite imperative 'Talk nicely!' for *Tu ne parles pas comme ça!* ['You don't talk like that!'] or such a syntactically correct negative as 'He didn't do anything' (rather than 'He ain't done nothing/nuffin'/nowt').

The dynamic element of language noted by Hatim and Mason has here been overlooked or reduced by the translator. The increased cohesion of the TT and the reduction in some of the evaluative and interpersonal lexical items means that the identity constructed by the ST sociolect is less coherent. Also, the function it plays in binding the three main characters against the outside world is blurred.

Discussion of case studies

These brief cases studies have shown how discourse and register analysis can explain how texts construct meaning. House's model is perhaps designed more for the uncovering of 'errors' in a formal written TT: the analysis of the *Kaspar Hauser* example pointed out many such mismatches but not necessarily the reasons for the reworking. The reasons are likely to do with the unusual on-screen constraints, such as the numbers of words that can fit on the screen, the need to keep the TT words legible when superimposed on the German text, and probably the commission's views on what was acceptable to the TT audience. Investigation into the specific translation commission for this text may uncover some interesting issues.

The brief case study of *La haine* indicates the potential of Hatim and Mason's flexible approach to analysis. An analysis of the lexicogrammar and discourse semantics of the characters' speech can explain the construction of their sociolect. The initial findings concerning the translation of informal grammatical patterns in the film would seem to corroborate Hatim and Mason's comments about the difficulties posed to translators by the dynamic element of communication. The characters' aggressive sociolect clearly reflects their sociocultural environment, yet it undergoes shifts in the TT. However, on many occasions the violence of the speech is communicated in the sound track, even if the TT receiver cannot understand the words. This is indicative of the complex nature of film translation, with its audio and visual input, which a text-based discourse analysis may struggle to explain.

Summary

The discourse and register analysis approaches described in this chapter are based on the model of Hallidayan systemic functional linguistics which links microlevel linguistic choices to the communicative function of a text and the sociocultural meaning behind it. House's (1977, 1997) model of register analysis is designed to compare an ST–TT pair for situational variables, genre, function and language, and to identify both the translation method employed ('covert' or 'overt') and translation 'errors'. It has been criticized for its confusing and 'scientific' jargon; however, it provides a systematic means of uncovering some important considerations for the translator.

Works by both Baker (1992) and Hatim and Mason (1990, 1997) bring together a range of ideas from pragmatics and sociolinguistics that are relevant for translation and translation analysis. Baker's analysis is particularly useful in focusing on the thematic and cohesion structures of a text. Hatim and Mason, also working within the Hallidayan model, move beyond House's register analysis and begin to consider the way social and power relations are negotiated and communicated in translation. This ideological level is further developed in the culturally oriented theories discussed in chapters 8 and 9. First, in chapter 7, we look at other theories that attempt to place translation in its sociocultural context.

Further reading

For a more detailed introduction to the workings of systemic functional linguistics see Eggins (1994) and G. Thompson (1995). Halliday (1994) is the most detailed account, but it is very complex. Leech and Short (1981) is a well-known application of the model for the analysis of literary prose. See also Simpson (1993) for a related model for the analysis of modality, transitivity and narrative point of view. See Halliday and Hasan (1976) for cohesion. See Gutt (1991: 46–9) for criticisms of House's register analysis and Fawcett (1997: 80–4) for a more balanced assessment.

For discourse analysis based on specific languages, see Delisle (1982; for French and English), Taylor (1990; for Italian and English) and Steiner and Ramm (1995; for German and English). Bell's *Translation and Translating* (1991) outlines the systemic functional model clearly but refers little to translation. For analysis of thematic structure from a functional sentence perspective, see Enkvist (1978) and Firbas (1986, 1992).

For pragmatics, see Leech (1983) and Levinson (1983); see also Austin (1962) and Grice (1975). For language as social semiotic, see Halliday (1978).

Discussion and research points

1 'Unlike the scientifically (linguistically) based analysis, the evaluative judgement is ultimately *not* a scientific one, but rather a reflection of a social, political, ethical, moral or personal stance' (House 1997: 116). How far do you agree with this statement and what implications does it have for the evaluation of translations?

2 Carry out a register analysis on an ST–TT pair using House's model. What differences, if any, are there in text function? What 'mismatches' or errors are there? Is it a covert or overt translation? What might be motivating any differences you note? How useful is House's model for understanding the translation process that has produced the TT?

3 The text in box 6.4 is part of a speech by Vice President of the European Commission Sir Leon Brittan to the European Parliament in Strasbourg on 3 May 1999. After following up the relevant recommended reading, carry out a Hallidayan analysis of this text focusing (a) on thematic and information structures and (b) on cohesive patterns.

Box 6.4

> Let me now turn to bananas. The Commission decided last week – with the consent of the Council of Ministers – not to appeal on either the substance of the issue or the so-called systemic question, but we do intend to pursue the latter issue, the systemic issue, in the panel which you brought against Section 301 of the US Trade Act. We also intend to pursue it in the dispute settlement understanding review and if necessary in the next trade round.
>
> On the substance of the issue, our intention now is to change our regime in order to comply with the WTO [World Trade Organization] panel ruling. I believe that everybody has agreed that our objective has to be conformity with the WTO. But this will not be easy. We intend to consult extensively with all the main players with the objective of achieving a system which will not be threatened by further WTO challenges. I discussed this issue in Washington two weeks ago with the US agriculture secretary among others. My meetings were followed by discussions at official level. Subsequently, the Council asked the Commission to put forward proposals for amending the banana regime by the end of May in the light of further contracts with the US and other parties principally concerned.

How useful do you consider such an analysis to be for a translator? One of the criticisms of the Hallidayan model is that it is biased towards English. Try translating the text into your mother tongue or main foreign language. How applicable is the linguistic analysis to your TL?

The official translations of this speech are available on the European Parliament website (http://www2.europarl.eu.int/omk/omnsapir.so/debats). Compare how the translators have dealt with cohesion and thematic structure.

4   'Grice's maxims seem to reflect directly notions which are known to be valued in the English-speaking world, for instance sincerity, brevity, and relevance' (Baker 1992: 237). Consider Grice's maxims with relation to the languages in which you work. What examples can you find of different maxims? How can a translator deal with any differences?

5   Follow up what Baker and Blum-Kulka say about cohesion and coherence. What examples can you find from your own languages to support the assertion that explicitation of cohesive ties is a universal feature of translation? How do translators tend to deal with literary and other texts that are deliberately lacking in conventional cohesion or coherence?

6   Read the cases studies in Hatim and Mason's *The Translator as Communicator*. How far do you agree with Venuti's criticisms (see section 6.5 above) that such linguistics-oriented models are 'conservative'?

7   Case study 2 above is a discussion of *La haine*, in particular the problem of the semiotics of sociolect and the difficulties of translating it. How would or did your own TL deal with the translation of this film? Find examples of other films and novels containing dialects or sociolects. Is there a pattern to the way that they are translated? What does this indicate about the discourse of those involved in the translation process?

7 Systems theories

Key concepts

- Even-Zohar's polysystem theory (1970s) sees translated literature as part of the cultural, literary and historical system of the TL.
- Toury (1995) puts forward a methodology for descriptive translation studies (DTS) as a non-prescriptive means of understanding the 'norms' at work in the translation process and of discovering the general 'laws' of translation.
- In DTS, equivalence is functional–historical and related to the continuum of 'acceptability' and 'adequacy'.
- Other systems approaches include the Manipulation School.

Key texts

Chesterman, A. (1997) *Memes of Translation*, Amsterdam and Philadelphia, PA: John Benjamins, chapter 3.

Even-Zohar, I. (1978/2000) 'The position of translated literature within the literary polysystem', in L. Venuti (ed.) (2000), pp. 192–7.

Gentzler, E. (1993) *Contemporary Translation Theories*, London and New York: Routledge, chapter 5.

Hermans, T. (ed.) (1985a) *The Manipulation of Literature*, Beckenham: Croom Helm.

Hermans, T. (1999) *Translation in Systems*, Manchester: St Jerome, chapters 6 to 8.

Toury, G. (1978/2000) 'The nature and role of norms in literary translation', in L. Venuti (ed.) (2000), pp. 198–211.

Toury, G. (1995) *Descriptive Translation Studies – And Beyond*, Amsterdam and Philadelphia, PA: John Benjamins.

7.0 Introduction

In chapters 5 and 6 we saw how linguistics broadened out from static models in the 1960s to an approach which incorporates first skopos theory and then register and discourse analysis, relating language to its sociocultural function. In the 1970s, another reaction to the static prescriptive models was polysystem theory (see section 7.1), which saw translated literature as a system operating in the larger social, literary and historical systems of the target culture. This was an important move, since translated literature had up to that point mostly been dismissed as a derivative, second-rate form. Polysystem theory fed into developments in descriptive translation studies (see section 7.2), a branch of translation studies that has been crucial in the last twenty years and which aims at identifying norms and laws of translation. Developments in the study of norms are discussed in section 7.3 (work by Chesterman), and work by systems theorists of the related Manipulation School is described in section 7.4.

7.1 Polysystem theory

Polysystem theory was developed in the 1970s by the Israeli scholar Itamar Even-Zohar borrowing ideas from the Russian Formalists of the 1920s, who had worked on literary historiography (see further reading section). A literary work is here not studied in isolation but as part of a literary system, which itself is defined as 'a system of functions of the literary order which are in continual interrelationship with other orders' (Tynjanov 1927/71: 72). Literature is thus part of the social, cultural, literary and historical framework and the key concept is that of the **system**, in which there is an ongoing dynamic of 'mutation' and struggle for the primary position in the literary canon.

Although building on work by the Formalists, Even-Zohar reacts against 'the fallacies of the traditional aesthetic approach' (Even-Zohar 1978: 119), which had focused on 'high' literature and had disregarded as unimportant literary systems or genres such as children's literature, thrillers and the whole system of translated literature. Even-Zohar (p. 118) emphasizes that translated literature operates as a system:

1. in the way the TL selects works for translation;
2. in the way translation norms, behaviour and policies are influenced by other co-systems.

Even-Zohar focuses on the relations between all these systems in the overarching concept to which he gives a new term, the **polysystem**, which is defined by Shuttleworth and Cowie (1997: 176) as follows:

> The polysystem is conceived as a heterogeneous, hierarchized conglomerate (or system) of systems which interact to bring about an ongoing, dynamic process of evolution within the polysystem as a whole.

The hierarchy referred to is the positioning and interaction at a given historical moment of the different strata of the polysystem. If the highest position is occupied by an innovative literary type, then the lower strata are likely to be occupied by increasingly conservative types. On the other hand, if the conservative forms are at the top, innovation and renewal are likely to come from the lower strata. Otherwise a period of stagnation occurs (Even-Zohar 1978: 120). This 'dynamic process of evolution' is vital to the polysystem, indicating that the relations between innovatory and conservative systems are in a constant state of flux and competition. Because of this flux, the position of translated literature is not fixed either. It may occupy a primary or a secondary position in the polysystem. If it is primary, 'it participates actively in shaping the centre of the polysystem' (Even-Zohar 1978/2000: 193). It is likely to be innovatory and linked to major events of literary history as they are taking place. Often, leading writers produce the most important translations and translations are a leading factor in the formation of new models for the target culture, introducing new poetics, techniques and so on. Even-Zohar gives three major cases when translated literature occupies the primary position:

1   when a 'young' literature is being established and looks initially to 'older' literatures for ready-made models;
2   when a literature is 'peripheral' or 'weak' and imports those literary types which it is lacking. This can happen when a smaller nation is dominated by the culture of a larger one. Even-Zohar sees that 'all sorts of peripheral literature may in such cases consist of translated literature' (p. 194). This happens at various levels. For instance, in modern Spain smaller regions such as Galicia import many translations from the dominant Spanish form Castilian, while Spain itself imports canonized and non-canonized literature from the English-speaking world;
3   when there is a critical turning point in literary history at which established models are no longer considered sufficient, or when there is a vacuum in the literature of the country. Where no type holds sway, it is easier for foreign models to assume primacy.

If translated literature assumes a secondary position, then it represents a peripheral system within the polysystem. It has no major influence over the central system and even becomes a conservative element, preserving conventional forms and conforming to the literary norms of the target system. Even-Zohar points out (p. 196) that this secondary position is the 'normal' one for translated literatures. However, translated literature itself is stratified (p. 195). Some translated literature may be secondary while others, translated from major source literatures, are primary. An example Even-Zohar gives is of the Hebrew literary polysystem published between the two world wars, when translations from Russian were primary but translations from English, German and Polish were secondary.

Even-Zohar (pp. 196–7) suggests that the position occupied by translated literature in the polysystem conditions the translation strategy. If it is primary, translators do not feel constrained to follow target literature models and are more prepared to break conventions, They thus often produce a TT that is a close match in terms of adequacy, reproducing the textual relations of the ST. This in itself may then lead to new SL models. On the other hand, if translated literature is secondary, translators tend to use existing target-culture models for the TT and produce more 'non-adequate' translations

(p. 197). The term 'adequate' is developed in the discussion of Toury's work in section 7.2 below.

Genztler (1993: 120–1 and 124–5) stresses the way polysystem theory represents an important advance for translation studies. The advantages of this are several:

1   Literature itself is studied alongside the social, historical and cultural forces.
2   Even-Zohar moves away from the isolated study of individual texts towards the study of translation within the cultural and literary systems in which it functions.
3   The non-prescriptive definition of equivalence and adequacy allows for variation according to the historical and cultural situation of the text.

This last point offers translation theory an escape from the repeated linguistic arguments that had begun to follow insistently the concept of equivalence in the 1960s and 1970s (see chapter 3).

However, Gentzler (pp. 121–3) also outlines criticisms of polysystem theory. These include:

1   overgeneralization to 'universal laws' of translation based on relatively little evidence;
2   an over-reliance on a historically based 1920s' Formalist model which, following Even-Zohar's own model of evolving trends, might be inappropriate for translated texts in the 1970s;
3   the tendency to focus on the abstract model rather than the 'real-life' constraints placed on texts and translators;
4   the question as to how far the supposed scientific model is really objective.

Despite these objections, polysystem theory has had a profound influence on translation studies, moving it forward into a less prescriptive observation of translation within its different contexts.

7.2 Toury and descriptive translation studies

Working with Even-Zohar in Tel Aviv was Gideon Toury. After his early polysystem work on the sociocultural conditions which determine the translation of foreign literature into Hebrew, Toury focused on developing a general theory of translation. In chapter 1, we considered Toury's diagrammatic representation of Holmes's 'map' of translation studies. In his influential *Descriptive Translation Studies – And Beyond* (Toury 1995: 10), Toury calls for the development of a properly systematic descriptive branch of the discipline to replace isolated free-standing studies that are commonplace:

> What is missing is not isolated attempts reflecting excellent intuitions and supplying fine insights (which many existing studies certainly do), but a systematic branch proceeding from clear assumptions and armed with a methodology and research

techniques made as explicit as possible and justified within translation studies itself. Only a branch of this kind can ensure that the findings of individual studies will be intersubjectively testable and comparable, and the studies themselves replicable.

(Toury 1995: 3)

Toury goes on to propose just such a methodology for the branch of descriptive translation studies (DTS).

For Toury (1995: 13), translations first and foremost occupy a position in the social and literary systems of the target culture, and this position determines the translation strategies that are employed. With this approach, he is continuing and building on the polysystem work of Even-Zohar and on earlier versions of his own work (Toury 1978, 1980, 1985, 1991). Toury (1995: 36–9 and 102) proposes the following three-phase methodology for systematic DTS, incorporating a description of the product and the wider role of the sociocultural system:

1   Situate the text within the target culture system, looking at its significance or acceptability.
2   Compare the ST and the TT for shifts, identifying relationships between 'coupled pairs' of ST and TT segments, and attempting generalizations about the underlying concept of translation.
3   Draw implications for decision-making in future translating.

An important additional step is the possibility of repeating phases (1) and (2) for other pairs of similar texts in order to widen the corpus and to build up a descriptive profile of translations according to genre, period, author, etc. In this way, the norms pertaining to each kind of translation can be identified with the ultimate aim (as more descriptive studies are performed) of stating laws of behaviour for translation in general. The concepts of norms and laws are further discussed in sections 7.2.1 and 7.2.2 below.

The second step of Toury's methodology is one of the most controversial areas. The decisions on which ST and TT segments to examine and what the relationships are between them is an apparatus which Toury (1995: 85) states should be supplied by translation theory. Yet, as we have seen in chapters 4 and 5, linguistic translation theory is far from reaching a consensus as to what that apparatus should be. Most controversially, in earlier papers (1978: 93, 1985: 32), Toury still holds to the use of a hypothetical intermediate invariant or *tertium comparationis* (see page 49 for a discussion of this term) as an 'Adequate Translation' (AT) against which to gauge translation shifts. However, at the same time he also admits (1978: 88–9) that, in practice, no translation is ever fully 'adequate'; for this contradiction, and for considering the hypothetical invariant to be a universal given, he has been roundly criticized (see, e.g., Gentzler 1993: 131–2, Hermans 1999: 56–7).

In his 1995 book, Toury drops the invariant concept. What remains in his model is a 'mapping' of the TT onto the ST which 'yields a series of (ad hoc) coupled pairs' (Toury 1995: 77). This is a type of comparison which Toury admits (p. 80) is inevitably 'partial [and] indirect' and which will undergo 'continuous revision' during the very analytical process itself. The result is a flexible and non-prescriptive, if also less than rigorously systematic, means of comparing ST and TT. The flexibility leads to different aspects of texts being examined in Toury's series of case studies. Thus, in one study (pp. 148–65) it is the addition of rhymes and omission of passages in the Hebrew translation of a German fairy tale; in another study it is conjoint phrases in literature translated into Hebrew (see section 7.2.3 below).

7.2.1 The concept of *norms* of translation behaviour

The aim of Toury's case studies is to distinguish trends of translation behaviour, to make generalizations regarding the decision-making processes of the translator and then to 'reconstruct' the norms that have been in operation in the translation and make hypotheses that can be tested by future descriptive studies. The definition of **norms** used by Toury is:

> the translation of general values or ideas shared by a community – as to what is right or wrong, adequate or inadequate – into performance instructions appropriate for and applicable to particular situations.
>
> (Toury 1995: 55)

These norms are sociocultural constraints specific to a culture, society and time. An individual is said to acquire them from the general process of education and socialization. In terms of their 'potency' Toury places norms between rules and idiosyncrasies (p. 54). He considers translation to be an activity governed by norms, and these norms 'determine the (type and extent of) equivalence manifested in actual translations' (p. 61). This suggests the potential ambiguity of the term 'norm': although Toury uses it, first, as a descriptive analytical category to be studied through regularity of behaviour (norms are 'options that translators in a given socio-historical context select on a regular basis'; Baker 1997a: 164), they appear to exert pressure and to perform some kind of prescriptive function.

Although Toury focuses initially on the analysis of the translation *product*, he emphasizes (p. 174) that this is simply in order to identify the decision-making *processes* of the translator. His hypothesis is that the norms that have prevailed in the translation of a particular text can be reconstructed from two types of source:

1 from the **examination of texts**, the products of norm-governed activity. This will show up 'regularities of behaviour' (p. 55) (i.e. trends of relationships and correspondences between ST and TT segments). It will point to the processes adopted by the translator and, hence, the norms that have been in operation;

2 from the explicit **statements** made about norms by translators, publishers, reviewers and other participants in the translation act. However, Toury (p. 65) warns that such explicit statements may be incomplete or

biased in favour of the role played by the informants in the sociocultural system and are therefore best avoided (see chapter 9 for further discussion of this point).

Toury (pp. 56–9) sees different kinds of norms operating at different stages of the translation process. The basic **initial norm** refers to a general choice made by translators (figure 7.1). Thus, translators can subject themselves to the norms realized in the ST or to the norms of the target culture or language. If it is towards the ST, then the TT will be **adequate**; if the target culture norms prevail, then the TT will be **acceptable** (p. 57). The poles of adequacy and acceptability are on a continuum since no translation is ever totally adequate or totally acceptable. Shifts – obligatory and non-obligatory – are inevitable, norm-governed and 'a true universal of translation' (p. 57).

Other, lower order, norms described by Toury are **preliminary norms** (p. 58) and **operational norms** (pp. 58–9). Preliminary norms can be displayed as in figure 7.2. **Translation policy** refers to factors determining the selection of texts for translation in a specific language, culture or time. Toury does not pursue this area in his case studies. **Directness of translation** relates to whether translation occurs through an intermediate language (e.g. Finnish to Greek via English). Questions for investigation include the tolerance of the TT culture to this practice, which languages are involved and whether the practice is camouflaged or not.

Operational norms (figure 7.3) describe the presentation and linguistic matter of the TT. **Matricial norms** relate to the completeness of the TT. Phenomena include omission or relocation of passages, textual segmentation, and the addition of passages or footnotes. **Textual–linguistic norms** govern the selection of TT linguistic material: lexical items, phrases and stylistic features (compare Nord's list in chapter 5).

The examination of the ST and TT should reveal shifts in the relations between the two that have taken place in translation (compare shift analysis in chapter 4). It is here that Toury introduces the term 'translation equivalence' (p. 85), but he is at pains to emphasize that it is different from the traditional notion of equivalence (see chapter 3). Toury's is a

Figure 7.1

Toury's initial norm and the continuum of adequate and acceptable translation

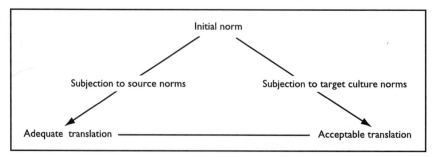

Figure 7.2
Preliminary norms

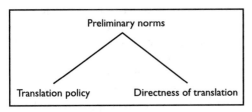

Figure 7.3
Operational norms

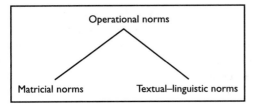

'functional–relational concept', by which he means that equivalence is assumed between a TT and an ST. This is very important because analysis does not then focus prescriptively on whether a given TT or TT-expression is 'equivalent' to the ST or ST-expression. Instead it focuses on how the assumed equivalence has been realized and is a tool for uncovering 'the underlying concept of translation ... [the] derived notions of decision-making and the factors that have constrained it' (p. 86).

As noted above, DTS aims to reconstruct the norms that have been in operation during the translation process. However, Toury stresses (p. 67) that norms are a 'graded notion' since 'a translator's behaviour cannot be expected to be fully systematic'. In addition, these norms are of different intensity, ranging from behaviour that is mandatory (maximum intensity) to tendencies that are common but not mandatory and to behaviour that is tolerated (minimum intensity) (pp. 67–9). We discuss this further in sections 7.2.4 and 7.3.

7.2.2 'Laws' of translation

Toury hopes that the cumulative identification of norms in descriptive studies will enable the formulation of probabilistic 'laws' of translation and thence of 'universals of translation'. The tentative laws he proposes are:

1   The **law of growing standardization** (pp. 267–74), which states that 'in translation, textual relations obtaining in the original are often modified, sometimes to the point of being totally ignored, in favour of [more] habitual options offered by a target repertoire' (p. 268). This refers to the

disruption of the ST patterns in translation and the selection of linguistic options that are more common in the TL. Thus, for example,
there will a tendency towards a general standardization and loss of variation in style in the TT, or at least an accommodation to target culture
models. This is especially the case if, as commonly occurs, translation
assumes a weak and peripheral position in the target system.

2   The **law of interference** (1995: 274–9), which sees interference from ST
to TT as 'a kind of default'. Interference refers to ST linguistic features
(mainly lexical and syntactical patterning) being copied in the TT, either
'negatively' (because they create non-normal TT patterns) or 'positively'
(the existence of features in the ST that will not be non-normal in the TT
makes them more likely to be used by the translator). Toury (p. 278)
considers tolerance of interference to depend on sociocultural factors
and the prestige of the different literary systems: there is greater tolerance when translating from a prestigious language or culture, especially
if the target language or culture is 'minor'. These laws are further
discussed in section 7.2.4 below.

7.2.3 Toury's model in action

Toury (1995) presents a series of case studies, including an 'exemplary' study
of conjoint phrases in Hebrew TTs. Conjoint phrases or binomials are pairs
of near-synonyms that function together as a single unit. Examples Toury
gives from English are *able and talented* and *law and order*; and, from German,
nie und nimmer. He discusses (pp. 103–4) the significance of such phrases in
Hebrew literature, indicating that their use is prevalent in old written Hebrew
texts from the Bible onwards and in Hebrew texts from the end of the
eighteenth century onwards, when the language was struggling to adapt to
modern writing and was under the influence of imported literary models.
However, the preference for conjoint phrases has declined over the past fifty
years, now that Hebrew is a more confident and central literature. Nevertheless, Toury (p. 105) suggests that the number of such phrases in Hebrew
translations tends to be higher than in Hebrew STs and that translations also
contain more newly coined or 'free' combinations (rather than fixed
phrases). He supports this with examples from Hebrew translations of children's literature, of Goethe and of a story by Heinrich Böll (*Ansichten eines
Clownes*). In the latter case, the translator's very frequent use of conjoint
phrases to translate single lexical items in German produces a TT that is
almost 30 per cent longer than the ST. The effect, in a translation published
in 1971, is also to make the Hebrew seem very dated.

From these findings, Toury puts forward a possible generalization to be
tested in future studies across languages and cultures. The claim (p. 111) is
that frequent use of conjoint phrases, particularly in place of single lexical
items in the ST, 'may represent a universal of translation into systems which
are young, or otherwise "weak"'. The consideration of translated literature as

part of a hierarchical system shows the way DTS interlinks with polysystem theory.

The final stage of Toury's model is the application of the findings. An example is his own translation of Mark Twain's *Connecticut Yankee in King Arthur's Court*, where Toury says he has deliberately used frequent conjoint phrases in Hebrew in order to create 'a parodistic air of "stylistic archaism"' (p. 112).

7.2.4 Discussion of Toury's work

Toury's methodology for DTS seems to be an important step towards setting firm foundations for future descriptive work. Gentzler lists four aspects of Toury's theory that have had an important impact on translation studies:

1　the abandonment of one-to-one notions of correspondence as well as the possibility of literary/linguistic equivalence (unless by accident);
2　the involvement of literary tendencies within the target cultural system in the production of any translated text;
3　the destabilization of the notion of an original message with a fixed identity;
4　the integration of both the original text and the translated text in the semiotic web of intersecting cultural systems.

(Gentzler 1993: 133–4)

Nevertheless, Toury's TT-oriented position is questioned by Hermans (1995: 218) in a review of Toury's earlier (1980) book. Certainly, Toury's stance risks overlooking, for example, ideological and political factors such as the status of the ST in its own culture, the source culture's possible promotion of translation of its own literature and the effect that translation might exert back on the system of the source culture. These are areas which will benefit from employing concepts from reception theory, notably consideration of the way in which a new literary work influences its audience (see chapter 9).

Furthermore, criticisms which Genztler makes of the earlier polysystem work (see section 7.1) can also be levelled at Toury: there is still a wish to generalize (or even overgeneralize) from case studies, since the 'laws' Toury tentatively proposes are in some ways simply reformulations of generally-held (though not necessarily proven) beliefs about translation. It is also debatable to what extent a semi-scientific norm/law approach can be applied to a marginal area such as translation, since the norms described are, after all, abstract and only traceable in Toury's method by examining the results of the often subconscious behaviour that is supposedly governed by them.

One might also question whether the translator's decision-making really is sufficiently patterned as to be universalized. Hermans (1999: 92), for example, asks how it is possible to know all the variables relevant to translation and to find laws relevant to all translation. Toury's two laws themselves are also to some extent contradictory, or at least pull in different directions: the law of growing standardization depicts TL-oriented norms, while the law of interference is ST-oriented. Findings from my own descriptive studies (Munday 1997) suggest that the *law of interference* needs to be modified, or even a new law proposed, that of *reduced control over linguistic realization in translation*. This would bring together some of the varied factors which affect the translation process and make the concept of norms and laws in translation more complex than is suggested by some of Toury's studies. These factors include the effect of ST patterning, the preference for clarity and avoidance of ambiguity in TTs and real-life considerations for the translator, such as the need to maximize the efficiency of thought processes and the importance of decision-making under time pressure (compare Levý's minimax strategy, discussed in chapter 4). When taking real-life considerations into account, it is worth noting that systems theorists in general have restricted their work to literary translation. However, Toury's inclusion of sociocultural factors in and around the translation process might well lend itself to the examination of the translation of non-fiction or technical texts.

Toury's ambivalence towards the notion of equivalence has also been discussed by Hermans (1999: 97), who furthermore highlights (p. 77) the confusion inherent in Toury's proposed terms 'adequate' and 'acceptable' because of their evaluative connotations in other contexts. Hermans prefers 'TT-oriented' and 'ST-oriented'. Finally, the ad-hoc nature of the ST–TT mapping inevitably means that Toury's model is not fully objective or replicable. The alternative is Holmes's (1988a: 80) suggestion of an extensive 'repertory of features' approach, even though this is, as we have seen in chapter 4, potentially 'arduous and tedious'.

7.3 Chesterman's translation norms

Toury's concept of norms is focused mainly on their function as a descriptive category to identify translation patterns. However, as we noted in section 7.2.1, even such supposedly non-prescriptive norms attract approval or disapproval within society. Likewise, Andrew Chesterman (1997: 68) states that all norms 'exert a prescriptive pressure'.

Chesterman himself (pp. 64–70) proposes another set of norms, covering the area of Toury's initial and operational norms (see figure 7.3 above). These are (1) product or expectancy norms and (2) process or professional norms:

1 **Product** or **expectancy norms** 'are established by the expectations of readers of a translation (of a given type) concerning what a translation (of this type) should be like' (p. 64). Factors governing these norms include the predominant translation tradition in the target culture, the discourse conventions of the similar TL genre, and economic and ideological considerations. Chesterman makes two important points about these norms:

   (a) Expectancy norms allow evaluative judgements about translations since readers have a notion of what is an 'appropriate' or 'acceptable' translation of the specific text variety and will approve of a translator who conforms to these expectations (p. 65).

(b) Expectancy norms are sometimes 'validated by a norm-authority of some kind' (p. 66). For example, a teacher, literary critic and publisher's reader can confirm the prevalent norm by encouraging translations that conform with that norm. This may be, for instance, that a translation should meet TL criteria of readability and fluency (see chapter 9). Alternatively, a literary critic may criticize a translation that offends the norm, and this criticism may damage the reception of that book amongst ordinary readers. Of course, as Chesterman notes (p. 66), there may sometimes be a clash between the norm 'authorities' and society in general.

(2) **Professional norms** 'regulate the translation process itself' (p. 67). They are subordinate to and determined by expectancy norms. Chesterman proposes three kinds of professional norm:

(a) **The accountability norm** (p. 68): This is an **ethical** norm, dealing with professional standards of integrity and thoroughness. The translator will accept responsibility for the work produced for the commissioner and reader.

(b) **The communication norm** (p. 69): This is a **social** norm. The translator, the communication 'expert', works to ensure maximum communication between the parties (compare Holz-Mänttäri's model of translational action in chapter 5).

(c) **The 'relation' norm** (pp. 69–70): This is a **linguistic** norm which deals with the relation between ST and TT. Again, in terms similar to those discussed in chapter 5, Chesterman rejects narrow equivalence relations and sees the appropriate relation being judged by the translator 'according to text-type, the wishes of the commissioner, the intentions of the original writer, and the assumed needs of the prospective readers' (p. 69).

These professional norms are validated partly by norm authorities such as other professionals and professional bodies and partly by their very existence (p. 70). They include new areas not covered by Toury, and therefore they may be useful in the overall description of the translation process and product.

7.4 Other models of descriptive translation studies: Lambert and van Gorp and the Manipulation School

With the influence of Even-Zohar's and Toury's early work in polysystem theory, the International Comparative Literature Association held several meetings and conferences around the theme of translated literature. Particularly prominent centres were in Belgium, Israel and the Netherlands, and the first conferences were held at Leuven (1976), Tel Aviv (1978) and Antwerp (1980).

The key publication of this group of scholars, known as the Manipulation School or Group, was the collection of papers entitled *The Manipulation of Literature: Studies in Literary Translation* (1985a), edited by Theo Hermans. In his introduction, 'Translation studies and a new paradigm', Hermans summarizes the group's view of translated literature:

> What they have in common is a view of literature as a complex and dynamic system; a conviction that there should be a continual interplay between theoretical models and practical case studies; an approach to literary translation which is descriptive, target-organized, functional and systemic; and an interest in the norms and constraints that govern the production and reception of translations, in the relation between translation and other types of text processing, and in the place and role of translations both within a given literature and in the interaction between literatures.
>
> (Hermans 1985b: 10–11)

The link with polysystem theory and DTS can be seen to be strong and the Manipulation School proceeded on the basis of 'a continual interplay between theoretical models and practical case studies'.

A key point at that time was the exact methodology for the case studies. The paper by José Lambert and Hendrik van Gorp (1985), 'On describing translations', draws on Even-Zohar's and Toury's early work and proposes one such scheme for the comparison of the ST and TT literary systems and for the description of relations within them. Each system comprises a description of author, text and reader. Lambert and van Gorp divide the scheme into four sections (Lambert and van Gorp 1985: 52–3):

1. **Preliminary data**: information on title page, metatexts (preface, etc.) and the general strategy (whether the translation is partial or complete). The results should lead to hypotheses concerning levels 2 and 3.
2. **Macro-level**: the division of the text, titles and presentation of the chapters, the internal narrative structure and any overt authorial comment. This should generate hypotheses about the micro-level (level 3).
3. **Micro-level**: the identification of shifts on different linguistic levels. These include the lexical level, the grammatical patterns, narrative, point of view and modality. The results should interact with the macro-level (level 2) and lead to their 'consideration in terms of the broader systemic context'.
4. **Systemic context**: here micro- and macro-levels, text and theory are compared and norms identified. Intertextual relations (relations with other texts including translations) and intersystemic relations (relations with other genres, codes) are also described.

Lambert and van Gorp (p. 47) accept that 'it is impossible to summarize all relationships involved in the activity of translation' but suggest a systematic scheme that avoids superficial and intuitive commentaries and 'a priori judgments and convictions'. Like Hermans, they stress the link between the individual case study and the wider theoretical framework:

> It is not at all absurd to study a single translated text or a single translator, but it is absurd to disregard the fact that this translation or this translator has (positive or negative) connections with other translations and translators.
>
> (Lambert and van Gorp 1985: 51)

Since that paper was written, DTS has moved on, not least with Toury's 1995 work. Scholars such as the late André Lefevere moved away from polysystem terminology to consider the role of ideology and patronage in the system of translated literature. Pointers for future work in the theory of descriptive studies are given by Hermans:

> The discipline generally, but the descriptive school in particular, urgently needs to take account of developments in some of the more vigorous intellectual and social movements of our time, including gender studies, poststructuralism, postcolonial and cultural studies, and the new interdisciplinarity of human sciences.
>
> (Hermans 1999: 159–60)

We examine Lefevere's work and the contribution of these other movements to translation studies in chapters 8 and 9.

Case study

The text for this case study is the hugely successful children's book *Harry Potter and the Philosopher's Stone* by J. K. Rowling[1] and its translations into Italian (*Harry Potter e la pietra filosofale*[2]) and Spanish (*Harry Potter y la piedra filosofal*[3]). Following Toury's three-phase methodology, we shall:

1 place the TTs in their TT cultural systems;
2 'map' TT segments onto the ST equivalents;
3 attempt to draw some generalizations regarding the translation strategies employed and the norms at work.

Comparing two translations of the same ST, albeit in different languages, allows findings to be checked and helps to avoid jumping to conclusions based on a single isolated study.

1 Both the Italian and Spanish TTs are presented and accepted as translations, the translators' names and the original titles being published on
   the copyright pages. The Italian also has the translator's name on the title
   page. Both TTs are direct translations from English. Even though both
   target cultures have strong native children's literature traditions themselves, the decision to select this book for translation is not surprising
   given its huge success in the UK and the USA where at one time it was
   the best-selling book in the country among both adults and children.
      The fact that the books are translations is not stressed, however. The

blurb on the back cover of the Spanish TT, for example, quotes comments from reviews in the UK and Italy and emphasizes the book's relevance to 'all children of all ages'. The Italian TT also incorporates illustrations by an Italian illustrator, Serna Riglietti, cited along with the translator on the title page, where the book is described as a *romanzo* 'novel'. The use of this word indicates the way in which the book is marketed as adult literature in Italy. There is a strong suggestion, therefore, that the Spanish and Italian publishers are prepared to make modifications, even perhaps including a modification of the genre, in order to ensure its full acceptability, including to more sophisticated adult readers.

2   The TTs are full translations of the ST with no major additions, omissions or footnotes. The choice of ST–TT pairs to examine is ad hoc in Toury's model. In the case of *Harry Potter*, one of the most striking features of the book (and indeed of much children's literature) concerns the names of characters and elements related to the school of magic and sorcery of which Harry Potter is a pupil. The school itself has the sonorous and Anglo-Saxon sounding name of *Hogwarts*. Along the old British grammar school model, it is divided into houses with suggestive names such as *Slytherin*, *Gryffindor* and *Ravenclaw*. The names of the characters are similarly sonorous and suggestive: *Hagrid*, *Hedwig*, *Snape*, *Draco Malfoy*, *Argus Filch* and the headmaster *Albus Dumbledore*.

The two TTs deal with these names in very different ways. The Spanish TT, almost without exception, retains these names in the translation, although the first time *Draco Malfoy* appears, the translator adds an explanation of his name in brackets: 'Draco (dragón) Malfoy'. On the other hand, the Italian TT, although transferring some of the names such as *Hogwarts*, *Hagrid* and *Hedwig* directly into the TT, makes an attempt at translating the sense of others: *Slytherin* is *Serpeverde*, *Ravenclaw* is *Pecoranera*, Snape is *Piton*, *Argus Filch* is *Argus Gazza* and so on. Where the sound of the name is more important and where the original would be difficult for the TT readers to pronounce (as happens with *Gryffindor*) the Italian translator adapts (in this case to *Grifondoro*). She goes further with the headmaster's name: he becomes *Albus Silente*, and one of his titles, *Supreme Mugwamp*, is rendered by the colloquial and humorous *supremo Pezzo Grosso*. Even though this is not a neologism, it is markedly different from the neutral and formal Spanish *jefe supremo*.

Names of crucial features of life in the school – such as the ball-game *Quidditch* and the term *Muggles* for non-magicians – are retained in Spanish, although italicized to emphasize their foreignness. In Italian, *Quidditch* is retained, but *Muggles* is replaced by the neologism *Babbani*. Some of the most playful names are those of the authors in the list of textbooks which the children receive before the start of term. Typical is '*Magical Theory by Adalbert Waffling*'. The Spanish does not change the author's name, while the Italian attempts to suggest the play on words with *Adalbert Incant*. Even more imaginatively, the Italian TT changes the author's name in '*The Dark Forces* by *Quentin Trimble*' to *Dante Tremante*, using the rhyme of the Italian, the sense of *tremante* ('trembling') and, of course, the allusion to Dante and his inferno.

3   From these findings certain generalizations can be proposed concerning the translation norms that have been in operation: the Spanish adopts an ST-oriented translation strategy, retaining the lexical items of the English original, even when this means that the TT reader will encounter pronunciation problems and/or not understand the allusion; the Italian adopts a TT-oriented translation strategy, modifying many of the names to create new humorous sound patterns, plays on words and illusions. One amusing play on words is the name of the Italian translator, given on the title page as Marina Astrologo.

This descriptive comparison of two translations suggests that different norms are at work in the two target cultures (or at least in the translations). It also provides research questions that can be addressed in future studies: Do translations of modern children's literature into Spanish generally tend to reinforce ST lexical patterns? Does translation strategy depend on the translator, the publisher, the SL? Do translations of this literature into Italian usually demonstrate a TL orientation? If so, does this suggest that Italian culture gives central position to its own culture, forcing imports to adapt to it? How has this varied over time? Do other genres show the same trend?

Discussion of case study

The advantages of Toury's methodology are that an attempt is made to place translation within its target-culture context, it is relatively simple to carry out, and it is replicable. Other studies can then follow up the findings and a better picture can gradually be formed about the translation of the genre of modern children's literature, the way this has varied over the years, the translation strategies into Italian and Spanish, their relation to what might have been assumed to be the more dominant English culture, and so on. A framework has thus been set up enabling researchers from almost any background to contribute in a meaningful way to our knowledge of translation. Nevertheless, some objections could be raised. The choice of ST–TT coupled pairs is still far from systematic. While the study of the translation of proper names produces interesting findings and names might be expected to be the most culturally bound items, this does not necessarily mean that the overall translation strategy is the same. It may well be preferable, as suggested by Holmes, to develop a check-list of features to examine, even if that list is not as comprehensive as some of the taxonomies we reviewed in chapters 4 and 5. The placing within the target-culture context is also inevitably limited. Focus could be shifted to look more deeply at the interaction between culture, ideology and text, and to look at the translators and publishing industry themselves. These topics are discussed in the next two chapters.

Summary

Even-Zohar's polysystem theory moves the study of translations out of a static linguistic analysis of shifts and obsession with one-to-one equivalence and into an investigation of the position of translated literature as a whole in the historical and literary systems of the target culture. Toury then focuses attention on finding a methodology for descriptive translation studies. His TT-oriented theoretical framework combines linguistic comparison of ST and TT and consideration of the cultural framework of the TT. His aim is to identify the patterns of behaviour in the translation and thereby to 'reconstruct' the norms at work in the translation process. The ultimate aim of DTS is to discover probabilistic laws of translation, which may be used to aid future translators and researchers. The exact form of ST–TT comparison remains to be determined; scholars of the related Manipulation School led an interplay of theoretical models and case studies in the 1980s, among which was Lambert and van Gorp's systematic 'scheme' for describing translations. Chesterman has later developed the concept of norms.

Further reading

For a summary of the influence of the Russian Formalists on polysystem theory, read Genztler (1993: 118–15). Selected writings in English translation are to be found in Matejka and Pomorska (1971). For further reading on polysystem theory see Even-Zohar (1978, 1990). For further discussion on norms, see Komissarov (1993), Hermans (1996), Nord (1997) and Pym (1998). For the Manipulation School and other descriptive approaches, see the collection of papers in Hermans (1985a). Also refer back to chapter 4 to van Leuven-Zwart (1989, 1990). Related work by Lefevere is discussed in chapter 8.

Discussion and research points

1   'Translation is no longer a phenomenon whose nature and borders are given once and for all, but an activity dependent on the relations within a certain cultural system' (Even-Zohar 1978/2000: 197). What are the implications of this comment for translation and translation studies? How far do you agree with it?

2   Consider the position of translation in the polysystem of your own country. Does it occupy a primary or secondary position? Have there been noticeable changes over the years? What about translated literature's own polysystem? Are there variations according to genre, SL, etc.?

3   Look at the different case studies given in Toury's book. What elements do they have in common? What studies could you carry out to test or extend these findings?

4   One of the severest criticisms of Toury's earlier work concerned his use of the

invariant or *tertium comparationis*. How well do you consider Toury overcomes this problem with his 'coupled pairs' approach in his 1995 book?

5 Carry out a descriptive study of the translation of *Harry Potter and the Philosopher's Stone* in another TL. Are your findings similar to those given in the case study in this chapter? What generalizations can you then make about the translation process? What hypotheses can you propose and how would you seek to investigate them further?

6 With reference to Toury's work of the 1970s and 1980s, Gentzler (1993: 133) claims that 'recent translation studies has found itself effectively using Toury's model in spite of his theoretical contradictions'. What evidence can you find to support or dismiss this claim? Read the various papers presented in *The Manipulation of Literature* (Hermans 1985a). How far do they differ from Toury's approach?

7 Follow up the discussion of norms in Toury (1978/2000, 1995), Komissarov (1993), Hermans (1996, 1999), Chesterman (1997), Nord (1997) and Pym (1998). How far are these scholars discussing the same concept? Can they be merged? How useful are norms in describing translation process and product? Are there other elements or norms which you feel they have omitted?

8 Systems theories have focused exclusively on literary translation. How far do you feel these theories can work for non-fiction and for technical texts?

8 Varieties of cultural studies

Key concepts

- The 'cultural turn': This is the term used in translation studies for the move towards the analysis of translation from a cultural studies angle.
- Lefevere, working originally from within systems theory, examines translation as 'rewriting' and the ideological tensions around the text.
- Simon and the Canadian feminists' translation 'project': Making the feminine visible.
- Postcolonial translation theories: Translation has played an active role in the colonization process and the image of the colonized.
- Call by Niranjana for an 'interventionist' approach by translators.
- Cultural theorists writing on translation have various agendas of their own.

Key texts

Bassnett, S. (1980, revised edition 1991) *Translation Studies*, London and New York: Routledge.

Bassnett, S. and A. Lefevere (eds) (1990) *Translation, History and Culture*, London and New York: Pinter.

Bassnett, S. and H. Trivedi (eds) (1999) *Postcolonial Translation: Theory and Practice*, London and New York: Pinter.

Cronin, M. (1996) *Translating Ireland: Translation, Languages, Cultures*, Cork: Cork University Press.

Lefevere, A. (1992a) *Translation, Rewriting and the Manipulation of Literary Fame*, London and New York: Routledge.

Niranjana, T. (1992) *Siting Translation: History, Post-structuralism, and the Colonial Context*, Berkeley, CA: University of California Press.

Simon, S. (1996) *Gender in Translation: Cultural Identity and the Politics of Transmission*, London and New York: Routledge.

Spivak, G. (1993/2000) 'The politics of translation', in L. Venuti (ed.) (2000), pp. 397–416.

Vieira, E. (1999) 'Liberating Calibans: Readings of Antropofagia and Haroldo de Campos' poetics of transcreation', in S. Bassnett and H. Trivedi (eds), pp. 95–113.

8.0 Introduction

In their introduction to the collection of essays *Translation, History and Culture*, Susan Bassnett and André Lefevere dismiss the kinds of linguistic theories of translation we examined in chapters 3 to 6, which, they say, 'have moved from word to text as a unit, but not beyond' (Bassnett and Lefevere 1990: 4). Also dismissed are 'painstaking comparisons between originals and translations' which do not consider the text in its cultural environment.[1]

Instead, Bassnett and Lefevere go beyond language and focus on the interaction between translation and culture, on the way in which culture impacts and constrains translation and on 'the larger issues of context, history and convention' (p. 11). They examine the image of literature that is created by forms such as anthologies, commentaries, film adaptations and translations, and the institutions that are involved in that process. Thus, the move from translation as text to translation as culture and politics is what Mary Snell-Hornby (1990), in her paper in the same collection, terms 'the cultural turn'. It is taken up by Bassnett and Lefevere as a metaphor for this cultural move and serves to bind together the range of case studies in their collection. These include studies of changing standards in translation over time, the power exercised in and on the publishing industry in pursuit of specific ideologies, feminist writing and translation, translation as 'appropriation', translation and colonization, and translation as rewriting, including film rewrites.

Translation, History and Culture constitutes an important collection and the beginning of a decade or more when the cultural turn has held sway in translation studies. In this chapter, we consider three areas where cultural studies has influenced translation studies in the course of the 1990s: translation as rewriting, which is a development of systems theory (section 8.1); translation and gender (section 8.2) and translation and postcolonialism (section 8.3). The ideology of the theorists themselves is discussed in section 8.4.

8.1 Translation as rewriting

André Lefevere worked in comparative literature departments in Leuven (Belgium) and then in the USA at the University of Texas, Austin. His work in translation studies developed out of his strong links with polysystem theory and the Manipulation School (see chapter 7). Although some may argue that Lefevere sits more easily among the systems theorists, his later work on translation and culture in many ways represents a bridging point to the cultural turn. They are most fully developed in his book *Translation, Rewriting and the Manipulation of Literary Fame* (Lefevere 1992a).

Lefevere focuses particularly on the examination of 'very concrete factors' that systemically govern the reception, acceptance or rejection of literary texts; that is, 'issues such as power, ideology, institution and manipulation'

(Lefevere 1992a: 2). The people involved in such power positions are the ones Lefevere sees as 'rewriting' literature and governing its consumption by the general public. The motivation for such rewriting can be ideological (conforming to or rebelling against the dominant ideology) or poetological (conforming to or rebelling against the dominant/preferred poetics). An example given by Lefevere (p. 8) is of Edward Fitzgerald, the nineteenth century translator (or 'rewriter') of the Persian poet Omar Khayyam. Fitzgerald considered Persians inferior and felt he should 'take liberties' in the translation in order to 'improve' on the original, at the same time making it conform to the expected Western literary conventions of his time.

Lefevere (p. 9) claims that 'the same basic process of rewriting is at work in translation, historiography, anthologization, criticism, and editing.' This bringing-together of studies of 'original' writing and translations shows translation being incorporated into general literary criticism. However, it is translation that is central to Lefevere's book:

> Translation is the most obviously recognizable type of rewriting, and . . . it is potentially the most influential because it is able to project the image of an author and/or those works beyond the boundaries of their culture of origin.
>
> (Lefevere 1992a: 9)

Lefevere describes the literary system in which translation functions as being controlled by three main factors, which are: (1) professionals within the literary system, (2) patronage outside the literary system and (3) the dominant poetics.

(1) **Professionals within the literary system**: These include critics and reviewers (whose comments affect the reception of a work), teachers (who often decide whether a book is studied or not) and translators themselves (as in the Fitzgerald example above), who decide on the poetics and at times the ideology of the translated text. These control factors are discussed more fully in chapter 9.

(2) **Patronage outside the literary system**: These are 'the powers (persons, institutions) that can further or hinder the reading, writing, and rewriting of literature' (p. 15). Patrons may be:

- an influential and powerful individual in a given historical era (e.g. Elizabeth I in Shakespeare's England, Hitler in 1930s Germany, etc.);
- groups of people (publishers, the media, a political class or party);
- institutions which regulate the distribution of literature and literary ideas (national academies, academic journals and, above all, the educational establishment).

Lefevere (p. 16) identifies three elements to this patronage:

(a) **The ideological component**: This constrains the choice of subject and the form of its presentation. Lefevere adopts a definition of ideology that is not restricted to the political. It is, more generally and perhaps less clearly, 'that grillwork of form, convention, and belief which orders our actions'.[2] He sees patronage as being basically ideologically focused.

(b) **The economic component**: This concerns the payment of writers and rewriters. In the past, this was in the form of a pension or other regular emolument from a benefactor. Nowadays, it is more likely to be royalty payments and translator's fees. Other professionals, such as critics and teachers are, of course, also paid or funded by patrons (e.g. by newspaper publishers, universities and governments).

(c) **The status component**: This occurs in many forms. In return for economic payment from a benefactor or the literary press, the beneficiary is often expected to conform to the patron's expectations. Similarly, membership of a particular group involves behaving in a way conducive to supporting that group: Lefevere gives the example of the Beat poets using the City Lights bookstore in San Francisco as a meeting point in the 1950s.

Patronage (p. 17) is termed **undifferentiated** if all three components are provided by the same person or group as would be the case with a totalitarian ruler. In that case, the patron's efforts are directed at maintaining the stability of the system. Patronage is **differentiated** when the three components are not dependent on each other. Thus, a popular best-selling author may receive high economic rewards but accrue little status in the eyes of the hierarchy of the literary system.

3 **The dominant poetics**: Lefevere (p. 26) analyzes this into two components:

(a) **Literary devices**: These include the range of genres, symbols, leitmotifs and prototypical situations and characters.

(b) **The concept of the role of literature**: This is the relation of literature to the social system in which it exists. The struggle between different literary forms is a feature of polysystem theory. Lefevere takes this idea further and looks at the role of institutions in determining the poetics:

> Institutions enforce or, at least, try to enforce the dominant poetics of a period by using it as the yardstick against which current production is measured. Accordingly, certain works of literature will be elevated to the level of 'classics' within a relatively short time after publication, while others are rejected, some to reach the exalted position of a classic later, when the dominant poetics has changed.
>
> (Lefevere 1992a: 19)

Lefevere sees 'clear indication of the conservative bias of the system itself and the power of rewriting' regarding those 'canonized' classics that never lose their status yet are reinterpreted or 'rewritten' to conform to changes in dominant poetics. This is the case, for example, with the Greek classics, which continue to exert influence on western European literature.

Lefevere notes that 'the boundaries of a poetics transcend languages, and ethnic and political entities' (p. 30). As an example, he describes a poetics shared by many languages and groups across Africa. He sees the dominant poetics as tending to be determined by ideology: for instance, the early spread of Islam from Arabia led to the poetics of Arabic being adopted by other languages such as Persian, Turkish and Urdu.

8.1.1 Poetics, ideology and translation

A key claim is made by Lefevere concerning the interaction between poetics, ideology and translation:

> On every level of the translation process, it can be shown that, if linguistic considerations enter into conflict with considerations of an ideological and/or poetological nature, the latter tend to win out.
>
> (Lefevere 1992a: 39)

For Lefevere, the most important consideration is the ideological one, which in this case refers to the translator's ideology, or the ideology imposed upon the translator by patronage. The poetological consideration refers to the dominant poetics in the TL culture. Together these dictate the translation strategy and the solution to specific problems (p. 41). An example given by Lefevere (pp. 41–2) is taken from Aristophanes's *Lysistrata*, where Lysistrata asks the allegorical female peace character to bring the Spartan emissaries to her, adding 'En mē dido tēn cheira, tēs sathēs age' [lit. 'If he doesn't give you his hand, take him by the penis'].

Lefevere lists English translations over the years that have rendered *penis* variously as *membrum virile, nose, leg, handle, life-line* and *anything else*, often accompanied by justificatory footnotes. According to Lefevere, such euphemistic translations are 'to no small extent indicative of the ideology dominant at a certain time in a certain society'[3] (p. 41) and they 'quite literally become the play' for the TT audience that cannot read the ST (p. 42).

This is very much the case in Lefevere's discussion (pp. 59–72) of the diary of Anne Frank, a young Dutch Jewish schoolgirl in hiding with her family during the Second World War. Anne Frank had begun to rewrite the diary for possible publication before her family was arrested and sent to a concentration camp, where Anne died. Lefevere describes how the 1947 Dutch edition of the diary – prepared in conjunction with (and 'rewritten' by) Anne's father Otto – doctors the image of the girl by, for example, omitting paragraphs relating to her sexuality. 'Unflattering' descriptions of friends and family are also cut as are sentences referring to several people who collaborated with the Germans, the latter omissions made at the request of the individuals named.

Lefevere then examines the German translation published in 1950. This was put together by Anneliese Schütz, a friend of Otto Frank, and contains both errors of comprehension and alterations to the image of Germans and

Germany. Lefevere (pp. 66–9) lists many of these discrepancies, including instances where derogatory remarks about Germans are omitted or toned down. References to the Germans' treatment of the Jews are also altered. The following is a clear example:

> er bestaat geen groter vijandschap op de wereld dan tussen Duitsers en Joden
> [there is no greater enmity in the world than between Germans and Jews]

> eine grössere Feindschaft als zwischen *diesen* Deutschen und den Juden gibt es nicht auf der Welt
> [there is no greater enmity in the world than between *these* Germans and the Jews]
> (Lefevere 1992a: 66)

According to Lefevere, the decision to translate *Duitsers* by *diesen Deutschen* (rather than by simply *den Deutschen* ['the Germans']) was taken by Schütz in conjunction with Otto Frank because that is what Anne 'meant' to say and also so as not to affect sales in post-war Germany by insulting all Germans. Such rewriting, before and during translation, is, in Lefevere's eyes, down to ideological pressures.

8.2 Translation and gender

The interest of cultural studies in translation has inevitably taken translation studies away from purely linguistic analysis and brought it into contact with other disciplines. Yet this 'process of disciplinary hybridization' (Simon 1996: ix) has not always been straightforward. Sherry Simon, in her *Gender in Translation: Cultural Identity and the Politics of Transmission* (1996), criticizes translation studies for often using the term culture 'as if it referred to an obvious and unproblematic reality' (p. ix). Lefevere (1985: 226), for example, had defined it as simply 'the environment of a literary system'.

Simon approaches translation from a gender-studies angle. She sees (p. 1) a language of sexism in translation studies, with its images of dominance, fidelity, faithfulness and betrayal. Typical is the seventeenth century image of *les belles infidèles*, translations into French that were artistically beautiful but unfaithful (Mounin 1955), or George Steiner's male-oriented image of translation as penetration in *After Babel* (see chapter 10). The feminist theorists see a parallel between the status of translation, which is often considered to be derivative and inferior to original writing, and that of women, so often repressed in society and literature. This is the core of feminist translation theory, which seeks to 'identify and critique the tangle of concepts which relegates both women and translation to the bottom of the social and literary ladder' (p. 1). But Simon takes this further in the concept of the committed **translation project**:

> For feminist translation, fidelity is to be directed toward neither the author nor the reader, but toward the writing project – a project in which both writer and translator participate.
> (Simon 1996: 2)

Simon gives examples of Canadian feminist translators from Quebec who seek to emphasize their identity and ideological stance in the translation project. One of these, Barbara Godard, theorist and translator, is openly assertive about the manipulation this involves:

> The feminist translator, affirming her critical difference, her delight in interminable re-reading and re-writing, flaunts the signs of her manipulation of the text.
>
> (Godard 1990: 91)

Simon also quotes the introduction to a translation of Lise Gauvin's *Lettres d'une autre* by another committed feminist translator, Susanne de Lotbinière-Harwood. The latter explains her translation strategy in political terms:

> My translation practice is a political activity aimed at making language speak for women. So my signature on a translation means: this translation has used every translation strategy to make the feminine visible in language.
>
> (de Lotbinière-Harwood, quoted in Gauvin 1989: 9; also cited in Simon 1996: 15)

One such strategy discussed by Simon is the treatment of linguistic markers of gender. Examples quoted from de Lotbinière-Harwood's translations include using a bold 'e' in the word *one* to emphasize the feminine, capitalization of M in *HuMan Rights* to show the implicit sexism, the neologism *auther* (as opposed to *author*) to translate the French *auteure*, and the female personification of nouns such as *aube* (*dawn*) with the English pronoun *she* (Simon p. 21).

Other chapters in Simon's book revalue the contribution women translators have made to translation throughout history, discuss the distortion in the translation of French feminist theory and look at feminist translations of the Bible. Among the case studies are summaries of the key literary translation work carried out by women in the first half of the twentieth century. Simon (pp. 68–71) points out that the great classics of Russian literature were initially made available in English in translations produced mainly by one woman, Constance Garnett. Her sixty volumes of translation include almost the entire work of Turgenev, Tolstoy, Dostoevsky, Chekov and Gogol. Similarly, key works of literature in German were translated by women translators: Jean Starr Untermeyer, Willa Muir (in conjunction with her husband Edwin) and Helen Lowe-Porter.[4]

The important role played by women translators up to the present is emphasized by Simon's reference to the feminist Suzanne Jill Levine, the translator of Guillermo Cabrera Infante's *Tres tristes tigres*. In contrast to the self-effacing work of some of the earlier translators mentioned above, Levine collaborated closely with Infante in creating a 'new' work, as we discuss in chapter 9. From the feminist perspective, however, it is not only Levine's self-confidence but also her awareness of a certain 'betrayal' – translating a male discourse that speaks of the woman betrayed – that fascinates Simon. She hints (p. 82) at the possible ways Levine may have rewritten, manipulated and 'betrayed' Infante's work in her own feminist project.

Simon's focus centres on underlining the importance of the cultural turn in translation. In the conclusion to her book, she insists on how 'contemporary feminist translation has made gender the site of a consciously transformative project, one which reframes conditions of textual authority' (p. 167) and summarizes the contribution of cultural studies to translation as follows:

> Cultural studies brings to translation an understanding of the complexities of gender and culture. It allows us to situate linguistic transfer within the multiple 'post' realities of today: poststructuralism, postcolonialism and postmodernism.
>
> (Simon 1996: 136)

Simon thus links gender and cultural studies to the developments in **postcolonialism**. The exact scope of postcolonialism is open to some debate; however, it is generally used to cover studies of the history of the former colonies, studies of powerful European empires, resistance to the colonialist powers and, more broadly, studies of the effect of the imbalance of power relations between colonized and colonizer. The consequent crossover between different contemporary disciplines can be seen by the fact that essays by Simon and by Lefevere appear in collections of postcolonial writings on translation, and Simon herself makes extensive reference to the postcolonialist Spivak, as we describe in the next section.

8.3 Postcolonial translation theory

In the concluding chapter of her book on translation and gender, Simon draws together issues of gender and postcolonialism as seen in the work of the Bengali critic and translator Gayatri Chakravorty Spivak. In particular, Simon highlights (pp. 145–7) Spivak's concerns about the ideological consequences of the translation of 'Third World' literature into English and the distortion this entails. Spivak has addressed these questions in her seminal essay 'The politics of translation' (1993/2000), which brings together feminist, postcolonialist and poststructuralist approaches. Tensions between the different approaches are highlighted, with Spivak speaking out against Western feminists who expect feminist writing from outside Europe to be translated into the language of power, English. Such translation, in Spivak's view, is often expressed in '**translationese**', which eliminates the identity of politically less powerful individuals and cultures:

> In the act of wholesale translation into English there can be a betrayal of the democratic ideal into the law of the strongest. This happens when all the literature of the Third World gets translated into a sort of with-it translatese, so that the literature by a woman in Palestine begins to resemble, in the feel of its prose, something by a man in Taiwan.
>
> (Spivak: 1993/2000: 399–400)

Spivak's critique of Western feminism and publishing is most biting when she suggests (p. 405) that feminists from the hegemonic countries should show real solidarity with women in postcolonial contexts by learning the language in which those women speak and write. In Spivak's opinion, the 'politics of translation' currently gives prominence to English and the other 'hegemonic' languages of the ex-colonizers. Translations into these languages from Bengali too often fail to translate the difference of the Bengali view because the translator, albeit with good intentions, over-assimilates it to make it accessible to the Western readers. Spivak's own translation strategy[5] necessitates the translator intimately understanding the language and situation of the original. It draws on poststructuralist concepts of rhetoric, logic and the social; this topic is further discussed in chapter 10.

Spivak's work is indicative of how cultural studies, and especially post-colonialism, has over the past decade focused on issues of translation, the transnational and colonization. The linking of colonization and translation is accompanied by the argument that translation has played an active role in the colonization process and in disseminating an ideologically motivated image of colonized peoples. Just as, in the previous section, we saw a parallel which feminist theorists have drawn between the conventional male-driven depiction of translations and of women, so has the metaphor been used of the colony as an imitative and inferior translational copy whose suppressed identity has been overwritten by the colonizer. Translation's role in disseminating such ideological images has led Bassnett and Trivedi (1999: 5) to refer to the 'shameful history of translation'.

The central intersection of translation studies and postcolonial theory is that of **power relations**. Tejaswini Niranjana's *Siting Translation: History, Post-structuralism, and the Colonial Context* presents an image of the post-colonial as 'still scored through by an absentee colonialism' (Niranjana 1992: 8). She sees literary translation as one of the discourses (the others being education, theology, historiography and philosophy) which 'inform the hegemonic apparatuses that belong to the ideological structure of colonial rule' (p. 33). Niranjana's focus is on the way translation into English has generally been used by the colonial power to construct a rewritten image of the 'East' that has then come to stand for the truth. She gives other examples of the colonizer's imposition of ideological values. These vary from missionaries who ran schools for the colonized and who also performed a role as linguists and translators, to ethnographers who recorded grammars of native languages. Niranjana sees all these groups as 'participating in the enormous project of collection and codification on which colonial power was based' (p. 34). She specifically attacks translation's role within this power structure:

> Translation as a practice shapes, and takes shape within, the asymmetrical relations of power that operate under colonialism.
>
> (Niranjana 1992: 2)

Furthermore, she goes on to criticize translation studies itself for its largely

Western orientation and for three main failings that she sees resulting from this (pp. 48–9):

1   that translation studies has until recently not considered the question of power imbalance between different languages;
2   that the concepts underlying much of Western translation theory are flawed ('its notions of text, author, and meaning are based on an unproblematic, naively representational theory of language');
3   that the 'humanistic enterprise' of translation needs to be questioned, since translation in the colonial context builds a conceptual image of colonial domination into the discourse of Western philosophy.

Niranjana writes from an avowedly poststructuralist perspective. The latter forms the basis of chapter 10 where we consider the influence of the deconstructionists such as Derrida. This overlapping is indicative of the interaction of different aspects of cultural studies and of the way in which they interface with translation studies. It also informs Niranjana's recommendations for action, which are:

1   In general, that the postcolonial translator must call into question every aspect of colonialism and liberal nationalism (p. 167). For Niranjana, this is not just a question of avoiding Western metaphysical representations; it is a case of 'dismantl[ing] the hegemonic West from within', deconstructing and identifying the means by which the West represses the non-West and marginalizes its own otherness (p. 171). In this way such repression can then be countered.
2   Specifically, Niranjana calls for an 'interventionist' approach from the translator. 'I initiate here a practice of translation that is speculative, provisional and interventionist', she proclaims (p. 173) in her analysis of translations of a spiritual *vacana* poem from Southern India. She attacks existing translations (including one by the celebrated A. K. Ramanujan) as 'attempting to assimilate Śaivite poetry to the discourses of Christianity or of a post-Romantic New Criticism' (p. 180), analogous to nineteenth century native responses to colonialism. Her own suggested translation resists the 'containment' of colonial discourse by, amongst other things, reinscribing the name of the poet's god Guhēśvara and the *linga* representation of light, and by avoiding similes that would tone down the native form of metaphorization (pp. 182–6).

Asymmetrical power relationships in a postcolonial context also form the thread of the important collection of essays entitled *Postcolonial Translation: Theory and Practice*, edited by Susan Bassnett and Harish Trivedi (1999). In their introduction (p. 13) they see these power relationships being played out in the unequal struggle of various local languages against 'the one master-language of our postcolonial world, English'. Translation is thus seen as the battleground and exemplification of the postcolonial context; there is a close linkage of **translational** to **transnational**, the latter term referring both to those postcolonials living 'between' nations as emigrants (as in the example of Salman Rushdie, described in Bhabha 1994) and, more widely, as the 'locational disrupture' that describes the situation of those who remain in the melting pot of their native 'site':

> In current theoretical discourse, then, to speak of postcolonial translation is little short of tautology. In our age of (the valorization of) migrancy, exile and diaspora, the word 'translation' seems to have come full circle and reverted from its figurative literary meaning of an interlingual transaction to its etymological physical meaning of locational disrupture; translation seems to have been translated back to its origins.
>
> (Bassnett and Trivedi 1999: 13)

Postcolonial translation studies takes many forms, as can be seen by the studies contained in Bassnett and Trivedi's book. Several are based on the theory and practice of translation from an Indian perspective: 'Indian literary traditions are essentially traditions of translation', says Devy (1999: 187), and studies are included of the work of celebrated translators B. M. Srikantaiah (Viswanatha and Simon 1999) and A. K. Ramanujan (Dharwadker 1999). In the latter case, Dharwadker reacts against Niranjana's attack on Ramanujan, stating that Ramanujan had worked from an earlier and different version of the poem, that Niranjana ignores the translator's commentary on the poem, and that the goal of the translation was to orient the Western reader to cross-cultural similarities.

8.3.1 Brazilian cannibalism

Another important postcolonial movement in translation has come from Brazil. It is based on the metaphor of anthropophagy or cannibalism which emerged in the 1920s with Oswald de Andrade's *Manifesto Antropófago*, drawing on the famous story of the ritual cannibalization of a Portuguese bishop by native Brazilians. From the 1960s, with the poetical work of the de Campos brothers, the metaphor has been used by the strong Brazilian translation-studies community to stand for the experience of colonization and translation: the colonizers and their language are devoured, their life force invigorating the devourers, but in a new purified and energized form that is appropriate to the needs of the native peoples.

A summary of the Brazilian cannibalist movement and its debt to Haroldo de Campos is given by one of its leading proponents, Else Vieira, in her paper 'Liberating Calibans' (Vieira 1999):

> Cannibalism is a metaphor actually drawn from the natives' ritual whereby feeding from someone or drinking someone's blood, as they did to their totemic 'tapir', was a means of absorbing the other's strength, a pointer to the very project of the Anthropophagy group: not to deny foreign influences or nourishment, but to absorb and transform them by the addition of autochtonous input. Initially using the metaphor as an irreverent verbal weapon, the *Manifesto Antropófago* stresses the repressive nature of colonialism . . .

In the overt attempt at freeing Brazilian culture from mental colonialism, the *Manifesto* redirects the flow of Eurocentric historiography. The New World, by means of the permanent 'Caraíba' revolution, becomes the source of revolutions and changes; the Old World is pronounced indebted to the New World because without it 'Europe would not even have its poor declaration of the rights of man.'

(Vieira 1999: 98–9)

Once again, then, the postcolonial world is one of change and struggle. However, in this case, it is former colonizers who are strengthened by the energy of the struggle. In terms of translation this means a 'translational project' (Vieira, p. 106) that is marked by creation and re-creation, absorbing the ST and revitalizing it through nourished TTs that employ an energized and different form of the colonizer's language that belongs to the postcolony.

The way that the Brazilian cannibalists, notably Haraldo de Campos, set about achieving this was, somewhat ironically, strongly influenced by Western thinkers, especially the experimental work of Ezra Pound and Walter Benjamin, and the concept of the transformational strength of 'pure' language (see chapter 10). For the moment, however, it is important to be aware that these different postcolonial writings on translation have found their echo within Europe, specifically in the Irish context.

8.3.2 The Irish context

The translation of Irish literature is the subject of two recent book-length studies: Michael Cronin's *Translating Ireland* (1996) and Maria Tymoczko's *Translation in a Postcolonial Context* (1999a). In this section we focus on Cronin's more politically assertive work.

Cronin (p. 3) takes issue with Niranjana and other writers on translation and postcolonialism because of their 'simple opposition of Europe and the New World or Europe and the Colony' and because of their neglect of the 'internal colonialism' within Europe itself. Cronin himself concentrates on the role of translation in the linguistic and political battle between the Irish and English languages, examining how Irish translators throughout history have discussed and presented their work in prefaces, commentaries and other writings. Of particular interest is his description of this process from historical, political and cultural angles and the way translation is seen, at different times, to serve the interests of both colonizer and colonized. The role of language in the subjugation of Ireland by the English is evident in the 1537 Act for the English Order which was designed to make the Irish speak English. Cronin uses the metaphor of translation to draw a parallel with what was happening physically to the Irish:

Translation at a cultural level – the embrace of English acculturation – is paralleled by translation at a territorial level, the forcible displacement and movement of populations.

(Cronin 1996: 49)

On the other hand, Cronin (pp. 49–51) quotes the English poet Edmund Spenser, writing in 1596, who supported the power of the conqueror, but nevertheless appreciated English translations of Irish poems. This appreciation of Irish literature in translation counters the barbarian Irish stereotype of the time.

Cronin (pp. 67–71) goes on to describe how, in the seventeenth century, translation into English was promoted by new forms of patronage (the education system, the landed aristocracy, the church and the large numbers of new settlers) which gave economic and political incentives for the use of English. In the eighteenth and nineteenth centuries, translations into English were produced by Irish scholars in an attempt to oppose views of Irish history and literature produced by England and to defend their own culture. This, as Cronin points out (p. 92), ironically assisted in the strengthening of the English language in Ireland. Translation continues to be a political issue in modern postcolonial Ireland where the Irish and English languages co-exist.

The translation into the other European languages of literature written in both Irish and English by Irish writers is now financially supported by the Arts Council in Ireland. Cronin's quoting (p. 174) of the Council's Laurence Cassidy reveals the economic power over culture that remains with the former colonial power:

> It is of the most crucial importance that an independent country with an independent literature in two languages takes onto itself its own representation of that literature and doesn't leave it to London [publishing] houses who are really only promoting the authorial end and the economic end of the process and are not concerned about the Irish image.

In this way, the political stance of Cronin's book demonstrates that the postcolonial power relations within translation do not just operate on a globally North–South or West–East scale.

8.4 The ideologies of the theorists

Cultural studies has taken an increasingly keen interest in translation. One consequence of this widening of the ambit of translation studies is that it has brought together scholars from a wide range of backgrounds. Yet it is important to remember that cultural theorists themselves have their own ideology and agendas that drive their own criticisms. Thus, the feminist translators of the Canadian project are very open about flaunting their manipulation of texts. Sherry Simon is also explicit in stating that the aim of her book on gender and translation is 'to cast the widest net around issues of gender in translation . . . and, through gender, to move translation studies closer to a cultural studies framework' (Simon 1996: ix). This has inevitably entailed an attack on linguistic theories of translation. Such aims can be traced back a long way. As early as 1980, Susan Bassnett was openly dismissive of linguistic theories of translation in her influential survey *Translation Studies*.

To be sure, these new cultural approaches have widened the horizons of translation studies with a wealth of new insights, but there is also a strong element of conflict and competition between them. For example, Simon (1996: 95), writing from a gender-studies perspective, describes the distortion of the representation in translation of the French feminist Hélène Cixous, since many critics only have access to that portion of her work that is available in English. However, Rosemary Arroyo (1999), writing from a postcolonial angle, claims that Cixous's own appropriation of the Brazilian author Clarice Lispector 'is in fact an exemplary illustration of an aggressively "masculine" approach to difference' (Arroyo 1999: 160).

Such differences of perspective are inevitable and even to be welcomed as translation and translation studies continue to increase their influence. In many ways, it is part of the rewriting process described by Lefevere. And the anthologizing, canonizing process can be seen everywhere. The present book, for example, cannot avoid rewriting and to some extent manipulating other work in the field. The cultural turn might also be described as an attempt by cultural studies to colonize the less established field of translation studies.

Additionally, postcolonial writers have their own political agenda. Cronin, for instance, posits the potential for English-speaking Irish translators to 'make a distinctive contribution to world culture as a non-imperial English-speaking bridge for the European audiovisual industry' (Cronin 1996: 197). This, he feels, can be achieved 'using appropriate translation strategies', although he does not give details except for 'the need to protect diversity and heterogeneity'. The promotion of such translation policies, albeit from the perspective of the 'minority' cultures, still involves a political act and a manipulation of translation for specific political or economic advantage.

Case study

This case study concerns *The Last Flicker* (1991), the English translation of Gurdial Singh's Punjabi novel *Marhi Da Deeva* (1964).[6] Punjabi and English have shared an unequal and problematic power equation owing to a long history of British rule in India and the imposition of the English language during that time. In more recent years, the native literature of the Punjab has become more valued, and no writer more so than Gurdial Singh, joint winner of India's prestigious Jnanpith Literary Award in 1999.

It is significant first of all that his novel should have been selected for translation, albeit twenty-seven years after the publication of the ST. This fact immediately raises the status of a novel in its source culture. Its enormous success in its other translations, in Hindi and Russian, may have assisted its publication in English, which coincided with the release in India of a film based on the novel. There may be other political and cultural reasons too: the publisher of the translation, Sahitya Akademi, is the national organization set up by the government of India 'to co-ordinate liter-ary activities and to promote through them the cultural unity of India'.[7] In this instance, therefore, English is being used as a tool both nationally and internationally.

The translation is by Ajmer S. Rode, a Punjabi settled in Canada. The facts that the book has been translated by a fellow countryman, but one who is settled in a Western country, that it has been promoted by a central govern-ment organization and that it is written in the hegemonic language of English immediately raise a complex range of cultural issues concerning the power structures at play in and around the text and translator.

A further factor is added by the setting of the novel in an isolated village in the Malwa region of Punjab. The poorly educated characters converse with each other in the local Malwai dialect of Punjabi. Their colloquial dialogue constitutes a crucial element of the fictional discourse, with the third person narrator portraying characters and situations through the character's speech rhythms and the cultural environment they evoke.

In the English translation, the dialogue shows a mix of registers: there are archaic insults (*wretched dog!*) and others that combine slight archaism with the reference points of rural life (*that oaf, big-boned like a bullock*), alongside modern American expletives (*asshole, Goddam dumb ox, fucking God, fucking piece of land, king shit!, bullshit, bloody big daddies*) and speech markers (*huh, yeah, right?*). Lexis such as *Goddam, bullshit, fucking God*, etc., clearly points to a cultural context very different to the one within which the novel was con-ceived, uprooting the characters from rural Punjab and giving them the speech accents of street-smart urban North America.

The mixing of registers in the translation also affects kinship markers. Culturally loaded as they often are, they are sometimes replaced by their nearest English equivalents and on other occasions are retained in their ori-ginal form for emphasis. For instance, *Bapu*, a term used for father or an elder, is preserved in its original form while the overtly Americanized *mom* and Anglicized *aunty* replace *Maa* and *Chachi/Tayyi*.[8] Kinship culture in Punjab is inextricably bound up with notions of hierarchy and status-consciousness, as well as revealing the emotional bonds between characters. At times, the emotional bonds are indicated by Americanized terms of endearment, such as the use of *honey* by a father to refer to his daughter. This points to a disruption in translation of a central theme from the source culture.

Nevertheless, it is also true that this kind of text would pose problems for any translator. The translation of a Punjabi regional novel for the inter-national audience will inevitably involve spatial and cultural dislocation. What the translator has done is to translate the regional and social dialect of a small village community with the sociolect of urban working-class North America, where he has lived for several years. This may prove problematic for those reading the text in English in India, since the indicators of the dislocation towards the hegemonic Anglo-Saxon culture – as Spivak or

Niranjana might call it – would be very noticeable. Yet the mix of registers also serves to make apparent that we are reading a translation. The result is not exactly the 'with-it translatese' bemoaned by Spivak or the dominant Anglo-American domesticating translations castigated by Venuti (1995; see chapter 9); it is rather a dislocationary translation practice that brings into sharp relief the clash of different cultures. The characters are dislodged from their source culture, but they are also made to come alive and challenge the English-language reader. This is the kind of complex interventionist approach the translator has carried out, but he leaves himself open to the criticism that he has chosen to superimpose the sociolect of the hegemonic power.

Interestingly enough, the translation of *Marhi Da Deeva* was followed by the translation of two other Singh novels: *Addh Chanini Raat* (*Night of the Half-Moon*, Madras: Macmillan, 1996) and *Parsa* (National Book Trust, 1999); these translations bring Singh to the attention of an even wider audience and are perhaps indicative of the success of the first translation.

Discussion of case study

This case study, which looks at the language of the TT and sees cultural implications in the choices made, has examined a case where a novel from a minority language has been translated into the hegemonic international language (English) under the auspices of a centralized national organization (the Sahitya Akademi). The language of the characters becomes mingled with that of the colonizer, and their identity – embedded in their Punjabi cultural milieu – is blurred. While postcolonial theories help to understand the power relations that operate around the translation process, it is also clear from this brief analysis of *The Last Flicker* that a whole range of interacting factors are at work. These include the perhaps inevitable dislocation of the source culture, the dislocation of the Punjabi translator in Canada and the location of the patronage within India itself. It would now be interesting to compare the translation strategies employed in the other novels. The aim would be to see how far this translation strategy is due to translation policy or to the way literary translators function in general. The latter is an issue that will be considered in the next chapter.

Summary

This chapter has focused on the varieties of cultural studies in translation studies. Linguistic theories of translation have been sidelined and attention has centred on translation as cultural transfer and the interface of translation with other growing disciplines within cultural studies. Those examined in this chapter have been:

- section 8.1: translation as rewriting, developed from systems theories and pioneered by André Lefevere, studying the power relations and ideologies existing in the patronage and poetics of literary and cultural systems that interface with literary translation;

- section 8.2: translation and gender, with the Canadian feminist translation project described by Sherry Simon, making the feminine visible in translation;
- section 8.3: translation and postcolonialism, with examples from Spivak, Niranjana and Cronin comparing the 'dislocature' of texts and translators working in former colonies of the European powers or in their languages.

Niranjana in particular highlights the power relations in the translation of the colonized peoples and takes translation studies to task for its Western philosophical and ideological bias. Finally, Brazilian cannibalism, as exemplified by de Campos and Vieira, employs the metaphor of devouring the colonizer to energize the native Brazilian tradition. The next chapter turns to examine the role of translators themselves at the cultural interface.

Further reading

For an introduction to cultural studies, read Easthope (1991) or During (1999). For translation as rewriting, read additionally Lefevere (1981, 1985, 1993) and the collection of essays edited by Alvarez and Africa-Vidal (1996) for translation as a political act. Related discussion of issues of patronage follows in chapter 9. For an introduction to gender issues, read Butler (1990) and Buikema and Smelik (1995). For translation and gender, read Godard (1990) and, for the first sign that gay issues are beginning to enter the translation forum, read Harvey (1998/2000; see also chapter 11). For an introduction to postcolonialism, read Said (1978). In addition, for translation and postcolonialism read Cheyfitz (1991), Bhabha (1994), and Robinson (1997a), and for Brazilian cannibalism read de Campos (1992) and Vieira (1997).

Discussion and research points

1   Lefevere sees translation 'as potentially the most influential' (1992a: 9) form of rewriting. How far do you agree with him? Compare this with examples taken from other forms of rewriting (film adaptations, anthologization, historiography, etc.).
2   Lefevere identifies three factors (the professionals, patronage and poetics) which control the literary system. Examine how each functions in your own culture and which, if any, seems to be most important. Are there other factors you would add?
3   Should women writers ideally be translated by women only? What about male writers? Look at published translations and their prefaces to see how often this could become an issue.
4   Look for examples from translations in various times and locations that reveal a gender bias. How is that bias revealed? Is there a pattern to these examples? How might the translator have acted differently?

5   How far do you feel Barbara Godard is justified in 'flaunting her manipulation of the text' for feminist purposes, or Niranjana is justified for her 'interventionist' approach?
6   What research work has been carried out on postcolonialism and translation in your own country and language(s)? Do the results tie in with those discussed here?
7   How far do you agree with Niranjana that translation studies has been overly dominated by Western theories? If this is true, how can or should the situation be changed?
8   'Co-existence implies translating the culture and (political, religious, emotional) language of the other into a language and culture that is strengthened by the presence of the other. The alternative to translation is the muteness of fear' (Cronin 1996: 200). How far does this statement hold for the linguistic policies of your own country? What examples have you come across of translation involving a power difference between the two languages and cultures?

Chapter 8

9 Translating the foreign: the (in)visibility of translation

Key concepts

- Venuti: the 'invisibility' of the translator in the modern publishing world.
- Venuti: 'foreignizing' vs. 'domesticating' translation, and the 'call for action'.
- Berman: the 'negative analytic' and deformation of translation.
- Literary translators' accounts of their work: 'ear' and 'voice'.
- The power network of the publishing industry.
- The reception of translation – reception theory and translation reviewing.

Key texts

Berman, A. (1984/92) L'épreuve de l'étranger: Culture et traduction dans l'Allemagne roman-tique, Paris: Éditions Gallimard; translated (1992) by S. Heyvaert as The Experience of the Foreign: Culture and Translation in Romantic Germany, Albany: State University of New York.

Berman, A. (1985b/2000) 'Translation and the trials of the foreign', translated by L. Venuti, in L. Venuti (ed.) (2000), pp. 284–97. (Originally published as 'La traduction comme épreuve de l'étranger', Texte (1985): 67–81).

Felstiner, J. (1980) Translating Neruda: The Way to Macchu Picchu, Stanford, CA: Stanford University Press.

Levine, S. (1991) The Subversive Scribe: Translating Latin American Fiction, St Paul, MN: Graywolf Press.

Venuti, L. (ed.) (1992) Rethinking Translation: Discourse, Subjectivity, Ideology, London and New York: Routledge.

Venuti, L. (1995) The Translator's Invisibility: A History of Translation, London and New York: Routledge.

Venuti, L. (1998) The Scandals of Translation: Towards an Ethics of Difference, London and New York: Routledge.

9.0 Introduction

Chapter 8 examined varieties of cultural studies that have focused on transla-tion. In this chapter, we concentrate on other research that deals with cultural difference and with the interface between the source culture and the foreign, linking ideology and dominant discourse to translation strategies.

Section 9.1 focuses on key areas of the influential work of Lawrence Venuti, notably the 'invisibility' of translation and the translator in Anglo-American culture (section 9.1.1) and the 'domesticating' and 'foreignizing' translation strategies which are available to the translator (section 9.1.2). Section 9.1.3 considers work by Antoine Berman that follows a similar line, Berman's 'negative analytic' attacking the homogenization of the translation of literary prose.

The remainder of the chapter considers other related areas and players in the translation process. Thus, in section 9.2 a description is given of what practising literary translators say about their practices, in order to see if their own view of their work tallies with Venuti's and Berman's theories. Section 9.3 deals with crucial aspects of the powerful publishing industry and section 9.4 discusses criticisms of Venuti. Finally, section 9.5 examines the reception of translations, notably the reviewing process, and what this reveals about cultural attitudes to translation in general. Following this, the case study illustrates one method of investigating these ideas by analyzing the reviews of a translated text.

9.1 Venuti: the cultural and political agenda of translation

Like the other cultural theorists discussed in chapter 8, Venuti insists that the scope of translation studies needs to be broadened to take account of the value-driven nature of the sociocultural framework. Thus he contests Toury's 'scientific' descriptive model with its aim of producing 'value-free' norms and laws of translation (see chapter 7):

> Toury's method ... must still turn to cultural theory in order to assess the significance of the data, to analyze the norms. Norms may be in the first instance linguistic or literary, but they will also include a diverse range of domestic values, beliefs, and social representations which carry ideological force in serving the interests of specific groups. And they are always housed in the social institutions where translations are produced and enlisted in cultural and political agendas.
>
> (Venuti 1998: 29)

In addition to governments and other politically motivated institutions, which may decide to censor or promote certain works (compare Lefevere's discussion of control factors in section 8.1), the groups and social institutions to which Venuti refers would include the various players in the publishing industry as a whole. Above all, these would be the publishers and editors who choose the works and commission the translations, pay the translators and often dictate the translation method. They also include the literary agents, marketing and sales teams and reviewers. The reviewers' comments indicate and to some extent determine how translations are read and received in the target culture. Each of these players has a particular position and role within the dominant cultural and political agendas of their time and place.

The translators themselves are part of that culture, which they can either accept or rebel against.

9.1.1 Venuti and the 'invisibility' of the translator

Invisibility is a term used by Venuti (1995: 1) 'to describe the translator's situation and activity in contemporary Anglo-American culture'. Venuti sees this invisibility as typically being produced:

1 by the way translators themselves tend to translate 'fluently' into English, to produce an idiomatic and 'readable' TT, thus creating an 'illusion of transparency';
2 by the way the translated texts are typically read in the target culture:

> A translated text, whether prose or poetry, fiction or non-fiction, is judged acceptable by most publishers, reviewers and readers when it reads fluently, when the absence of any linguistic or stylistic peculiarities makes it seem transparent, giving the appearance that it reflects the foreign writer's personality or intention or the essential meaning of the foreign text – the appearance, in other words, that the translation is not in fact a translation, but the 'original'.
>
> (Venuti 1995: 1)

Venuti (1998: 31) sees the most important factor for this as being 'the prevailing conception of authorship'. Translation is seen as derivative and of secondary quality and importance. Thus, the English practice since Dryden has been to conceal the act of translation so that, even now, 'translations are rarely considered a form of literary scholarship' (Venuti 1998: 32).

9.1.2 Domestication and foreignization

Venuti (1995: 19–20) discusses invisibility hand in hand with two types of translating strategy: domestication and foreignization. These strategies concern both the choice of text to translate and the translation method. Their roots are traced back by Venuti to Schleiermacher and his 1813 essay 'Über die verschiedenen Methoden des Übersetzens' (see chapter 2). Venuti (1995: 21) sees domestication as dominating Anglo-American translation culture. Just as the postcolonialists are alert to the cultural effects of the differential in power relations between colony and ex-colony, so Venuti (1995: 20) bemoans the phenomenon of domestication since it involves 'an ethnocentric reduction of the foreign text to [Anglo-American] target-language cultural values'. This entails translating in a transparent, fluent, 'invisible' style in order to minimize the foreignness of the TT. Venuti allies it with Schleiermacher's description of translation that 'leaves the reader in peace, as much as possible, and moves the author towards him' (Schleiermacher 1813/1992: 41–2; see chapter 2 of this book). Domestication further covers adherence to domestic literary canons by carefully selecting the texts that are likely to lend themselves to such a translation strategy (Venuti 1997: 241).

Foreignization, on the other hand, 'entails choosing a foreign text and developing a translation method along lines which are excluded by dominant cultural values in the target language' (Venuti 1997: 242). It is the preferred choice of Schleiermacher, whose description is of a translation strategy where 'the translator leaves the writer alone, as much as possible and moves the reader towards the writer' (Schleiermacher 1813/1992: 42). Venuti (1995: 20) considers the foreignizing method to be 'an ethnodeviant pressure on [target-language cultural] values to register the linguistic and cultural difference of the foreign text, sending the reader abroad'. It is 'highly desirable', he says, in an effort 'to restrain the ethnocentric violence of translation'. In other words, the foreignizing method can restrain the 'violently' domesticating cultural values of the English-language world. The foreignizing method of translating, a strategy Venuti also terms '**resistancy**' (1995: 305–6), is a non-fluent or estranging translation style designed to make visible the presence of the translator by highlighting the foreign identity of the ST and protecting it from the ideological dominance of the target culture.

In his later book *The Scandals of Translation* (1998), Venuti continues to insist on foreignizing or, as he also calls it, '**minoritizing**' translation, to cultivate a varied and 'heterogeneous discourse' (Venuti 1998: 11). One of the examples he gives of a minoritizing project is his own translation of works by the nineteenth-century Italian Tarchetti (pp. 13–20). The choice of works to translate is minoritizing since Tarchetti was a minor nineteenth-century Italian writer, a Milanese bohemian who further challenged the literary establishment by using the standard Tuscan dialect to write experimental and Gothic novels and by challenging the moral and political values of the day. As far as the language is concerned, the minoritizing or foreignizing method of Venuti's translation comes through in the deliberate inclusion of foreignizing elements, such as modern American slang, in a bid to make the translator 'visible' and to make the readers realize they are reading a translation of a work from a foreign culture. Venuti gives the extract shown in box 9.1 as an example of what he means by this approach.

Among the elements of this extract which Venuti considers to be distinctive of foreignization are the close adherence to the ST structure and syntax (e.g. the adjunct positions in the first sentence), the calques *soggiorno* as *sojourn*, *indurlo* as *induce him* and the archaic structure *nor could I ever*. In other passages (see Venuti 1998: 16–17), he juxtaposes both archaisms (e.g. *scapegrace*) and modern colloquialisms (e.g. *con artist*, *funk*), and uses British spellings (e.g. *demeanour*, *offence*) to jar the reader with a 'heterogeneous discourse'.

Venuti is happy to note (1998: 15) that some of the reviews of the translation were appreciative of his 'visible' translating strategy. However, he also adds (pp. 18–19) that some of the reviews attacked the translation for not being what, in Venuti's terms, would be domestication.

Box 9.1

Nel 1855, domiciliatomi a Pavia, m'era allo studio del disegno inuna scuola privata di quella città; e dopo alcuni mesi di soggiorno aveva stretto relazione con certo Federico M. che era professore di patologia e di clinica per l'insegnamento universitario, e che morì di apoplessia fulminante pochi mesi dopo che lo aveva conosciuto. Era un uomo amantissimo delle scienze, della sua in particolare – aveva virtù e doti di mente non comuni – senonché, come tutti gli anatomisti ed i clinici in genere, era scettico profondamente e inguaribilmente – lo era per convinzione, né io potei mai indurlo alle mie credenze, per quanto mi vi adoprassi nelle discussioni appassionate e calorose che avevamo ogni giorno a questo riguardo.

In 1855, having taken up residence at Pavia, I devoted myself to the study of drawing at a private school in that city; and several months into my sojourn, I developed a close friendship with a certain Federico M., a professor of pathology and clinical medicine who taught at the university and died of severe apoplexy a few months after I became acquainted with him. He was very fond of the sciences and of his own in particular – he was gifted with extraordinary mental powers – except that, like all anatomists and doctors generally, he was profoundly and incurably skeptical. He was so by conviction, nor could I ever induce him to accept my beliefs, no matter how much I endeavored in the impassioned, heated discussions we had every day on this point.[1]

(Venuti 1998: 15)

Although Venuti advocates foreignizing translation, he is also aware (1995: 29) of some of its contradictions, namely that it is a subjective and relative term that still involves some domestication because it translates an ST for a target culture and depends on dominant target-culture values to become visible when it departs from them. However, Venuti defends foreignizing translations. They 'are equally partial [as are domesticating translations] in their interpretation of the foreign text, but they do tend to flaunt their partiality instead of concealing it' (1995: 34). Importantly, it should also be pointed out at this point that domestication and foreignization are considered by Venuti (1999), in the introduction to the Italian translation of *The Translator's Invisibility*, to be 'heuristic concepts ... designed to promote thinking and research' rather than binary opposites: 'They possess a contingent variability, such that they can only be defined in the specific cultural situation in which a translation is made and works its effects.' This, according to Venuti, means that the terms may change meaning across time and location. What does not change, however, is that domestication and foreignization deal with 'the question of how much a translation assimilates a foreign text to the translating language and culture, and how much it rather signals the differences of that text'. This is a question which had already attracted the attention of the noted French theorist, the late Antoine Berman.

9.1.3 Antoine Berman: the 'negative analytic' of translation

Antoine Berman's major theoretical work – *L'épreuve de l'étranger: Culture et traduction dans l'Allemagne romantique* (1984), translated into English as *The Experience of the Foreign: Culture and Translation in Romantic Germany* (1992) – precedes and influences Venuti, who himself has recently produced an English translation of an important article by Berman. This article, 'La traduction comme épreuve de l'étranger' (1985), is entitled 'Translation and the trials of the foreign' in English (in Venuti 2000). The change from *experience* in the title of the book to *trials* in the article is perhaps indicative of Venuti's desire to challenge the reader by highlighting the challenge and trials that translation represents to the ST. Berman (2000: 284) describes it as an *épreuve* ('**trial**') in two senses:

1   a trial for the target culture in experiencing the strangeness of the foreign text and word;
2   a trial for the foreign text in being uprooted from its original language context.

Berman deplores the general tendency to negate the foreign in translation by the translation strategy of 'naturalization', which would equate with Venuti's later 'domestication'. 'The properly *ethical* aim of the translating act', says Berman (p. 285), is 'receiving the foreign as foreign', which would seem to have influenced Venuti's 'foreignizing' translation strategy. However, Berman considers (p. 286) that there is generally a 'system of textual deformation' in TTs that prevents the foreign coming through. His examination of the forms of deformation is termed 'negative analytic':

> The negative analytic is primarily concerned with ethnocentric, annexationist translations and hypertextual translations (pastiche, imitation, adaptation, free writing), where the play of deforming forces is freely exercised.
>
> (Berman 1985b/2000: 286)

Berman, who translated Latin American fiction and German philosophy, sees every translator as being inevitably and inherently exposed to these ethnocentric forces, which determine the 'desire to translate' as well as the form of the TT. He feels (p. 286) that it is only by psychoanalytic analysis of the translator's work, and by making the translator aware of these forces, that such tendencies can be neutralized. His main attention is centred on the translation of fiction:

> The principal problem of translating the novel is to respect its *shapeless polylogic* and avoid an arbitrary homogenization.
>
> (Berman 1985b/2000: 287)

By this, Berman is referring to the linguistic variety and creativity of the novel and the way translation tends to reduce variation. He identifies twelve 'deforming tendencies' (p. 288):

1   **Rationalization**: This mainly affects syntactic structures including punctuation and sentence structure and order. Berman also refers to the abstractness of rationalization, the translation of verbs by noun forms and the tendency to generalization.

2   **Clarification**: This includes explicitation, which 'aims to render "clear" what does not wish to be clear in the original' (p. 289).

3   **Expansion**: Like other theorists (for example, Vinay and Darbelnet; see chapter 4), Berman says that TTs tend to be longer than STs. This is due to 'empty' explicitation that unshapes its rhythm, to 'overtranslation' and to 'flattening'. These additions only serve to reduce the clarity of the work's 'voice'.

4   **Ennoblement**: This refers to the tendency on the part of certain translators to 'improve' on the original by rewriting it in a more elegant style. The result, according to Berman (p. 291), is an annihilation of the oral rhetoric and formless polylogic of the ST. Equally destructive is a TT that is too 'popular' in its use of colloquialisms.

5   **Qualitative impoverishment**: This is the replacement of words and expressions with TT equivalents 'that lack their sonorous richness or, correspondingly, their signifying or "iconic" features' (p. 291). By iconic or iconicity, Berman means terms whose form and sound are in some way associated with their sense. An example he gives is the word *butterfly* and its corresponding terms in other languages.

6   **Quantitative impoverishment**: This is loss of lexical variation in translation. Berman gives the example of a Spanish ST that uses three different synonyms for *face* (*semblante*, *rostro* and *cara*); rendering them all as *face* would involve loss.

7   **The destruction of rhythms**: Although more common in poetry, rhythm is still important to the novel and can be 'destroyed' by deformation of word order and punctuation.

8   **The destruction of underlying networks of signification**: The translator needs to be aware of the network of words that is formed throughout the text. Individually, these words may not be significant, but they add an underlying uniformity and sense to the text. Examples are augmentative suffixes in a Latin American text (*jaulón*, *portón*, etc.).

9   **The destruction of linguistic patternings**: While the ST may be systematic in its sentence constructions and patternings, translation tends to be 'asystematic' (p. 293). The translator likely adopts a range of techniques, such as rationalization, clarification and expansion which, although making the TT linguistically more homogenous, also render it more 'incoherent' because the systematicity of the original is destroyed.

10 **The destruction of vernacular networks or their exoticization**: This relates especially to local speech and language patterns which play an important role in establishing the setting of a novel. There is severe loss if these are erased, yet the traditional solution of exoticizing some of these terms by, for example, the use of italics, isolates them from the

co-text. Alternatively, seeking a TL vernacular or slang is a ridiculous exoticization of the foreign (compare the case study from Punjabi in chapter 8).

11   **The destruction of expressions and idioms**: Berman considers the replacing of an idiom or proverb by its TL 'equivalent' to be an 'ethnocentrism': 'to play with "equivalence" is to attack the discourse of the foreign work', he says (p. 295). Thus, an English expression from Conrad containing the name of the well-known insane asylum Bedlam, should not be translated by 'Charenton', a French insane asylum, since this would result in a TT that produces a network of French cultural references.

12   **The effacement of the superimposition of languages**: By this, Berman means the way translation tends to erase traces of different forms of language that co-exist in the ST. These may be the mix of peninsular and Latin American Spanishes in the work of Valle-Inclán, the proliferation of language influences in Joyce's *Finnegan's Wake*, different sociolects and idiolects, and so on. Berman (p. 296) considers this to be the 'central problem' in the translation of novels.

Counterbalancing the 'universals' of this negative analytic is Berman's 'positive analytic' (pp. 286, 296–7), his proposal for the type of translation required to render the foreign in the TT. This he calls '**literal translation**':

> Here 'literal' means: attached to the letter (of works). Labor on the letter in translation, on the one hand, restores the particular signifying process of works (which is more than their meaning) and, on the other hand, transforms the translating language.
>
> (Berman 1985b/2000: 297)

Berman's term is markedly different and more specific compared to the conventional use of literal translation discussed in chapter 2; his use of *literal* and *letter* and his reference to the 'signifying process' point to a Saussurean perspective and to a positive transformation of the TL. The term *literal* is also discussed by Venuti (1995: 146–7), who construes the *letter* as 'the range of signifying possibilities in the TL'.

Berman's work is important in linking philosophical ideas to translation strategies with many examples drawn from existing translations. His discussion of the ethics of translation as witnessed in linguistic 'deformation' of TTs is of especial relevance and a notable counterpoint to earlier writing on literary translation. Yet, despite Berman's concern for the foreign in translation, it is Venuti's work that has attracted more attention and aggressive reaction (see section 9.4). The following sections consider what Venuti says about various aspects of the sociocultural context (translators, publishers, reviewers), including his 'call to action'. This is related to observations that come from the perspective of the participants themselves, beginning with the literary translators.

9.2 *Literary translators' accounts of their work*

Although Toury (1995: 65; see also chapter 7 in this book) warns that explicit comments from participants in the translation process need to be treated with circumspection since they may be biased, such comments are at best a significant indication of working practices; at worst they at least reveal what the participants feel they ought to be doing. This section limits itself to English-language translators of Latin American fiction, but the ideas and arguments that are presented are representative of the writing of many other translators.

Venuti's 'call to action' (1995: 307–13), for translators to adopt 'visible' and 'foreignizing' strategies, is perhaps a reaction to those contemporary translators who seem to debate their work along lines appropriate to the age-old and vague terms which we discussed in chapter 2. For example, Rabassa (Hoeksema 1978: 12) discusses the relative exigencies of 'accuracy' and 'flow' in literary translation. The translators often consider that their work is intuitive and that they must listen to their '**ear**' (Rabassa 1984: 35, Felstiner 1980: 81). In similar vein, Peden (1987: 9), the translator of Sábato, Allende and Esquivel, listens to the '**voice**' of the ST. She defines this as 'the way something is communicated: the way the tale is told; the way the poem is sung' and it determines 'all choices of cadence and tone and lexicon and syntax' (p. 9). Felstiner, who translated Pablo Neruda's classic poem about Macchu Picchu, went as far as to listen to Neruda reading his poems so as to see the stresses and the emphases (Felstiner 1980: 51).

The 'invisibility' of translators is such that relatively few of them have written in detail about their practice. Two full-length works of import by contemporary literary translators of Latin American Spanish are John Felstiner's *Translating Neruda: The Way to Macchu Picchu* (1980) and Suzanne Jill Levine's *The Subversive Scribe: Translating Latin American Fiction* (1991). Felstiner (1980: 1) makes the important point that much of the work that goes into producing a translation 'becomes invisible once the new poem stands intact'. This includes the translator's own background and research as well as the process of composition. As far as the process is concerned, the British translator Peter Bush (1997: 129) describes how he often produces six or seven drafts of a translation. As the director of the British Centre for Literary Translation, Bush is behind the Centre's present project to collect an archive of translators' drafts and manuscripts in the interests of future research into that composition process.

Felstiner's account is also very interesting from the point of view of describing his immersion in the work and culture of the ST author, including visits to Macchu Picchu itself and his reading of Neruda's poem in that environment. However, Felstiner still uses age-old terms to describe 'the twofold requirement of translation': namely, 'the original must come through essentially, in language that itself rings true' (Felstiner 1980: 24). Phrases such as 'come through essentially' and 'ring true' are typical of the approaches of early translation theory discussed in chapter 2.

On the other hand, Levine sees herself (1991: xi) as a 'translator–collaborator' with the Cuban author Cabrera Infante, and as a 'subversive scribe', 'destroying' the form of the original but reproducing the meaning in a new form (p. 7). Levine sometimes creates a completely different passage in translation in order to give free rein to the English language's propensity to punning, surprising the reader with a mixture of the Latin American and the Anglo-Saxon. One example she gives (p. 15) from Cabrera Infante's *Tres tristes tigres* is the translation of the first line of the song Guantanamera ('Yo soy un hombre sincero') as 'I'm a man without a zero', playing on the sound of the words (*sincero* meaning 'sincere', but phonetically identical to *sin cero*, meaning 'without a zero'). She also (p. 23) invents humorous names of books and authors (such as I. P. Daley's *Yellow River* and *Off the Cliff* by (H)ugo First) to replace a list in the Spanish ST. This would appear to be a very domesticating approach, altering whole passages to filter out the foreign and to fit in with the target culture expectations. Yet the 'jarring' linguistic result in English, juxtaposed to a Latin American context, may go some way to creating what would be a 'foreignizing' reading. For Levine, adopting a feminist and poststructuralist view of the translator's work, the language of translation also plays an ideological role:

> A translation should be a critical act . . . creating doubt, posing questions to the reader, recontextualising the ideology of the original text.
>
> (Levine 1991: 3)

Translators have also become more vociferous about the injustices of the publishing process. Rabassa (Hoeksema 1978: 13–14) slates the 'translation police' of reviewers and 'nit-picking academics' who focus microscopically on errors in a translation, ignoring the literary value of the book as a whole. Bush (1997) details the professionalism of the literary translator, as reader, researcher and writer. He also points out (1997: 127) that literary translation is an economic activity, 'a cash nexus of relations' and 'an original subjective activity at the centre of a complex network of social and cultural practices'. This network is discussed in the next section.

9.3 The power network of the publishing industry

Venuti (1992: 1–3, 1998: 31–66) describes and laments the typical lot of the literary translator, working from contract to contract often for a usually modest flat fee, the publishers (rather than translators) initiating most translations and generally seeking to minimize the translation cost. Publishers, as Venuti shows (1995: 9–10), are very often reluctant to grant copyright or a share of the royalties to the translator. Venuti deplores this as another form of repression exercized by the publishing industry, but it is a repression that is far from uncommon because of the weakness of the translator's role in the network. Fawcett (1995: 189) describes this complex network as amounting to a 'power play', with the final product considerably shaped by editors and copy-editors. This most often results in a domesticating translation. Interviews with publishers confirm that it is often the case that the editor is not fluent in the foreign language and that the main concern is that the translation should 'read well' in the TL (Munday 1997: 170).

In some cases, the power play may result in the ST author being omitted from the translation process altogether: Kuhiwczak (1990) reports the dramatic fate of Milan Kundera's *The Joke*, whose first English translator and editor, working jointly, decided to unravel the ST's intentionally distorted chronology in an attempt to clarify the story for the readers. Kundera was sufficiently shocked and used his dominant position to demand a new translation. Venuti (1998: 6) questions Kundera's role, including the use of the previous translators' work without acknowledgement, claiming that 'Kundera doesn't want to recognize the linguistic and cultural differences that a translation must negotiate'.

Another key player in the process is the author's literary agent. In fact, little has been written (even if much has been said at literary translation conferences) about the role of agents in translation. Agents represent a range of authors and take a percentage of the writers' profits. They offer an ST to prospective target-language publishing houses, who then contact their preferred translators.

For many authors writing in other languages, the benchmark of success is to be translated into English. In fact, the decision whether or not to translate a work is the greatest power wielded by the editor and publisher. According to Venuti (1998: 48), publishers in the UK and USA tend to choose works that are easily assimilated into the target culture. The percentages of books translated in both countries are extremely low, comprising only around 2.5 per cent to 3 per cent of the total number of books published (Venuti 1995: 12–17). On the other hand, not only is the percentage of books translated in countries such as Germany and Italy much higher, but the majority of those translations are also from English (Venuti 1995: 14). Venuti sees the imbalance as yet another example of the cultural hegemony of Anglo-American publishing and culture, which is very insular and refuses to accept the foreign yet is happy for its own works to maintain a strong hold in other countries. Venuti had expressed this in damning terms in the introduction to *Rethinking Translation: Discourse, Subjectivity, Ideology*:

> It can be said that Anglo-American publishing has been instrumental in producing readers who are aggressively monolingual and culturally parochial while reaping the economic benefits of successfully imposing Anglo-American cultural values on a sizeable foreign readership.
>
> (Venuti 1992: 6)

Market forces reinforce and even determine these trends. Thus, the first print-run for a literary translation in the UK or the USA rarely exceeds 5000 (Venuti 1995: 12). For this reason many translations into English depend on grants from cultural bodies such as the Arts Council of England (Hale 1997: 193).

9.4 Discussion of Venuti's work

Venuti's analysis of the Anglo-American publishing hegemony might seem to tie in with the power relations of the postcolonial world (see chapter 8), but it has sparked wide debate and a backlash from some translation theorists (see, for example, criticisms in Hermans 1999: 1–3). Pym (1996) takes issue with Venuti's figures, noting that, although the percentages of translations published in the UK and the USA might seem low, they do in fact represent large numbers of books and that the numbers have increased as the number of published books has increased.

Despite Pym's sarcastic stance towards Venuti, he raises a number of pertinent issues. These include:

1   Will translation really change if translators refuse to translate fluently (Pym 1996: 166)? Pym (p. 174) notes that Venuti's 'call for action', for translators to demand increased visibility, is best exemplified by Venuti himself as a translator–theorist. Although Pym questions whether other translators survive by adopting this stance, there are cases, such as Pevear and Volokhonsky's new English translations of Dostoevksy, where a non-fluent strategy has been acclaimed (see Venuti 1997: 313).

2   Although Venuti concentrates on translation into English, the trend towards a translation policy of 'fluency' (or 'domestication') occurs in translations into other languages as well. Pym (p. 170) cites Brazil, Spain and France as examples. This would seem to suggest that translation is, at the current time, typically domesticating, irrespective of the relative power of source and target cultures.

3   Pym also asks if Venuti's 'resistancy' is testable. He relates it to Toury's law of tolerance of interference (see chapter 7), with fluency ('non-tolerance of interference') expected to occur generally in translation. Thus, suggests Pym (p. 171), it is not surprising that this phenomenon should occur in Anglo-American translation.

Nevertheless, Pym concedes (p. 176) that Venuti 'does enable us to talk about translators as real people in political situations, about the quantitative aspects of translation policies, and about ethical criteria that might relate translators to the societies of the future'. The linking of translation to political and ideological agendas has already been discussed in chapter 8. The sociocultural context was also mentioned by Toury (see chapter 7), but it is Venuti who investigates it in more depth and who links that context to specific translation strategies.

Venuti does not offer a specific methodology to apply to the analysis of translation. His numerous case studies of translation encompass a range of approaches, including discussion of translators' prefaces and analysis of extracts of ST–TT pairs in order to assess the translation strategy prevalent in a given context and culture. Nevertheless, Venuti's general premises about foreignizing and domesticating translation strategies, and about the invisibility of the translator and the relative power of the publisher and the translator, can be investigated in a variety of ways:

- by comparing ST and TT linguistically for signs of foreignizing and domesticating strategies;
- by interviewing the translators about their strategies and/or researching what the translators say they are doing, their correspondence with the authors and the different drafts of a translation if available;
- by interviewing the publishers, editors and agents to see what their aims are in publishing translations, how they choose which books to translate and what instructions they give to translators;
- by looking at how many books are translated and sold, which ones are chosen and into which languages, and how trends vary over time;
- by looking at the kind of contracts that are made for translation and how 'visible' the translator is in the final product;
- by seeing how literally 'visible' the fact of translation is, looking at the packaging of the text, the appearance or otherwise of the translator's name on the title page, the copyright assignation, translators' prefaces, etc.;
- by analyzing the reviews of a translation, author or period. The aim would be to see what mentions are made of the translators (are they 'visible'?) and by what criteria reviewers (and the literary 'élite') judge translations at a given time and in a given culture.

Reviews are examined more carefully in the remainder of this chapter.

9.5 The reception and reviewing of translations

The link between the workings of the publishing industry and the reception of a given translation is clearly made in Meg Brown's in-depth study of Latin American novels published in West Germany in the 1980s (Brown 1994). She stresses (p. 58) the role of reviews in informing the public about recently published books and in preparing the readership for the work. Brown adopts ideas from **reception theory**, including examining the way a work conforms to, challenges or disappoints the readers' aesthetic 'horizon of expectation'. This is a term employed by Jauss (1982: 24) to refer to readers' general expectations (of the style, form, content, etc.) of the genre or series to which the new work belongs.

One way of examining the reception is by looking at the reviews of a work, since they represent a 'body of reactions' to the author and the text (Brown 1994: 7) and form part of the sub-area of translation criticism in Holmes's 'map' (see chapter 1). Reviews are also a useful source of information concerning that culture's view of translation itself, as we saw in section

9.1.2, where Venuti (1998: 18–20) uses literary reviews as a means of assessing the reception of his foreignizing translation of Tarchetti. Venuti quotes reviews that criticize the translation specifically because of its 'jarring' effect. This links in with Venuti's observations (1995: 2–5) that most English-language reviews prefer 'fluent' translations written in modern, general, standard English that is 'natural' and 'idiomatic'.

Venuti considers such a concentration on fluency and the lack of discussion of translation as prime indicators of the relegation of the translator's role to the point of 'invisibility'. The TT is normally read as if the work had originally been written in the TL, the translator's contribution being almost completely overlooked. There are several reasons for the lack of focus in reviews on the process of translation. One of these, noted by the American reviewer Robert Coover and quoted in Ronald Christ (1982: 17), is that 'whenever cuts are requested by the publishers of a review, the first to go are usually the remarks about the translation'. Many reviewers are also not able to compare the ST with the TT (Christ 1982: 21) and restrict themselves to often critical comments on individual words. Ronald Christ's article is one of the few relatively detailed discussions of issues related to translation reviews. Another, by Maier (1990), looks at reviews of Latin American literature in general. Maier goes a step further by noting how North American reviewers diminish the foreignness of a translation 'by focusing almost exclusively on [its] potential role in English, comparing it to "similar" works in North American literature and evaluating the ease with which it can be read' (p. 19). She sees translation reviewing as being 'largely undeveloped' (p. 20) and makes a series of suggestions, among which is the need 'to incorporate the contributions of translation theory and translation criticism into the practice of reviewing'.

There is no set model for the analysis of reviews in translation. Indeed, much work still remains to be done on the subject. Adopting the analytical approach of Jauss (1982), reviews can be analyzed synchronically or diachronically. An example of a synchronic analysis would be an examination of a range of reviews of a single work; examples of a diachronic analysis would be an examination of reviews of books of an author or newspaper over a longer time period. My own work (Munday 1998) combines the two, describing diachronically the evolution of the reception of García Márquez's works in English before analyzing synchronically the reception of one particular work, *Strange Pilgrims*. Part of that synchronic analysis forms the case study below.

Case study

This case study investigates many of the areas discussed in this chapter by focusing on a single book in English translation. This is a collection of short stories (*Doce cuentos peregrinos*) by the Colombian Nobel Prize winner García Márquez which was published in Spanish by Mondadori España (Madrid) and Oveja Negra (Bogota) in 1992. Its English translation, *Strange Pilgrims*, by Edith Grossman, appeared in hardback in 1993, published by Alfred Knopf (New York) and Jonathan Cape (London), both imprints of Random House. Pertinent research questions in this case study are:

- How 'visible' is the translator in the reviews?
- How is the translation judged by English-language reviewers?
- Do their comments suggest that García Márquez's success is due to what Venuti might term 'ethnocentric domestication' and 'violence'?

Reviews of the translation show a marked difference in the reception in the USA and in the UK. In the USA, reviews adopt an adulatory tone. In some instances, they might have been motivated by a self-interest in promoting the book. Thus, an advance review in the publishing industry's *Booklist*[2] raves that 'every story here is marvelous'. The daily and weekly press are similarly enthusiastic: *Time*[3] sees 'the enchanting density of García Márquez at his best'; *The New York Review of Books*[4] considers most of the stories to be 'undoubted masterpieces'.

The book is almost overlooked as a work of translation, and this supports Venuti's claim about the invisibility of translators. *Booklist*, *The Atlantic Monthly*[5] and *Time* give no mention that the book has even been translated. *The New York Review of Books* includes a short accolade: 'the quality of the tales is greatly enhanced by Edith Grossman's admirable translation'. This last review is more detailed and incorporates a summary of García Márquez's standing. It also makes an attempt to analyze his style and it is here that the crucial point that it is a translation is most glaringly absent. The example selected by the reviewer (Bayley) as 'a characteristic Márquez sentence' is the first sentence from *Miss Forbes's Summer of Happiness*: 'When we came back to the house in the afternoon, we found an enormous sea serpent nailed by the neck to the door frame.' This is not, in fact, a complete Márquez sentence at all, since the longer ST sentence had been divided by the translator and the circumstantial adjuncts reordered. The reviewer's reaction to this sentence is a clear indication that, while the translator's identity may be obscured, her words are definitely interpreted as the ST author's words.

Bayley also endeavours to incorporate García Márquez into the accepted literary culture of the European and US world, comparing his 'sense of detail' to Kafka and to Kundera, 'which suggests not only that magic realism has spread throughout Europe, but that something very like it was, or has become, a part of the literary spirit of our age, in Europe and America'. The suggestion is that García Márquez and the Latin Americans have had a recent profound influence on Europe and the USA, but that magic realism may have been at the core of the contemporary 'literary spirit', rendering Latin America's contribution less vital.

An appropriation of Latin America's success can also be seen on the cover of the US Penguin paperback. The predictably upbeat blurb on the back cover ends with the following conclusion: '*Strange Pilgrims* is a triumph of narrative sorcery by one of our foremost magicians of the written word.' The choice of the possessive pronoun shows that García Márquez's nationality and identity have been subsumed into the *our* of general literary heritage. The passivity of Latin America is also suggested by the theme of the stories, summarized as 'Latin American characters adrift in Europe'. The cover for the British paperback edition, on the other hand, makes the characters more active: 'the surreal haunting "journeys" of Latin Americans in Europe'.

British reviews of the translation were not as adulatory as those in the US. In the *Times Literary Supplement*,[6] 'García Márquez is criticized for 'crowd-pleasing' since 'these are for the most part facile stories, too easy on the mind, soft-centred and poorly focused'. The *Independent*[7] considers them on the whole as 'slight', 'laboured', 'portentous' and 'disappointing'.

Turner Hospital, the reviewer in the *Independent*, launches an attack on both the author, for his 'leaden prose', and on the translator, for 'occasional ambiguous welters of pronouns'. The immediate question is how qualified is the reviewer to make such judgements about language? She talks about the 'metaphor and off-kilter lyricism of the novels', presumably referring to the English of the translations she has read. The 'off-kilter lyricism' may also suggest that the reviewer herself has a stereotype of García Márquez the magic realist and is disappointed not to find this in *Strange Pilgrims*. Her horizon of expectation has been disappointed. The criticism that there are 'ambiguous welters of pronouns' appears rather strange since the effect of the pronouns is to increase cohesion and to avoid potential ambiguity. This is a further indication that translator and reviewer are on different wavelengths in a 'discussion' which the translator can hardly win.

The reviews show that the translator's role, while not 'invisible', is rarely highlighted in the reviews. The generally small, superficial comments on the translator mirror the observations of Christ and Maier and the examples quoted by Venuti. The translation is indeed mostly read as if it had originally been written in English (compare the recipes for good translation given by translators such as Dryden in chapter 2). This impression is fostered by the sales pitch of the book. There is also a strong hint that García Márquez's whole image, as well as his language, may have undergone some form of cultural appropriation or domestication, especially in the US context.

Discussion of the case study

The case study looked at one area of the sociocultural systems around the translator. It has shown that a study of a wide range of reviews is both reasonably straightforward methodologically and informative about one literary 'élite's' reaction to translation. Venuti's comments about the invisibility of the translator and about the cultural hegemony of the Anglo-American publishing world seem to be borne out in the study.

However, this kind of study needs to be developed, incorporating other ideas described in the last two chapters. Thus, close analysis of the ST and TT would tell more about the translation strategy adopted by Edith Grossman; the publishers and other players can be interviewed; the results of the study can be compared with reviews of other books; finally, the reception of a text is also obviously much wider than that of reviewers, encompassing a wide range of readers in a variety of different institutions and cultural settings. Moreover, as we saw in the last chapter, the cultural aspect of translation goes far beyond an analysis of the literary reception of a text and is entangled in an intricate web of political and ideological relations.

Summary

This chapter has focused on questions of translation strategy and the role of the literary translator. The key term has been Venuti's 'invisibility'. This refers to how, in Anglo-American cultures, the foreign is made invisible both by publishing strategies and by the preference for a 'fluent' TT that erases traces of the foreign. Venuti discusses two strategies, 'domesticating' and 'foreignizing', favouring the latter in a policy of 'resistance' to the dominant 'ethnocentrically violent' values of publishers and literary reviewers. Berman, an important influence on Venuti, also discusses the need for translation strategies that allow the 'foreign' to be experienced in the target culture. Other participants in the translation process are discussed: practising translators, who often view their work in vague terms, publishers, who drive and are driven by market forces worldwide, and reviewers, who represent one form of the reception of the TT.

The work of Venuti and of Berman has links both to those cultural studies theorists discussed in chapter 8 and the philosophical approaches examined in the next chapter, where the concept of the foreign and its linguistic, hermeneutic and ethical relationship to the source is paramount.

Further reading

For influences on Venuti's work, see Schleiermacher (1813/1992) and the references in the next chapter on translation and philosophy. For more on Berman, see Berman (1985/99, 1995). For other translators' accounts of their own work, see Frawley (1984), Warren (ed.) (1989), Bush (1997), and Orero and Sager (1997). For the publishing industry, read Hale (1997). For reception theory see Jauss (1982) and Holub (1984), and for the reception of translation, including reviews, see Brown (1994) and Gaddis Rose (1997).

Discussion and research points

1   Translate a short literary text (perhaps the Tarchetti extract in section 9.1.2) into your TL. Translate it first using a domesticating strategy and then with a foreignizing strategy. In what areas do differences occur in the translations?

2   Read Venuti's own descriptions of foreignizing and domesticating strategies, and research some of the criticisms that have been made of the terms. Do you accept Venuti's assertions that these are not binary opposites? How useful are the terms as 'heuristic research tools'?

3   Examine how 'visible' translation is in your own culture. Do your findings tally with Venuti's analysis? How far do you agree with Venuti's statement (1992: 10) that 'any attempt to make translation visible today is necessarily a political gesture'?

4   Read in detail Berman's account of his negative analytic. Apply it to an analysis of a literary text and its translation. Which of Berman's categories seem to be the most prominent in your analysis? Are there other related phenomena which you feel need to be accounted for?

5   Toury considered translators' accounts of their activities to be unreliable. Look at Felstiner's and Levine's works and at Venuti's descriptions of his own translations. How far do you agree with Toury?

6   What do you understand by the terms 'ear' and 'voice'? Is it possible (or even desirable) to look at literary translation in the more precise theoretical terms we have seen in chapters 3 to 6?

7   Compare the results of the case study in this chapter with your own reading of the reviews of a translated book, or an author, or of a series of reviews in a given newspaper or literary magazine. How 'visible' are the translators in these reviews?

8   Maier calls for the incorporation of translation theory into reviews of translation. Attempt to put together your own model for translation reviews, incorporating elements of theory (from this and previous chapters). Try writing a critique of a TT with your model. How successful is it?

10 Philosophical theories of translation

Key concepts

- Hermeneutics (the theory of interpretation of meaning), linked to the German Romantics.
- Steiner's hermeneutic motion, the four moves of translation.
- Pound: the energy of language, using archaism to overturn the literary poetics of the time, an early foreignization.
- Benjamin: the 'pure' language of interlinear translation.
- Derrida: deconstruction and the undermining of basic premises of linguistic translation theory.

Key texts

Benjamin, W. (1969/2000) 'The task of the translator', translated by H. Zohn, in L. Venuti (ed.) (2000), pp. 15–25.

Derrida, J. (1985) 'Des tours de Babel', in J. F. Graham (ed.), French original pp. 209–48; English translation in the same volume by J. F. Graham, pp. 165–207.

Derrida, J. (forthcoming) 'What is a "relevant" translation?', translated by L. Venuti, *Critical Inquiry*.

Graham, J. F. (ed.) (1985) *Difference in Translation*, Ithaca, NY: Cornell University Press.

Pound, E. (1918/2000) 'Guido's relations', in L. Venuti (ed.) (2000), pp. 26–33.

Steiner, G. (1975, 3rd edition 1998) *After Babel: Aspects of Language and Translation*, London and Oxford: Oxford University Press.

10.0 Introduction

This book has so far considered literary, linguistic and cultural theories of translation. The present chapter moves on to look at modern philosophical approaches to translation that have sought out the essence of (generally literary) translation. The writings contained in this chapter have been selected for their considerable influence on translation studies over the second half of the twentieth century, including on scholars working in other traditions, such as Niranjana and the Brazilian cannibalists (chapter 8) and Venuti and Berman (chapter 9).

This chapter is an examination of the inter-attraction of translation and philosophy, and examines George Steiner's hermeneutic motion (section 10.1), Ezra Pound's energizing of language (section 10.2), Walter Benjamin's 'pure' language of translation (section 10.3), and Derrida and the deconstruction movement's relevance to translation (section 10.4). The further reading section suggests others that expand on those described here or bring a different angle to the subject.

10.1 Steiner's hermeneutic motion

The hermeneutic movement owes its origins to the German Romantics such as Schleiermacher (see chapter 2), and, in the twentieth century, to Heidegger.[1] However, it is George Steiner's hugely influential *After Babel* which is the key advance of the hermeneutics of translation. There Steiner (1975/98: 249) defines the **hermeneutic approach** as 'the investigation of what it means to "understand" a piece of oral or written speech, and the attempt to diagnose this process in terms of a general model of meaning'.

Originally published in 1975, with subsequent editions in 1992 and 1998, *After Babel* claims to be 'the first systematic investigation of the theory and processes of translation since the eighteenth century'. Steiner's initial focus is on the psychological and intellectual functioning of the mind of the translator, and he goes on to discuss the process of meaning and understanding underlying the translation process. When he returns to considering the 'theory' (always in inverted commas) of translation, it is to posit his own hermeneutically oriented and 'totalizing' model:

> A 'theory' of translation, a 'theory' of semantic transfer, must mean one of two things. It is either an intentionally sharpened, hermeneutically oriented way of designating a working mode of *all* meaningful exchanges, of the totality of semantic communication (including Jakobson's intersemiotic translation or 'transmutation'). Or it is a subsection of such a model with specific reference to interlingual exchanges, to the emission and reception of significant messages between different languages . . . The 'totalizing' designation is the more instructive because it argues the fact that all procedures of expressive articulation and interpretative reception are translational, whether intra- or interlingually.
>
> (Steiner 1998: 293–4)

Steiner's description of the hermeneutics of translation, 'the act of elicitation and appropriative transfer of meaning' (p. 312), is based on a conception of translation not as a science but as 'an exact art', with precisions that are 'intense but unsystematic' (p. 311). The **hermeneutic motion** which forms the core of Steiner's description (pp. 312–435) consists of four parts: (1) initiative trust; (2) aggression (or penetration); (3) incorporation (or embodiment); and (4) compensation (or restitution). The main points of each are as follows:

1 **Initiative trust** (pp. 312–13): The translator's first move is 'an investment of belief', a belief and trust that there is something there in the ST that can be understood. Steiner sees this as a concentration of the human way of viewing the world symbolically. In the case of translation, the translator considers the ST to stand for something in the world, a coherent 'something' that can be translated. For this reason, argues Steiner, nonsense rhymes and the like 'are untranslatable because they are lexically non-communicative or deliberately insignificant'. This position entails two risks described by Steiner:

    - the 'something' may turn out to be 'everything', as in the case of medieval translators and exegetists of the Bible who were overwhelmed by the all-embracing divine message;
    - it may be 'nothing', because meaning and form are inextricably interwoven and cannot be separated and translated.

2 **Aggression** (pp. 313–14): This is an 'incursive . . . extractive . . . invasive' move. Steiner looks to Heidegger for a basis of this view of comprehension as 'appropriative' and 'violent'. As in St Jerome's description of the translator bringing home the ST as a captive slave (see chapter 2), so Steiner uses the metaphor of an open-cast mine for the translator's seizure of the ST and extraction of meaning: 'The translator invades, extracts, and brings home. The simile is that of the open-cast mine left an empty scar in the landscape' (p. 314). Steiner considers that some texts and genres 'have been exhausted by translation' and that others have been translated so well they are now only read in translation (Steiner gives the example of Rilke's translations of the sonnets of Louise Labé).

    At times, Steiner describes the aggression involved as 'penetration' (pp. 314, 319). As we shall discuss in section 10.1.1, this metaphor has been strongly criticized by feminists for its violent male-centric sexual imagery.

3 **Incorporation** (pp. 314–16): This is the third movement in Steiner's hermeneutics. It refers to the ST meaning, extracted by the translator in the second movement, being brought into the TL, which is already full of its own words and meanings. Different types of assimilation can occur: Steiner considers the two poles to be 'complete domestication', where the TT takes its full place in the TL canon; or 'permanent strangeness and marginality'. The crucial point Steiner makes (p. 315) is that the importing of the meaning of the foreign text 'can potentially dislocate or relocate the whole of the native structure'. He suggests, with further metaphors, the two ways in which this process functions: as 'sacramental intake' or as 'infection'. In other words, the target culture either ingests and becomes enriched by the foreign text, or it is infected by it and ultimately rejects it. As an example of the latter, Steiner gives the infection which was provoked by French neo-classical eighteenth-century literary models and which were repelled by European Romanticism. The

struggle for supremacy between literary systems is similar to the concepts described by the polysystem theorists such as Even-Zohar (see chapter 7).

This struggle, 'the dialectic of embodiment' (Steiner, p. 315), also takes place within the individual translator:

> The dialectic of embodiment entails the possibility that we may be consumed. This dialectic can be seen at the level of individual sensibility. Acts of translation add to our means; we come to incarnate alternative energies and resources of feeling. But we may be mastered and made lame by what we have imported.
>
> (Steiner 1998: 315)

Thus, just as a culture can be unbalanced by the importation of certain translated texts, so too can a translator's energies be consumed by translation that saps the creative powers necessary for the production of his or her own works. Steiner sees such imbalance as stemming from a 'dangerously incomplete' hermeneutic motion (p. 316). Balance can only be restored by the act of compensation, the fourth movement.

4   **Compensation** (pp. 316–19) or the 'enactment of reciprocity' is 'the crux of the *métier* and morals of translation'. Steiner describes the aggressive appropriation and incorporation of the meaning of the ST which 'leaves the original with a dialectically enigmatic residue' (p. 316). Dialectic because, although there has been a loss for the ST, the 'residue' is positive. Steiner sees the ST as being 'enhanced' by the act of translation. **Enhancement** occurs immediately an ST is deemed worthy of translation, and the subsequent transfer to another culture broadens and enlarges the original. The ST enters into a range of diverse relationships with its resultant TT or TTs, metaphorized as the 'echo' and the 'mirror' (p. 317), all of which enrich the ST. For example, even if a TT is 'only partly adequate' (Steiner uses the term 'adequate' in a non-technical sense), the ST is still enhanced since its 'resistant vitalities' and 'opaque centres of specific genius' are highlighted in contrast to the TT.

Imbalance arises from 'an outflow of energy from the source and an inflow into the receptor altering both and altering the harmonics of the whole system' (pp. 317–18). Such imbalance needs to be compensated. At those points where the TT is lesser than the original, the TT makes the original's virtues 'more precisely visible'; where the TT is greater than the original, it nevertheless 'infers that the source-text possesses potentialities, elemental reserves as yet unrealized by itself' (p. 318). In this way, equity is restored. Steiner sees the requirement of equity as providing real and 'ethical' meaning to the concept of fidelity:

> The translator, the exegetist, the reader is *faithful to* his [sic] text, makes his response responsible, only when he endeavours to restore the balance of forces, of integral presence, which his appropriative comprehension has disrupted.
>
> (Steiner 1998: 318; author's emphasis)

Steiner is confident that this fluid, moral, balanced 'hermeneutic of trust' (p. 319) will allow translation theory to escape the 'sterile triadic model' (literal, free and faithful) which, as we saw in chapter 2, had marked theory for so long.

The rest of Steiner's chapter on the hermeneutic motion is devoted to detailed analysis of examples of literary translation within that context. Steiner points out particularly successful translations, such as Jean Starr Untermeyer's collaboration with Hermann Broch in her English translation of his *Der Tod des Vergil*, where, in Steiner's view (p. 337), the TT becomes 'in many ways indispensable to the original'. In the merging 'meta-syntax' of English and German, where the English follows the German so closely, Steiner sees a kind of 'interlinear' text, 'close to the poets' dream of an absolute idiolect' (p. 338). Similarly, in Hölderlin's translations of Pindar and Sophocles, it is the 'verbal interlinear, a mid-zone between antique and modern, Greek and German', which attracts Steiner's praise (p. 341). Here, too, Steiner differentiates himself from that earlier translation theory which had derided word-for-word or literal translation. Steiner's focus is on the word, 'which can be circumscribed and broken open to reveal its organic singularity' (p. 347).

If Steiner feels that real understanding and translation occur at the point where languages diffuse into each other, then the ability to move outside the self is key: 'This insinuation of self into otherness is the final secret of the translator's craft', he says (p. 378), speaking of Ezra Pound's translations from Chinese. Pound translated from Chinese without knowing very much of the language, and Steiner (pp. 379–80) sees this as an advantage, since remoteness from the ST and culture allows the translator to work without preconceptions or the complications of mutual contact. Here is perhaps the crucial issue discussed by Steiner, and one that is related to the other philosophical writings on translation examined in this chapter:

> The relations of the translator to what is 'near' are inherently ambiguous and dialectical. The determining condition is simultaneously one of elective affinity and resistant difference.
>
> (Steiner 1998: 381)

For Steiner, the question of difference, one that is central to Derrida's writing (see section 10.4), occurs in two ways: the translator experiences the foreign language differently from his or her mother tongue; and each pair of languages, source and target, differs and imposes its vivid differences on the translator and society. The experience on the translator is all-encompassing:

> To experience difference, to feel the characteristic resistance and 'materiality' of that which differs, is to re-experience identity.
>
> (Steiner 1998: 381)

This linguistic and cultural experiencing of **resistant difference** may make the original text impermeable. However, Steiner also sees this impermeability as being transcended by '**elective affinity**' (p. 398), that is, when the translator has been drawn to that text as a kindred spirit and recognizes himself or herself in it. When resistant difference and elective affinity are both present they create an unresolved tension, attracting and repelling the translator, which expresses itself in good translation:

> Good translation . . . can be defined as that in which the dialectic of impenetrability and ingress, of intractable alienness and felt 'at-homeness' remains unresolved, but expressive. Out of the tension of resistance and affinity, a tension directly proportional to the proximity of the two languages and historical communities, grows the elucidative strangeness of the great translation.
>
> (Steiner 1998: 413)

Thus, in Steiner's view, paradoxically, translation between two distant cultures and languages is 'trivial' (p. 413) because that tension, which expresses itself in great translation, is reduced.

10.1.1 Discussion of Steiner

The popularity of Steiner's work can be gauged by the fact that it is still being re-edited and reprinted twenty-five years after its initial publication. It is certainly a monumental work in the breadth of its literary references and has introduced many non-specialists to translation theory, even if it is now in many ways marginal to contemporary translation studies. However, its influence can be seen on more modern theorists such as Berman and Venuti (see chapter 9). Both emphasize the importing of the foreign into the target culture and, like Steiner, do not equate good translation with fluent domestication. Steiner's 'resistant difference' and 'elective affinity' are in an unresolved state of tension, mirrored by the pull of Venuti's domesticating and foreignizing strategies.

But, in many ways, *After Babel* is a book that is stuck in a past time. Steiner's extensive references to Chomsky's generative–transformational grammar as a support for a universalist view of language, and thus an all-embracing theory of translation, now seem dated. So too is the male-dominated language of the text, for which he has been severely criticized by feminist translation theorists such as Simon (1996) and Chamberlain. Chamberlain (1988/2000: 320–2) particularly takes Steiner to task for his metaphors of 'erotic possession', notably the second 'penetrative' step of the hermeneutic motion, and for basing his model for the restitutive step on Lévi-Strauss's *Anthropologie structurale* 'which regards social structures as attempts at dynamic equilibrium achieved through an exchange of words, women and material goods' (Steiner 1998: 319). Nevertheless, despite these criticisms, Steiner's book remains an important contribution to hermeneutics and the theory of the language of translation. We shall now look at two other main influences on the twentieth century, both of whom are considered in some detail by Steiner. These are Ezra Pound and Walter Benjamin.

10.2 Ezra Pound and the energy of language

Steiner (p. 249) refers to both Pound and Benjamin as belonging to the age of 'philosophic–poetic theory and definition' and to having made an important contribution to developing theories of relations between languages. In the case of the twentieth-century American modernist poet Ezra Pound, this was done through both the practice and criticism of translation.

Although Pound's focus may have altered throughout his long active years, he was always experimental, looking at the expressive qualities of language, seeking to energize language by clarity, rhythm, sound and form, rather than sense. His 'reading' of Chinese ideograms is typical of his imagist approach privileging the creative form of the sign, capturing the energy of the thing or event pictured. Pound's whole work was very much influenced by his reading of the literature of the past, including Greek and Latin, Anglo-Saxon and Italian poetry. In his translations, he sought to escape from the rigid strait-jacket of the Victorian/Edwardian English tradition by experimenting with an archaicizing (and not necessarily clear) style which Venuti (1995: 34) links to his own foreignizing strategy. He notes Pound's close translation of the Anglo-Saxon text *The Seafarer*, where Pound imitates the original meter and calques ST words such as *bitre breostceare / bitter breast-cares* and *corna caldast / corn of the coldest*.

Pound's own writing on translation is sometimes idiosyncratic in its informality, a counterpoint to the archaicizing of his translations. In 'Guido's relations' (Pound 1929/2000), an essay related to his own translation of Guido Cavalcanti, an Italian poet from the thirteenth century who wrote in the *dolce stil nuovo* ('sweet new style'), Pound discards the possibility of translating into a Victorian or even a thirteenth-century English idiom:

> The ultimate Britons were at that date unbreeched, painted in woad, and grunting in an idiom far more difficult for us to master than the Langue d'Oc of the Planta-genets or the Lingua di Si.
>
> (Pound 1929/2000: 32)

Instead, Pound advocates an innovative solution, using what he terms 'pre-Elizabethan English', because of its 'clarity and explicitness' in bringing out the difference of the Italian text. His own translation in that mode is inevit-ably permeated by what is the now archaic language and spelling of that era (*makying, clearnesse*, etc.). Pound himself (p. 33) puts forward objections to this strategy, namely that a serious poem may in this way be rendered merely 'quaint', that thirteenth-century Italian is to a modern reader much less archaic in 'feel' than is fourteenth- or fifteenth-century English, and that it is doubtful whether such a solution is any more 'faithful' than his earlier attempts.

Pound's experimentalism and challenging of the poetic doctrine of his time continue to provide inspiration for many later translators and theorists who read his ideas into their own work. Thus, his use of translation is described as 'a tool in the cultural struggle' (Genztler 1993: 28) and his conscious archaicizing and foreignizing in translation leads to his 'marginalization' (Venuti 1995: chapter 5). His view of translation as criticism and his own form of 'creative' translation have also heavily influenced Brazilian poets including Haroldo de Campos, whose role in the Brazilian cannibalist movement was discussed in the postcolonialist section in chapter 8 (section 8.3). The current Brazilian translation theorist Else Vieira describes the link between Pound and the ideas of de Campos:

> The translation of creative texts, de Campos argues, is always recreation, the opposite of a literal translation, but always reciprocal; an operation in which it is not only the meaning that is translated but the sign itself in all its corporeality (sound properties, visual imagetics, all that makes up the iconicity of the aesthetic sign) . . . With Pound, translation is seen as criticism, insofar as it attempts theoretically to anticipate creation, it chooses, it eliminates repetitions, it organizes knowledge in such a way that the next generation may find only the still living part. Pound's well-known 'Make it new' is thus recast by de Campos as the revitalization of the past via translation.
>
> (Vieira 1999: 105)

For the Brazilian translation scholars, this revitalization is to be found in the taking of the life energies of the ST and their re-emergence in a nourished TT. Pound therefore continues to be 'reborn' or 'regested' in many guises.

10.3 The task of the translator: Walter Benjamin

Walter Benjamin's 1923 essay 'Die Aufgabe des Übersetzers' (Benjamin 1923/2000), translated into English as 'The task of the translator' by Harry Zohn in 1969 (Benjamin 1969/2000), also adopts an experimental view of translation. It originally formed an introduction to Benjamin's own German translation of Baudelaire's *Tableaux Parisiens*[2] but has come to be one of the seminal philosophical texts on literary translation.

Central to Benjamin's paper is the notion that a translation does not exist to give readers an understanding of the 'meaning' or information content of the original. Translation exists separately but in conjunction with the original, coming after it, emerging from its 'afterlife' but also giving the original 'continued life' (Benjamin 1969/2000: 16). This recreation assures survival of the original work, once it is already out in the world, in 'the age of its fame'[3] (p. 17).

According to Benjamin, what good translation does is to 'express the central reciprocal relationship between languages' (p. 17). It reveals inherent relationships which are present but which remain hidden without translation. It does this not by seeking to be the same as the original but by 'harmonizing' or bringing together the two different languages. In this expansive and creative way, translation both contributes to the growth of its own language (by the appearance in the TL of the new text) and pursues the goal of a 'pure' and higher language. This 'pure language' is released by the co-existence and complementation of the translation with the original (pp. 18–29). The strategy to achieve this is through a 'literal rendering' which allows the 'pure language' to shine through:

> A real translation is transparent; it does not cover the original, does not block its light, but allows the pure language, as though reinforced by its own medium, to shine upon the original all the more fully. This may be achieved, above all, by a literal rendering of the syntax which proves words rather than sentences to be the primary element of the translator.
>
> (Benjamin 1969/2000: 21)

The capacity to release this 'pure' language is singular to translation:

> It is the task of the translator to release in his own language that pure language which is under the spell of another, to liberate the language imprisoned in a work in his re-creation of that work.
>
> (Benjamin 1969/2000: 22)

The metaphors of liberation from imprisonment are the complete opposite of the kind of images we saw used by earlier translators such as St Jerome, who sought to march the ST meaning into captivity (see chapter 2). For Benjamin (p. 22), this only occurs if the translator allows the TL to be 'powerfully affected by the foreign tongue'. Literalness of syntax and the freedom of pure language come together in interlinear translation, and the 'ideal' translation, in Benjamin's opinion (p. 23), is an interlinear version of the Bible.

Benjamin's stress on allowing the foreign to enter the translation language harks back to Schleiermacher's concept of 'foreignization' and of bringing the reader to the foreign text (see chapter 2). But his style is diffuse and his philosophical idea of creating a 'pure' language by harmonizing the two languages is an ideal but abstract concept. This abstraction and search for a higher 'truth' through the form of language rather than the translation of 'meaning' has meant that Benjamin, with this one short preface, has, in the field of translation studies, exerted considerable influence on later postmodernists and deconstructionists such as Derrida, as we discuss in section 10.4.

10.4 Deconstruction

Christopher Norris, in his introductory book *Deconstruction: Theory and Practice* (1991), describes deconstruction in the following way:

> Deconstruction works at the . . . giddy limit, suspending all that we take for granted about language, experience and the 'normal' possibilities of human communication.
>
> (Norris 1991: xi)

It seeks to undo both a given order of priorities *and* the very system of conceptual opposition that makes that order possible . . . Deconstruction is . . . an activity of reading which remains closely tied to the texts it interrogates.

(Norris, 1991: 31)

Allied to the postmodern and poststructuralist movements, deconstruction involves a questioning of language and the very terms, systems and concepts which are constructed by that language. Deconstruction rejects the primacy of meaning fixed in the word and instead foregrounds or 'deconstructs' the ways in which a text undermines its own assumptions and reveals its internal contradictions.

The movement owes its origins to the 1960s and France and its leading figure is the French philosopher Jacques Derrida. The terminology employed by Derrida is complex and shifting, like the meaning it dismantles. The term *différance* is perhaps the most significant; it plays on the two meanings of the verb *différer* (*defer* and *differ*), neither of which totally encompasses its meaning, and its spelling shift (*différence* to *différance*) is a visual, although silent, indication of a blurring of the signifier and the dislocation or deferral of meaning. This is emphasized in Norris's concise description of the importance of Derrida's term:

Where Derrida breaks new ground . . . is in the extent to which 'differ' shades into 'defer'. This involves the idea that meaning is always *deferred*, perhaps to the point of an endless supplementarity, by the play of signification. *Différance* not only designates this theme but offers in its own unstable meaning a graphic example of the process at work.

(Norris 1991: 32)

Deconstruction is thus beginning to dismantle some of the key premises of linguistics, starting with Saussure's clear division of signified and signifier and any concept of being able to define, capture or stabilize meaning. Whereas Saussure's sign stood for the concept (see chapter 3), and whereas Saussure's linguistics was based on language as a differential system, *différance* suggests a location at some uncertain point in space and time between differ and defer. Clearly, such questioning of basic concepts of signifying and meaning has exceptional consequences for translation, which deconstructionists have approached through their reading and commentary of Benjamin's 'The task of the translator'. Prime among these readings is Jacques Derrida's 'Des tours de Babel' (1985).

The very title of the paper is a play on words, *tours* potentially having the sense of 'turn', 'turn of phrase', 'towers' (of Babel); *des tours* additionally has the same sound as *détour(s)* (with the sense of 'detour(s)'). Thus, from the very beginning there is a questioning of the basis of the language of the translation, rejecting the theories of meaning and translation that are based on 'the unity and identity of language'. Derrida interrogates Jakobson's division of interlingual, intralingual and intersemiotic translation (see chapter 1), pointing out the illogicality of Jakobson's definition of 'interlingual translation or translation proper', with the word translation being used as a translation of itself.

Derrida then embarks on a complex rereading and commentary on Benjamin's text. Importantly, he calls into question, by this act which he terms 'translating . . . the translation of another text on translation' (p. 175), many of the other premises on which translation theory has been based. These include the impossibility of fully describing and explaining the translation process by language. In addition, and most importantly, Derrida redefines Benjamin's 'pure language' as *différance* (Venuti 1992: 7) and deconstructs the distinction between source and target texts, seeing not only that the commentary is a translation of a translation, but also that original and translation owe a debt to each other; they also owe a mutual dependence and survival, once the translation act or Babelian performance has taken place.

Derrida addresses the issue of translation most openly in his 1998 lecture 'Qu'est-ce qu'une traduction relevante?', translated by Lawrence Venuti as 'What is a relevant translation?' (Derrida forthcoming). Derrida, speaking before an audience of translators, is here treating a term – 'relevance' – that is primarily used in translation theory by Gutt (1991/2000). Although Derrida does not directly mention Gutt's work, he criticizes the concept of **relevance** in translation. This is because, in Derrida's view, a relevant translation relies on the supposed stability of the signified–signifier relationship (it is 'that which presents itself as the transfer of an intact signified through the inconsequential vehicle of any signifier whatsoever' (Derrida forthcoming), and aims at total transparency (what would be 'domestication' in modern translation terminology).

The title of Derrida's paper involves a play on words as he discusses his own translation of a line from Portia in Shakespeare's *The Merchant of Venice*, 'when mercy seasons justice'. Derrida renders *seasons* as *relève* ('seasons/ spices up') as well as 'relieves' and many other meanings: 'quand le merci relève la justice'. His analysis is particularly interesting because it draws on age-old terms such as word-for-word and sense-for-sense translation and the related notion of letter and spirit which we examined in chapter 2. While it can be argued that Derrida's knowledge of translation theory is restricted, his cultural and religious critique of the text adds a depth and currency that enhance the description of the translation process. He does this by linking these translation strategies to the culture and the religious ideologies depicted in the play: just as the 'letter' is associated with Judaism and 'spirit' to Christianity, so Portia's interpretation or 'relevant' translation of Shylock's words shows the 'mercy' of dominant Christian discourse assimilating the 'justice' of Judaism. Derrida's own translation strategy is not 'relevant' but instead seeks to uncover this assimilation. The choice of *relève* assists this all the more because it contains an intertextual reference: it had been used by Derrida in 1967 to translate the supposedly 'untranslatable' Hegelian term *Aufhebung*, which has the double meaning of 'elevation' and 'replacement'. Just as Derrida had been attempting at that time to reveal the contradiction within Hegelian dialectics, so here he uncovers and deconstructs the dominant discourse of power.

In addition to the importance of this essay – with Derrida openly tackling issues of translation theory – there is the interesting question of the methods used to translate it into English. Here there is collaboration between Derrida and a translation scholar, Venuti. Venuti's translation often resorts to underlinings and the retaining of technical terms from the original between parentheses: especially the term (relève). Furthermore, Venuti adds an introduction or commentary to his translation – another step of rewriting, or translating or supplementing, as Lewis would call it (see below) – in which Venuti describes his own translating strategy:

> In translating Derrida's lecture I sought to implement his reflections on translation, as well as the concepts and practices that those reflections have inspired in the work of other theorists and translators. This meant adhering as closely as possible to his French, trying to reproduce his syntax, lexicon, and typography by inventing comparable effects – even when they threaten to twist the English into strange new forms.
>
> (Venuti in Derrida: forthcoming)

As well as being a foreignizing strategy, this may also be considered an example of the kind of **abusive fidelity** which Lewis (1985/2000) advocates in his essay on the translation of Derrida, 'The measure of translation effects' (Lewis 1985/2000). It appears in the same volume as Derrida's 'Des tours de Babel'. Lewis makes use of contrastive stylistics and applied discourse analysis in the discussion of translation from French into English and identifies a trend in English towards 'more explicit, precise, concrete determinations, for fuller more cohesive delineations' (p. 267). He notes that translators have traditionally tended to conform to fluent patterns or 'use-values' in the TL (p. 270). He argues for a different translation strategy, which he calls 'abusive fidelity'. This involves risk-taking and experimentation with the expressive and rhetorical patterns of language, supplementing the ST, giving it renewed energy: this is 'the strong, forceful translation that values experimentation, tampers with usage, seeks to match the polyvalencies or pluralivocities or expressive stresses of the original by producing its own' (p. 270). To translate Derrida, where the signifier–signified distinction is deconstructed, requires 'a new axiomatics of fidelity, one that requires attention to the chain of signifiers, to syntactic processes, to discursive structures, to the incidence of language mechanisms on thought and reality formation'.

Lewis sees the need for the translator to compensate for the inevitable losses in translation, the loss of the abuse that is present in the original. The abuse that is needed in the translation, says Lewis (p. 271), is not just any abuse, but needs to 'bear upon the key operator or a decisive textual knot' in the text and to 'resist' the domesticating 'use-values'. Based on the kinds of features identified as characterizing French–English translation, and on the tensions between abuse and use, the original and the translation, Lewis

(p. 273) analyzes the shifts, or 'differences' as he calls them, that occur in the published English translation of Derrida's essay 'White mythology' (Derrida 1974). These include (pp. 273–9):

- punctuation changes: omitting italics, adding parentheses and inverted commas around important technical terms;
- the dropping of suffixes: a *métaphorique* becomes *metaphor* rather than *metaphorics*;
- the loss of precision in the translation of linguistic and philosophical terms: *effet*, *valeur* and *articulation* are rendered as *phenomenon*, *notion* and *joint*;
- changes to syntactic and discursive order;
- the failure to recreate the play on the word *tour*: the translation given is *metaphor* rather than *turn*.

For these reasons, Lewis considers that the English translation of 'White mythology' fails to achieve abusive fidelity because the abuses of the French text disappear. The 'performative dimension' (p. 280) of Derrida's language, which deconstructs the ideas of the text, is not present in the English. A different strategy is required: the **experimental translation strategy** proposed by Lewis may be especially relevant in tackling some of the difficulties of the translation of philosophical texts of this kind where the language plays such a role in deconstructing the premises upon which language stands. His approach is also of special interest because it borrows elements from contrastive discourse analysis to examine philosophical translation, along the lines of the interdisciplinary studies that we consider in chapter 11.

Although some may bemoan the complexity of the writing and the practical applications of their approach, the deconstructionists have brought new ways of reading to translation and have interrogated some long-held beliefs, such as the primacy and stability of meaning and the sign.

Case studies

Case study I

The first case study attempts to see how far the translation strategy of a celebrated poet and translator seems to be explained by Steiner's model of the hermeneutic process. The text in question is the Irish poet Seamus Heaney's modern verse translation of the Anglo-Saxon epic poem *Beowulf*.[4] On publication in the UK in 1999, it was greeted with much critical acclaim and was soon the winner of the prestigious Whitbread Award. An important section of the book is Heaney's preface, relating the process of translation and his construction of a modern language for an old epic whose origins lie more than a thousand years before.

Heaney (1999: x) describes the strange relation the poem holds for present-day students of English who struggle to grasp the meaning and to gain a sufficiently rudimentary understanding of the Anglo-Saxon language and of the Scandinavian culture it depicts. The temporal and cultural displacement felt by a modern reader of the translation is described by Heaney (p. xii) in terms derived from his immersion in the Anglo-Saxon language:

> In spite of the sensation of being caught between a 'shield-wall' of opaque references and a 'word-hoard' that is old and strange, such readers are also bound to feel a certain 'shock of the new'. This is because the poem possesses a mythic potency. Like Shield Sheafson (as Scyld Scēfing is known in this translation), it arrives from somewhere beyond the known bourne of experience, and having fulfilled its purpose (again like Shield) it passes once more into the beyond.
>
> (Heaney 1999: xii)

The terms *shield-wall* and *word-hoard* derive from the language of the translation, itself modelled on the Anglo-Saxon rather than the Latin. And the 'mythic potency' referred to could also relate to the language. Although the name of *Scyld Scēfing* is modernized, it retains the strangeness of another time and place. Furthermore, Heaney's mystical image of the travelling force of the poem, from beyond the 'bourne of experience', indicates that there is more to this poem than verses sung and words on a page.

Heaney's language in the extract above nevertheless reveals that he has trust that there is meaning in the original poem, the first step in Steiner's hermeneutic motion. Despite the temporal and cultural displacement, despite the poem arriving from 'beyond the known bourne of experience', despite, that is, its 'resistant difference', Heaney is taken up by its power and is willing to attempt a translation. One might say that Heaney's enthusiasm for the Anglo-Saxon text demonstrates elective affinity. The tension that creates with the resistant difference leads to the creation of a great translation.

The strangeness of the poem, the tension of heathen past and modern reader, is highlighted by Heaney's metaphors for bringing the foreign to the present. Thus, he tells (p. xiii) of bringing the poem from the misty landscape of Anglo-Saxon England to the 'global village of the third millennium'; also, he equates the intercalated stories in the poem with modern-day channel-surfing. Such metaphors are rather different, modern versions of Steiner's 'open-cast mine', yet the idea of extracting and transporting remains. This can be equated to the act of aggression that is Steiner's second movement.

The temporal and spatial dislocation in the preface is paralleled by the dislocation of the language. Heaney (p. xvi) notes the contrast in the original poem between the Christian English of the time and the earlier heathen vernacular culture, a contrast which problematizes the search for a suitable 'voice' in the translation. Heaney has here extracted the meaning from the text, but he is struggling to find a language with which to incorporate it into the target language, the third movement of the hermeneutic motion. Yet Heaney finds that voice in his own past: 'I consider *Beowulf* to be part of my voice-right', he says, coining a new term and linking his own past to the language and culture of the poem. The link lies in Heaney's background as a

Catholic in Northern Ireland, with his English scored through by the influence of the Irish language that he had to learn. As a student, he discovered that the word *lachtar*, which was still part of the English idiom of his older Irish relatives, was in fact derived from Irish. This was 'like a rapier point of consciousness pricking me with an awareness of language-loss and cultural dispossession, and tempting me into binary thinking about language' (p. xxiv). This description of dispossession and suppression of language seems to resemble the postcolonialist arguments which we discussed in chapter 9, where, for example, Cronin gives an account of the struggle between the dominant English language and culture and the native Irish. It also in many ways fits Steiner's account of the meaning and words of the original coming into the new language and causing dislocation.

However, Heaney goes beyond this level; he recounts (pp. xxv–vi) how he 'escaped' from this cultural determination by what he terms 'illumination by philology'. This happened when he came to translate and realized that the Old English word *þolian* ('to suffer') that appears in Beowulf still existed, as *thole*, in the rural area of Ireland where Heaney grew up. For him this was his 'right of way' into the voice and music of the TT: he had a voice that was familiar to him; the heavy speech of the poor farm workers in the fields that fitted the Anglo-Saxon narrative. To this Heaney adds archaic words such as *bawn* ('fort'), used in Elizabethan English and deriving from the Irish *bó-dhún*, meaning 'a fort for cattle'. The result is a challenging and re-energizing of the language of the English translation with elements from the past and from an alternative culture. This very closely resembles Steiner's description of the fourth movement, that of compensation: the translation is being infused by the influence of another language so that it comes alive, it works in the new time frame and, by its strategies and success, it enhances the original Anglo-Saxon poem and provides balance to the interpretive process.

The translation strategy also fulfils a personal need: this underpinning of the translation with his own biography and language is 'one way for an Irish poet to come to terms with that complex history of conquest and colony, absorption and resistance, integrity and antagonism' (p. xxx). The tension between the elective affinity Heaney feels for the poem and the temporal resistant distance is therefore resolved by elements of the translator's linguistic and cultural background that link the source and target culture.

Discussion of case study I

The case study sets out to see how far philosophical approaches to translation are to be found in modern translation practice. Heaney's preface shows indications of the way that a search for language, and therefore a questioning of the language of earlier translations, plays an integral part in the construction of a modern *Beowulf*. Imbuing the language of that translation with conscious links both to the past culture (Anglo-Saxon and Scandinavian) and to a culture and language in conflict (Irish), the language of the translator, himself caught between the past and present, transferring a myth into a dominant language which he then disrupts with the voice of his own past, bears strong relation to Steiner's hermeneutic motion as well as echoing some of the arguments of the postcolonial theorists discussed in chapter 8. Steiner's model, based on a theory of interpretation, is able to explain quite closely the working practice of an acclaimed modern literary translator.

Case study 2

This case study deals with a text whose very language seemed designed to resist translation. The text in question is a short story, *Níneve*, by the contemporary Argentine author and translator Héctor Libertella.[5] It is based on the true story of the British archaeologist Sir Henry Rawlinson, which I originally translated for a collection of Latin American fiction in translation. Libertella uses language to illustrate, question and undermine the archaeologists' attempts to understand the inscriptions. It is interesting to see how far the kind of approach to translation adopted by Derrida and Lewis in section 10.4 is 'relevant' in discussing such a text.

The central themes of the story are illusion and deceit, which are conveyed with an array of wordplays and word confusions – such as *efectivo demente* ('effective demented/of mind') for *efectivamente* ('effectively/indeed') – in the Spanish. When such wordplays do not function in English, one possibility was to seek compensation at other points, tying in the sense of the wordplays and dis lo cation with the very form of the words on the page. Since a central strand of the story is the piecing together of old texts and the deciphering of ancient hieroglyphs, this is a not infrequent occurrence. In the following passage, Sir Rawlinson – or 'Sir Henry' as he is known in English texts of the time – is feverishly examining one such inscription:

> prolongando por estas líneas su mirada Sir Rawlinson las releyó mil veces, hasta donde lo permitieron sus ojos distraídos, y por la pura repetición acabó agotándolas y agotando un punto más cuanto leía otra vez. Y otra vez.

> extending his gaze over these lines, Sir Henry re read them a thous and times, as far as his dis tracted eyes allowed him, and by dint of pure re petition petition he eventually ex hausted the lines and ex hausted one letter more every time he re read them. And re red them.

The central idea in this passage is of repetition and rereading, of exhausting the deceptive, partially deciphered text at each reading. *Re* is one of the prefixes that is on other occasions dislocated by Libertella (e.g. *re partimos*, *re pone*). In the above passage, I used this technique even when it was not in the Spanish, to give *re petition*, *re read* and so on. To re emphasize this re petitive process on the page I added 're petition *petition*'. The disappearance of each *punto* as Sir Henry reads can also be visually represented in the English text, translating *punto* as *letter* and the phrase 're *read* them' (past tense) losing one letter to become 're *red* them' the second time, preserving the sound but surprising the reader visually, just as the red clay tablets surprise and deceive the archaeologists. Plot, pun and image (real and metaphoric) co in side here.

Discussion of case study 2

Deceit is revealed in Libertella's ST by a language that twists and turns and dislocates itself. The translation strategy that I employed bears some resemblance to Lewis's 'abusive fidelity'. Namely, it strives to recreate the energy of the ST by experimentation, involving some risk-taking and refusing, in part, to accept the normal 'use-values' of the TL (the dislocation of the *re* prefixes, the prefix representation of the loss of the *punto* in the phrase *re red*, and so on). It is important that such a translation strategy should not merely be purely comic wordplays but should 'bear upon the key operator . . . or decisive textual knots', as Lewis puts it. The focus of my translation, therefore, is on the way the inscription escapes deciphering, on the slipperiness of its meaning, on themes that run throughout the text. Libertella is illustrating these by his attack on the 'use-values' of Spanish, and the translator needs to be creative in constructing or deconstructing a similar attack in English.

Just as Derrida blurs the ST–TT distinction in his reading of Benjamin, so there are elements in the Libertella texts which merge. The very name of the archaeologist needs to be put together from the two texts: 'Sir Rawlinson' in the Spanish, 'Sir Henry' in the English. He is located somewhere between or across these two texts, texts which illustrate the deceit of the language more strongly, perhaps, when examined side by side. The translation highlights the deception, 'abusing' the fidelity to the original in, for example, the shift from *read* to *red*, where the reader is surprised by the introduction of the new element of colour, absent in the Spanish yet suggestive of the red clay tablets and of Sir Henry's tired, red and yet hungry eyes.

Nevertheless, such an experimental translation strategy demands a certain 'leap of faith' from the reader to accept that the translator's experimentation is not just facile wordplay. This may be easier when the text in question is philosophical; however, I would argue, for Libertella's *Níneve*, that more conventional strategies cannot hope to recreate the energy of the original. Finally, it is significant that the translation of *Níneve* was not included in the final collection precisely because the publisher felt that its experimentation would prove undigestible to the target audience. This is further illustration of the ultimate power of the publisher which we saw in chapter 9.

Summary

This chapter has considered a number of theorists whose work is philosophical in nature. Steiner draws upon the German hermeneutic tradition in *After Babel* (1975), his monumental description of literary translation, which at the time brought translation to the attention of many non-specialists. His 'hermeneutic motion' examines the interpretation of meaning. Ezra Pound's translations and criticisms emphasize the way that language can energize a text in translation, while Walter Benjamin's 'The task of the translator' talks densely and poetically about the release of a 'pure' language through 'literal' translation. Finally Derrida 'deconstructs' some of the long-held certainties of translation, including the opposition between source and target language and the stability of the linguistic sign. This calling into question of the principles of linguistic translation theory raises issues of a new order for translation studies.

Further reading

Philosophical approaches to translation cover a wide field. For an analysis of Steiner, read Larose (1989). For Pound's writing on translation, see Pound (1951, 1953, 1954); for the Brazilian cannibalists, influenced by Pound, see Vieira (1997, 1999) and de Campos (1992). Venuti (1995) examines Pound's work in considerable detail. Benjamin's essay has influenced a large number of other theorists, including Niranjana (1992). The latter discusses Benjamin and Derrida in some depth.

Norris (1991) is a readable introduction to deconstruction. Graham (1985) contains other significant papers besides Derrida's 'Des tours de Babel'. See also Derrida (1972/82) and Bennington and Derrida (1993) for the concept of *différance*, and the introduction to Venuti (1992) for a description of the poststructuralist reading of translation.

See Palmer (1969) for an introduction to hermeneutics; see also Schleier-macher (1813/1992) and Heidegger (1962, 1971). Many of the German originals, including Benjamin's 'Die Aufgabe des Übersetzers', are to be found in Störig (ed.) (1963). Finally, Guenthner and Guenthner-Reutter (eds) (1978) have edited an interesting collection of papers on philosophy and meaning in translation, and Andrew Benjamin has an important, although complex, volume entitled *Translation and the Nature of Philosophy* (1989).

Discussion and research points

1   Steiner's hermeneutic motion proposes an analysis of the translator's interpretative act. Look up some of the references to the German Romantic movement to see the origins of hermeneutics.
2   Try to analyze a translation of your own using Steiner's terminology. Compare your findings with the case study of Heaney's preface to *Beowulf*.
3   Read the feminist criticisms of Steiner in Chamberlain (1988/2000) and Simon (1996). How far do you agree with their comments? Do you feel the controversy over gender issues negates Steiner's contribution to translation theory?
4   Read some of Pound's own translations and poems. Identify his translation strategies. Try adopting some of these in your own translations of poetry. What kinds of results do you achieve?
5   Look at how other theorists such as Niranjana and Derrida have read Benjamin's 'The task of the translator'. Why do you think the essay has had such an influence?

6   Philosophical texts contain specialized terminologies and experimental structures. What form do you think a philosophical translation of a philosophical text might take? Have a look at published translations of works by authors such as Benjamin, Borges, Heidegger and Derrida to see what strategies have been employed. How far do they seem to follow Lewis's idea of 'abusive fidelity'?

7   Look at prefaces written by other literary translators. How many of them seem to consider their work in a philosophical way?

11 Translation studies as an interdiscipline

Key concepts

- Translation studies: a new discipline that is still faced with obstacles.
- Snell-Hornby's integrated approach to translation studies: a move towards interdisciplinarity.
- Examples of contemporary interdisciplinary research, combining linguistic, literary and cultural theory.
- Future perspectives: will translation studies combine or fragment?
- The challenge of the internet age, changing the practice of translation and translation studies.

Key texts

Harvey, K. (1998/2000) 'Translating camp talk: Gay identities and cultural transfer', in L. Venuti (ed.) (2000), pp. 446–67.

McCarty, W. (1999) 'Humanities computing as interdiscipline'. Online: http://ilex.cc. kcl.ac.uk/wlm/essays/inter/

Pym, A. (1998) *Method in Translation History*, Manchester: St Jerome, chapters 11 and 12.

Snell-Hornby, M. (1988, revised 1995), *Translation Studies: An Integrated Approach*, Amsterdam and Philadelphia, PA: John Benjamins.

Snell-Hornby, M., F. Pöchhacker and **K. Kaindl** (eds) (1994) *Translation Studies: An Interdiscipline*, Amsterdam: John Benjamins.

11.0 Introduction

The concluding chapter of this book tackles the status of translation studies. Section 11.1 discusses the remaining hurdles faced by translation studies in academia. It also discusses the subject's increased potential as an 'interdiscipline'. The rest of the chapter examines work in translation studies that has attempted to merge different approaches: Snell-Hornby's 'integrated approach' (section 11.2), interdisciplinary studies by a number of scholars who combine literary, cultural and linguistic approaches (section 11.3), focusing on Harvey's study of the translation of camp (section 11.3.1). Section 11.4 discusses some of the possibilities, but also the dangers, for the future of translation studies, including the role of new technologies. Finally, the case study is intended to demonstrate one method of performing an interdisciplinary study.

11.1 Discipline, interdiscipline or sub-discipline?

In chapter 1 of this book we considered Holmes's mapping of the new discipline of translation studies. We described how translation studies has developed, initially with courses as a part of other disciplines such as modern languages, contrastive linguistics and comparative literature. Yet, despite the boom in interest in the field at the end of the twentieth century, there still remains a reluctance within some sections of the academic world to place translation studies on an equal footing with longer-established disciplines. Thus, for example, in the UK neither the research assessment exercise nor the Arts and Humanities Research Board currently has a category of 'translation studies', forcing scholars in the field to class themselves according to other disciplines (linguistics, cultural or media studies, etc.) or as a miscellaneous 'other' category when applying for support for research.

Perhaps because of this, some moves in recent years have been towards establishing links across disciplines. Such interdisciplinary approaches break down barriers and reflect the rapid exchange of knowledge in an increasingly globalized and information-rich society. Translation studies is an example *par excellence* of a field which can bring together approaches from a wide range of language and cultural studies, modifying them for its own use and developing new models specific to its own requirements.

The growth of such interdisciplines can be seen across the board: examples produced by a search for the term **interdiscipline** on web search engines include archaeastronomy (the study of the astronomy of given periods in the past associated with specific archaeological sites and peoples), the history of medicine, forensic linguistics (the establishment of, for example, the authorship of texts or statements using linguistic techniques, now increasingly used in court cases), communication studies and humanities computing. Willard McCarty, in his paper 'Humanities computing as interdiscipline' (1999), gives the following description of how he sees the role of an interdiscipline in academic society:

> A true interdiscipline is . . . not easily understood, funded or managed in a world already divided along disciplinary lines, despite the standard pieties . . . Rather it is an entity that exists in the interstices of the existing fields, dealing with some, many or all of them. It is the Phoenician trader among the settled nations. Its existence is enigmatic in such a world; the enigma challenges us to rethink how we organise and institutionalise knowledge.
>
> (McCarty 1999)

An interdiscipline therefore challenges the current conventional way of thinking by promoting and responding to new links between different types of knowledge and technologies. Increased recognition within the academic world will likely lead to greater funding and status and the interdiscipline may be viewed with suspicion by more established subject areas.

An interdiscipline can be studied and taught in its own right and can also promote cross-disciplinary co-operation. Viewing the hierarchy of disciplines as a systemic order, McCarty sees the 'conventional' disciplines having either a 'primary' or a 'secondary' relationship to a new interdiscipline. This kind of approach which McCarty proposes for humanities computing may also be relevant for translation and translation studies. Translation studies would itself be the Phoenician trader among longer-established disciplines, having a primary relationship to disciplines such as linguistics (especially semantics, pragmatics and applied and contrastive linguistics), modern languages and language studies, comparative literature, cultural studies (including gender studies and postcolonial studies; see chapter 8) and philosophy (of language and meaning, including hermeneutics and deconstruction; see chapter 10). It is important to point out, however, that the relationship of translation studies to other disciplines is not fixed; this explains the changes over the years, from a strong link to contrastive linguistics in the 1960s to the present primacy of cultural studies.

Other, secondary, relationships come to the fore when dealing with the area of applied translation studies, such as translator training. For instance, specialized translation courses should have an element of instruction in the disciplines in which the trainees are planning to translate – such as law, politics, medicine and finance – as well as some input from information technology to cover issues in machine-assisted translation. In the study of the process of translating and interpreting, psychology and cognitive sciences also play a leading role.

The remainder of this chapter considers specific examples of how scholars in translation studies have moved towards interdisciplinarity over recent years. The first is Snell-Hornby's early attempt at integrating the analysis of translation.

11.2 Mary Snell-Hornby's 'integrated approach'

In her book *Translation Studies: An Integrated Approach* (1988, revised edition 1995), the Vienna-based scholar, teacher and translator Mary Snell-Hornby reviews and attempts to integrate a wide variety of different linguistic and literary concepts in an overarching 'integrated' approach to translation. Coming from a predominantly German-theoretical background, Snell-Hornby notably borrows the notion of prototypes for the categorizing of text types. Depending on the text type under consideration, she incorporates cultural history, literary studies, sociocultural and area studies and, for legal, economic, medical and scientific translation, the study of the relevant specialized subject. Her view of the field is illustrated by figure 11.1.

Snell-Hornby (1995: 31) explains that, horizontally, the diagram is to be read as a series of clines, from left to right, with no clear demarcations. This

Figure 11.1

Text type and relevant criteria for translation (from Snell-Hornby 1995: 32)

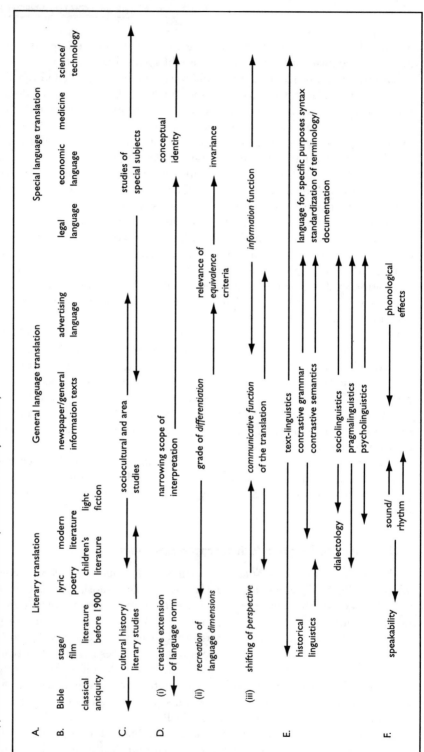

is complemented by a 'stratificational model' proceeding from the most general (A) to the most particular (F). In level A, she sets out to integrate 'literary', 'general' and 'special' translation into a single continuum, rather than isolating them according to separate 'conventional' areas of translation. Level B indicates prototypical basic text types, level C 'shows the non-linguistic disciplines ... which are inseparably bound up with translation', including knowledge of the sociocultural background. Level D then covers the translation process, including (i) understanding the ST, (ii) the TT focus and (iii) the communicative function of the TT. Level E covers areas of linguistics relevant to translation and level F, the lowest-order level, deals with phonological aspects, such as alliteration, rhythm and speakability of stage translation and film dubbing.

This is an interesting attempt to bring together diverse areas of translation and to bridge the gap between the commercial and artistic translations described by Schleiermacher in 1813 (see chapter 2). Yet one must question whether an attempt to incorporate all genres and text types into such a detailed single overarching analytical framework is really viable. Inconsistencies are inevitably to be found; for example:

- On level B, can all 'newspaper texts' really be lumped together as 'general language translation'?
- Why is 'advertising' placed further from the literary than is 'general', since it may well have far more in common with the creative language of lyric poetry?
- On level C, 'cultural history' may be just as relevant to the translation of a medical text as to a literary one.
- The 'studies of special subjects' may also be appropriate to the background of literary texts. For instance, it would be impossible to translate Saramago's *História do cerco de Lisboa* without researching the history of the crusades, and Thomas Mann's *Der Zauberberg* requires knowledge of the regimes of Alpine sanatoria in the 1920s.
- Similarly, 'speakability' need not be restricted to literary works: translations of foreign news broadcasts at the BBC World Service in Caversham are often designed to be read over the air, while translations of written speeches may also need to retain or recreate the rhythm or sound of the ST.

Even though we may quibble with Snell-Hornby's own form of categorization, the removal of rigid divisions between different types of language is to be welcomed. There is no necessity for translation studies to focus solely on the literary (as was so often the case until the last fifty years) or solely the technical (as has been more common with the text-type and functional analyzes we studied in chapters 5 and 6). Yet it would also be true to say that there is no reason to suppose that consideration of all kinds of language in a prototypical continuum necessarily produces more useful results for the analysis of translations and for translator training. A student wishing to be a commercial translator is likely to need a somewhat different training focus compared to one who would like to be a literary translator, even if each can benefit from studying the work of the other.

Snell-Hornby's assertion (p. 51) that breaking down the 'rigid divisions between literary and "other" language . . . is central to this study' nevertheless masks an important development that she presages. In her defence of translation studies as a new discipline, she sees translators and theorists working in the field as being 'concerned with a world *between* disciplines, languages and cultures' (p. 35; Snell-Hornby's emphasis). This kind of comment is a sign of the way current theorists have begun to consider translation studies in an interdisciplinary fashion. Snell-Hornby calls for translation studies to develop its own particular 'models and conventions' and to focus on the 'web of relationships' in the context of text, situation and culture rather than a classic linguistic approach of the individual word (p. 35).

This web of relationships is investigated by Snell-Hornby through various chapters and differing texts. After briefly covering recent translation theory, she deals in chapter 2 with 'translation as a cross-cultural event'. However, although she speaks of 'culture', she focuses particularly on the kinds of functional theories we considered in chapter 5 and on norms in a linguistic sense. In her second chapter (pp. 55–62) she discusses the translation of culturally embedded metaphors. A description of Belfast in a German newspaper contains the metaphor 'ein trostloses Meer verrusster Häuserreihen' [lit. 'a dreary sea of sooty ranks of houses']; Snell-Hornby discusses the incongruous connotations of translating *Meer* as *sea* in a collocation with *roofs*, preferring 'dreary view'. The focus of her analysis is on the function of the image in the text; the text is taken from literary language and a decision is made as to the relative frequency and 'normality' of the metaphor in question. This accords with later analysis in her book.

The last chapter, 'From special language to literary translation', examines 'style' in a variety of literary and specialized non-literary texts according to the following categories: (1) syntax; (2) semantics and lexis; (3) formal text presentation; and (4) translation strategies and methods. In these ways, Snell-Hornby is applying linguistic approaches to a literary translation problem. However, the 'cultural' aspect is limited to a consideration of the cultural-embeddedness of a given text or phrase. There is not a full examination of the cultural role of translation in the way that was discussed in chapters 8 and 9. The interdisciplinarity of the study is also limited: use is made of a range of linguistic and psychological theories (scenes-and-frames semantics, speech acts, prototype and gestalt theory, etc.), but always with the aim of supporting a relatively traditional close reading/text analysis.

11.3 Interdisciplinary approaches

The interdisciplinarity approach has gained ground in recent years. In 1991, Sonja Tirkkonen-Condit edited a collection of essays, *Empirical Research in Translation and Intercultural Studies* (Tirkkonen-Condit 1991). The very title of this book is indicative of the way translation has now established strong primary relationships to essentially non-linguistic disciplines. Snell-Hornby has co-edited a number of collections, including *Translation as Intercultural Communication* (Snell-Hornby et al. (eds) 1996) and *Translation Studies: An Interdiscipline* (Snell-Hornby et al. (eds) 1994). The latter work contains papers given at the 1992 translation conference at Vienna. The titles of these papers shows that they cover a wide range of subjects: history, transnational cultures, postmodernism, hermeneutics, intertextuality, philosophy, specialized terminology, medicine, law, linguistics and translation theory. However, although the papers as a whole cover a wide range of subjects, far fewer individual papers operate across disciplines. In some cases it seems that scholars have either been reluctant or unable to move beyond the confines of their specific specialism.

In more recent years, translation studies has gone beyond purely linguistic approaches to develop its own models, such as Toury's descriptive translation studies (see chapter 7). Hatim and Mason (chapter 6), working from within a framework of discourse analysis, have also brought cultural considerations into play by relating linguistic choices to the dominant ideology in texts such as the Unesco translation of the history of the indigenous peoples of the Americas (Hatim and Mason 1997: 15–24). Pym (1998) adopts the term 'interdisciplinary' and even 'intercultural' in describing the work of translation history and doubts whether translation studies can any longer be 'mapped' in the way Holmes had suggested. He describes two projects on which he was working simultaneously: the twelfth-century translation school of Toledo in Spain and flows of poetry in translation between France and Germany in the nineteenth century (Pym 1998: viii–ix). Both were interdisciplinary in the sense that the analysis incorporated cross-disciplinary methods, but the type of analysis varied considerably in the two projects: 'Medievalists were arguing about commas; modernists were busy defending social classes, genders and various ideas of progress or non-progress' (Pym 1998: ix). This emphasizes how a modern researcher investigating the history of translation is faced by widely diverging, although stimulating, phenomena.

Scholars approaching translation from a cultural perspective have begun to show evidence of cross-disciplinary research methods. Niranjana (1992), for example, examines the postcolonial from a poststructuralist perspective. Venuti (1995, 1998) draws on poststructualism, literary theory and criticism, historiography and philosophy and French discourse analysis. However, writing from the standpoint of the literary translator, he criticizes linguistic approaches because 'they project a conservative model of translation that would unduly restrict its role in cultural innovation and change' (Venuti

1998: 21). Tymoczko (1999b) combines a range of concepts from literary, linguistic and translation studies as she draws parallels between the literary translator and the postcolonial author writing in the colonizers' language for an international audience. In her opinion, both the literary translator and the postcolonial author are faced with the task of transposing a culture across a cultural and/or linguistic gap, and they both face choices that are inevitably ideologically driven. Translated texts and postcolonial writing thus share some of the same features of 'foreign' language and tend to explicate background information, the amount of which depends on the status of the two cultures and languages. Tymoczko continues by suggesting that the kinds of norms proposed by Toury (chapter 7) and the considerations of patronage and audience described by Lefevere (chapter 8) are just as useful when studying postcolonial literature. Other research, such as Harvey's described in the next section, combines the cultural with the analytic power of linguistic tools.

11.3.1 A combination of linguistic analysis and critical theory: Harvey (1998/2000)

Recent interdisciplinary research has involved combining linguistic methods of analysis of literature with a cultural-theory angle, enabling study of the social and ideological environment that conditions the exchange. One example is Keith Harvey's study 'Translating camp talk' (Harvey 1998/2000). Harvey draws on the theory of contact in language practice and on politeness to examine the homosexual discourse of camp in English and French texts and in translations. The theory of contact[1] is used by Harvey to examine the way 'gay men and lesbians work within appropriate prevailing straight (and homophobic) discourses' (p. 448), often appropriating language patterns from a range of communities. Thus, he describes (pp 449–52) the use of girl talk and Southern Belle accents (*Oh, my!*, *adorable*, etc.), French expressions (*ma bébé, comme ça*) and a mix of formal and informal register by gay characters in Tony Kushner's *Angels in America*.[2] Such characteristics are typical of camp talk in English. Harvey points out (p. 451) that French camp interestingly tends to use English words and phrases in a similar language 'game'.

Harvey also draws on the pragmatic theory of politeness (see Brown and Levinson 1987) and its notion of the 'face-threatening act' to analyze camp dialogue (pp. 452–3). He describes camp talk as face-threatening, because it openly calls for solidarity (thus imposing upon the addressee) and because of its tendency to use insults and ridicule (thus attacking the addressee's self image). Shifts in translation may be caused by a translator's lack of awareness of these strategies. An example given by Harvey from a novel by Richard Camus shows a TT that overly emphasizes camp by exaggerating the face-threatening act:

> ST: Tiens, Renaud, mais vous vous dévergondez!
> [lit. Hey, Renaud, but you are getting into bad ways!]
> TT: Hey, Renaud, you whore!

The formal *dévergondez* is translated by the vulgar insult *whore*, albeit typical of camp talk (Harvey, p. 453).

Importantly, Harvey links the linguistic characteristics of camp to cultural identity via **queer theory** (pp. 453–6). Camp is then seen not only as exposing the hostile values and thinking of 'straight' institutions, but also, by its performative aspect, as making the gay community visible and manifesting its identity.

Harvey brings together the various linguistic and cultural strands in his analysis of the translation of camp talk in extracts from two novels. The first (pp. 456–61) is the French translation of Gore Vidal's *The City and the Pillar*.[3] There are significant lexical and textual changes in the French translation:

- The same pejorative word, *tante/s* ('aunt/s'), is used for both the pejorative *pansies* and the more positive *queen*.
- The phrase *to be gay* is translated by the pejorative *en être* ('to be of it/ them'), concealing the gay identity.
- Gay camp collocations such as *perfect weakness* and *screaming pansies* are either not translated (*faible* [= 'weakness']) or else rendered by a negative collocation (*voyantes* [= 'showy']).

In general, therefore, markers of gay identity either disappear or are made pejorative in the TT. Harvey links these findings to issues of the target culture, discussing how, for instance, the suppression of the label *gay* in the translation 'reflects a more general reluctance in France to recognize the usefulness of identity categories as the springboard for political action' (p. 460) and a 'relative absence of radical gay (male) theorizing in contemporary France' (p. 461).

The second extract analyzed by Harvey is from the translation into American English of a novel by the Frenchman Tony Duvert. Here, he shows (pp. 464–5) how the translator's additions and lexical choices have intensified and made more visible some of the camp and turned a playful scene into one of seduction. Harvey suggests that the reason for such a translation strategy may be due to commercial pressures from the US publishers, who were supporting gay writing, and the general (sub)cultural environment in the USA which assured the book a better reception than it had enjoyed in France.

11.3.2 Discussion of interdisciplinary approaches

Much research in translation studies makes use of techniques and concepts from a range of backgrounds. Yet the construction of an interdisciplinary methodology is not straightforward, since few researchers possess the necessary expertise in a wide range of subject areas, and the original academic background of the individual researcher inevitably conditions the focus of their approach. Harvey warns against such bias and lays down a challenge to translation studies:

> What is required . . . in translation studies is a methodology that neither prioritizes broad concerns with power, ideology and patronage to the detriment of the need to examine representative examples of text, nor contents itself with detailed text-linguistic analysis while making do with sketchy and generalized notions of context.
>
> (Harvey 1998/2000: 466)

The type of study produced by Harvey represents an important step forwards in that it produces very interesting results by combining a '**linguistic toolkit**'[4] and a cultural studies approach. However, in order for such methodology to work, the researcher may have to abandon expectations of a comprehensive categorization of linguistic features. Instead, what is required is a dynamic, shifting interaction between relevant elements of the linguistic toolkit and cultural analysis.

11.4 The future: co-operation or fragmentation?

Translation studies is therefore already functioning, to borrow McCarty's term, at the interstices of existing fields and is developing a new interdisciplinary character. The question is how far this is a strength or a weakness for the field as a whole. Each of its subject areas is competing for prime position, with perhaps the most evident split being that between linguists and cultural theorists (see Baker 1997b: 277–80, Venuti 1998: 7–8). The former dominated in the 1950s and 1960s, while in the last decade linguistic theories have been marginalized by scholars moving within, or adopting the practices of, other disciplines. Some translation scholars, among them Bassnett and Lefevere (1990), have been scathingly dismissive of those working in linguistics. Given the range of interests and frictions represented in translation studies, one must wonder whether there might at some point not be a total fragmentation of the discipline and either a separation of the different strands or a consolidation of the previous disciplinary separation (modern languages, cultural studies, linguistics, etc.). A key question for contemporary researchers, faced with the proliferation of current work in translation studies, is how far they should specialize. What may be needed in the future is some greater degree of specialization and more collaboration on joint projects. For the moment, however, the kinds of interdisciplinary approach described in this chapter seem to be one way of bridging the gap between linguistics and cultural studies.

11.4.1 The role of changing technologies

The tools at the disposal of the translator and the theorist are altering. One of the reasons for this is the growth in the new technologies, which inevitably determine new areas of study and/or cause a re-examination of established ones. Corpus linguistics (the analysis of large amounts of electronically stored text) already facilitates the study of features of translated language (see Baker 1995, Laviosa 1998). Although the present applications of corpus linguistics are limited, the case study below suggests that it may have applications for, amongst others, descriptive translation studies, because the computer is able to analyze whole texts in a way that was impossible manually. Moreover, access to data of all sorts will be speeded up and new links forged. For example, online book shops have search facilities that enable the user to seek information on readership profiles and on genres such as 'translation' or 'translated fiction'. The results of such searches can give important insights into the reception of works, and this will inevitably differ from the findings of conventional research.

Clearly, there is a concern that those with limited access to new technology will be disadvantaged, but experience shows that contact, at least within the research community, is greatly facilitated. The availability and exchange of information – for example, through conference postings, calls for papers, websites of translation centres and individual researchers relaying details of their current projects and papers – all facilitate communication among scholars.

Finally, the internet is also changing the status and visibility of translators and translation. Not only can professional translators now easily work transnationally via email, but the need for translation itself is also increasing. Search engines now offer (sometimes rudimentary) automatic machine translation of individual pages and of whole websites in many major world languages, most often with English as the SL or TL. Perhaps the best-known automatic translation package is SYSTRAN's Babel Fish, used by the search engine AltaVista® (see http://babel.altavista.com or http://world.altavista.com). It can translate between at least thirteen language pairs and claims that over one million translations are generated in this way each day. Translation is thus available 'at the touch of a button' for internet users worldwide. However, it is a translation that conceals the human involvement and gives the impression of it being an easy and automatic process.

The developments outlined in this section might lead to further consolidation of English as the major global language of communication, but they also mean increased use of translation commercially. Furthermore, while information technology is bound to become more influential as a tool and subject of translation studies research in the future, the current wealth of ideas that is being generated within the field will no doubt also involve a re-evaluation and re-invigoration of older models. The following case study follows the line of interdisciplinary research described in this chapter. It brings together linguistic, literary and cultural analysis, supported by tools from corpus linguistics.

Case study

This case study demonstrates one interdisciplinary methodology for describing a translation: it concerns a short story by the Colombian Gabriel García Márquez, *El verano feliz de la señora Forbes*[5] (referred to in this chapter as VF), translated into English by Edith Grossman as *Miss Forbes's Summer of Happiness*[6] (referred to as MF).

There are severe practical and logistical obstacles to the analysis of a complete, lengthy translation. For this reason, even scholars such as van Leuven-Zwart, who puts together a model for the systematic evaluation of shifts (chapter 4), have tended to concentrate on extracts. One method of overcoming some of the difficulties is by using the computer-assisted analytical tools of **corpus linguistics** (for a detailed description of these, see Baker 1995, Stubbs 1996, Biber *et al.* 1998). If the texts are held in electronic form, concordances of any word or word strings, plus their corresponding translations, can be accessed in seconds. These tools thus immediately speed up access to data (*all* instances of a given term can be called up in a few seconds) and free the researcher to concentrate on close analysis of the phenomena.

The interdisciplinary methodology for this case study functions as follows:

1   A linguistic comparison of the texts is carried out. This can involve close comparison of the ST and TT to begin to see the translation strategies employed and a consideration of literary and narrative devices. For the present study, the linguistic construction of narratorial point of view is especially important, and the models followed are those of Simpson (1993) and Fowler (1996), both of whom are linked to chapter 6.

2   The analysis is computer-assisted. Initial findings from the reading of the text can be followed up through the whole story by concordancing. In addition, comparative word frequency lists can be scrutinized, which would give information about the kinds of lexical choices that have been made. Sentence structure can be analyzed, including sentence length and sentence-initial elements.

3   The results can then be set in their sociocultural framework. As in chapters 8 and 9, this sociocultural framework can draw on relevant concepts from reception theory and cultural studies. This can include the ideological and economic pressures at play, both from the forces of translation criticism and the participants in the publishing and translation world.

In the case of García Márquez's story, close reading reveals that there are no major additions or omissions within the TT, and the paragraph and sentence structure is almost always maintained. There is a certain trend towards explicitation, especially of cohesive links, and towards grammatical formalization, even in dialogue. Thus, questions such as '¿Y eso por qué?' (VF: 151) [lit. 'And that why?'] are expanded to 'Why would you do that?' (MF: 110).

Increased cohesion is also suggested from comparison of the word frequency lists: the number of possessive pronouns is much higher in the TT, and a close analysis reveals several instances where this is not due to systemic differences between the languages. Thus, 'la señora Forbes interrumpió *la* lección' (VF: 193) becomes 'Miss Forbes interrupted *her* lesson' (MF: 144).

Concordances can be produced of all sentence-initial items in the two texts. This helps in the analysis of narrative point of view, especially the order in which elements are presented to the reader.[7] The beginning of the first sentence is an example of this:

> Por la tarde, de regreso a casa, encontramos una enorme serpiente de mar clavada por el cuello en el marco de la puerta . . . (VF: 189)
> [lit. In the afternoon, on arrival at home, we found an enormous sea serpent nailed by the neck to the frame of the door . . .]
> When we came back to the house in the afternoon, we found an enormous sea serpent nailed by the neck to the door frame . . . (MF: 141).

In the TT, the specific time element *in the afternoon* has been right shifted and the action of returning slightly emphasized, changing a little the narrative point of view. In general, analysis of concordances reveals that the ST revolves rather more around time and place adjuncts in first position than does the TT. Similarly, the syntax is sometimes more complex in the English: the ST sentence continues 'y era negra y fosforescente y parecía un maleficio de gitanos . . . ' [lit. 'and it was black and phosphorescent and resembled a gypsy's curse'], translated as 'Black and phosphorescent, it looked like a Gypsy curse . . . '. Such shifts have an effect on the portrayal of the characters, since the ST structure, with the rather simple causal link y ('and'), is consistent with the workings of the child narrator's mind, whereas the TT breaks the sentence and begins again with a complex adjectival structure, 'black and phosphorescent'.

Although the translator often follows quite closely the lexical and syntactic patterns of the ST, the word order and cohesion shifts noted above seem to be TL-oriented. Increased cohesion, after all, is widely felt to be a universal feature of translation (see Blum-Kulka 1986/2000, Baker 1995, chapter 6 above). However, consideration of the wider cultural background adds an extra dimension to the analysis. García Márquez has been extremely successful commercially, not only in his native Colombia, and throughout the Spanish-speaking countries, but also worldwide. Sales of his best-known *One Hundred Years of Solitude* continue to be strong, even in English, which is a notoriously difficult market for foreign authors. Almost immediate publication in English is guaranteed for any new García Márquez work of fiction, and is contracted to the New York-based translator Edith Grossman, who has translated García Márquez's works since the mid-1980s. The same translation is used in the UK, albeit with a different cover. The enormous success of Grossman's translations – and of those of Gregory Rabassa, who preceded her in the role – may partially be due to some of the domesticating translation strategies she employs, such as increased cohesion and the rendering of children's speech into structures that probably more closely resemble her own and her readership's. Edith Grossman herself (personal correspondence) views the goal of her translation method in the following terms: 'to write as García Márquez would have done had he been writing in English', which is an echo of Dryden's observations on translating Latin poetry in seventeenth-century England ('make Virgil speak such English as he would himself have spoken, if he had been born in England, and in this present age'; see chapter 2).

The strategy may also be due to the publisher's general concern for a fluent text to avoid alienating the audience. The study of the reviews of the book that formed the case study of chapter 9 gave a strong indication that a modified image of García Márquez has been offered to the American audience. His Colombian background is downplayed both on the cover of the book and in the comments in the reviews. His status as a leading international literary figure is emphasized in the glowing reviews, there are few comments on the translation, and the observations concerning the style always refer to the English. It goes without saying that shifts similar to those noted in the 'Por la tarde . . . ' sentence above pass unnoticed by reviewers.

There may be several issues here: the success of García Márquez is in many ways being appropriated for the foreign audience (it is interesting that something similar occurs in the reviews in Spain); the discourse of Colombian Spanish is being translated into the dominant and transparent form of the political and economic power (the USA); and elements of García Márquez's background that do not fit easily with this new image, such as his non-fiction and socialist writings, tend not to be translated or, if they are, they tend to be given far less prominence and often suffer omissions. The latter has happened, for example, to the translation of his more recent article on the case of Elián González, a Cuban boy shipwrecked off the coast of Florida.[8] In the British English translation, both the text and, more particularly, the photographs that accompany the story relate the event from the dominant US perspective.[9]

Discussion of case study

This brief description of an interdisciplinary case study attempts to bring together forms of linguistic, corpus linguistic and cultural analysis. The results show some potential. They relate shifts at the linguistic level to effects on the narrative point of view and on the texture of the text. Most importantly, like Harvey's study in section 11.3.1, they attempt to consider the sociocultural environment around the translation process and the ideological and discourse motivations that may be encouraging the linguistic shifts. Nevertheless, it is clear that this approach is not without its dangers.

At present, computer-assisted analysis is limited in its capacity. It would be wrong to think that corpus linguistics can interpret findings or even provide analysts with all the data they might wish for. (It would be interesting, although not necessarily easy, for example, to be able to research semantic fields or to compare translation choices with those in a range of other similar translated fiction texts.) Close critical analysis is still required in order to interpret the findings, and the choice of linguistic model conditions that interpretation. Finally, the mapping of the linguistic phenomena onto ideological and discoursal constraints also reflects the ideology of the researcher. There may still be a tendency to seek out specific elements and to claim that they are caused by ideological conditions; not all would agree, for example, with the assessment above that the image of García Márquez has been 'appropriated' into US culture, nor that the translation strategy is necessarily the cause of this.

Summary

Academia has long tended to regard translation as a derivative activity and has been reluctant to accept translation studies as a new discipline. Much research in translation studies therefore continues to be conducted within a variety of departments. Snell-Hornby's 'integrated' approach is an attempt to overcome divisions between literary and linguistic analyzes of translation and is a pointer to the direction which translation studies is taking. Since then, the interdisciplinarity of translation studies has been emphasized, notably in collections of articles encompassing the wide range of the field, but now also in individual studies. These new studies, such as Harvey's, developing from a variety of other disciplines, are creating new methodologies appropriate for translation studies. This truly interdisciplinary approach may enable translation studies to play a leading role in universities, but there is also a counter-tendency towards fragmentation with cultural and linguistic approaches opposing each other. The growth of new technologies, in this as in other fields, is likely to have a major impact on the type and form of future research even if, at present, applications to the practice of translation remain somewhat problematic.

Further reading

For competing tendencies within translation studies, read Baker (1996, 1997b) and Venuti (1998: 8–9). For an example of another interdisciplinary study, see May's (1994) study of English-language translations of Russian literature. For corpus linguistics, see Stubbs (1996), Kennedy (1998) and Biber et al. (1998). For corpus linguistics and translation, see Baker (1995) and Laviosa (1998). For translation, minority languages and the internet, see Cronin (1998). A list of websites is also given in the appendix to this volume.

Discussion and research points

1   Look again at the Snell-Hornby typology of text types (figure 11.1 above). Consider its usefulness for texts that you yourself have translated or analyzed. How successfully do you feel Snell-Hornby achieves her aim of integrating literary and technical translation?

2   In his paper on humanities computing, McCarty (1999) makes the claim that an interdiscipline 'challenges us to rethink how we organise and institutionalise knowledge'. How far, and in what ways, does translation studies do this?

3   Do you consider translation studies to be a discipline, an interdiscipline or a sub-division of another discipline? What possible interdisciplinary links can be foreseen for translation studies in the coming years?

4   Look at the different interdisciplinary studies mentioned in this chapter. What elements does each theorist use and from which disciplines? How successful do you feel they are?

5   In what ways might the researcher's own ideology condition the choice of analytical tools and the relation to cultural theory?

6   Try to devise and carry out an interdisciplinary study of your own. What difficulties do you encounter in the planning, execution and writing-up of the study?

7   Try out different machine-translation software on a range of different texts. What are their strengths and weaknesses? Which give the best results? How do you see such software developing in the future?

8   What examples can you find of the new technologies changing the research practices of translation studies scholars?

Appendix: internet links

The following is a short list of some useful internet sites for research translation studies.

For up-to-date information on forthcoming conferences, recent publications and research

- *Boletín de Estudios de Traducción* (Spain): http://www.vc.ehu.es/campus/centros/filologia/deptos-f/depfi/firbet/
- *TRANSST: International Newsletter for Translation Studies* (Israel): http://spinoza.tau.ac.il/~toury/transst/

Journals

- *Babel* (the Netherlands): http://www.benjamins.nl/jbp/index.html
- *Cadernos de Tradução* (Brazil): http://www.cce.ufsc.br/cadernos/
- *Meta* (Canada): http://www.erudit.org/erudit/meta/
- *Target* (The Netherlands): http://www.benjamins.nl/jbp/index.html
- *The Translator* (UK): http://www.stjerome.co.uk/journal.htm
- *Translation Review* (USA): http://www.utdallas.edu/research/cts/tr/

Websites of organizations which often include useful links

- *British Centre for Literary Translation* (UK): http://www.uea.ac.uk/eas/intro/centre/bclt/bclt.htm
- *CETRA, the Leuven Research Centre for Translation, Communication and Cultures* (Belgium): http://www.arts.kuleuven.ac.be/cetra/#general
- *European Society for Translation Studies* (Finland): http://est.utu.fi/
- *Fédération Internationale des Traducteurs* (France): http://www.fit-ift.org/

Notes

2 TRANSLATION THEORY BEFORE THE TWENTIETH CENTURY

1 'Nec converti ut interpres, sed ut orator, sententiis isdem et earum formis tamquam figuris, verbis ad nostram consuetudinem aptis. In quibus non verbum pro verbo necesse habui reddere, sed genus omne verborum vimque servavi' (Cicero 46 BCE/1960 CE: 364). An extract from the English translation, by H. M. Hubbell, is also quoted in Robinson (1997b: 9).

2 Quoted in Robinson (1997b: 15).

3 In Robinson (1997b: 22–30).

4 'Ego enim non solum fateor, sed libera voce profiteor, me in interpretatione Graecorum, absque scripturis sanctis, ubi et verborum ordo et misterium est, non verbum e verbo, sed sensum exprimere de sensu' (St Jerome *Epistolae* Vol. II (395 CE/1565: 287)). The English translation is by Paul Carroll and is quoted in Robinson (1997b: 25).

5 Lambert (1991: 7) sees 'word-for-word' translation as referring to the process of translating morpheme by morpheme and gives the example of the Greek *syn-éid-ésis*, which was translated by the Latin *con-sci-entia*. By contrast, Lambert considers that 'sense-for-sense' refers to the translation of individual words or phrases 'according to their grammatical form and meaning in a given text', not according to the wider contextual meaning.

6 Reprinted in Störig (1963: 14–32). A modern colloquial American English translation is to be found in Robinson (1997b: 83–9). English translations of the German given here are my own.

7 Quoted in Störig (1963: 15).

8 'Rein und klar Deutsch' (quoted in Störig 1963: 20).

9 Literally, 'When the heart is full, the mouth overflows.'

10 'Man muß die Mutter im Hause, die Kinder auf der Gassen, den gemeinen Mann auf dem Markt drum fragen, und denselbigen auf das Maul sehen, wie sie reden und darnach dolmetschen; da verstehen sie es denn und merken, daß man Deutsch mit ihnen redet' (in Störig 1963: 21).

11 Cited in Bassnett (1980/91: 54), and given in full in Robinson (1997b: 95–7).

12 Reprinted in Störig (1963: 38–70). An abridged translation is given in Schulte and Biguenet (1992: 36–54) and a full translation is given in both Lefevere (1992b: 141–66) and Robinson (1997b: 225–38).

13 'Entweder der Uebersezer läßt den Schriftsteller möglichst in Ruhe, und bewegt den Leser ihm entgegen; oder er läßt den Leser möglichst in Ruhe, und bewegt den Schriftsteller ihm entgegen' (in Störig 1963: 47).

14 'Dem Leser durch die Uebersezung den Eindruck zu geben, den er als Deutscher

aus der Lesung des Werkes in der Ursprache empfangen würde' (in Störig 1963: 49).

15   Marcel Proust (1996) *In Search of Lost Time*, Vol. 1: *Swann's Way*, London: Vintage.

16   *Diploma in Translation: Notes for Candidates* (1990) London: Institute of Linguists. These notes were later modified for the 1996 examination, but the type of language used to describe translation varies little.

17   An additional fifth criterion is given for annotations that form part of paper 1, but need not detain us here.

18   Joan Kidd (1981, revised by Janet Doolaege 1990) *Guidelines for Translators*, document for Unesco translators, Paris: Unesco.

19   See note 15 above.

3 EQUIVALENCE AND EQUIVALENT EFFECT

1   *J. B. Phillips New Testament*, London: HarperCollins Bibles. 1st edition 1958, updated 1972, new edition 2000.

2   Newmark himself continues to teach such courses in the UK at the University of Surrey and previously taught at the Polytechnic of Central London (now University of Westminster).

3   See the further reading section for references to the work of these scholars, and chapter 5 for links to other work being conducted at the time by Reiss, Vermeer and Hölz-Manttäri in West Germany.

4 THE TRANSLATION SHIFT APPROACH

1   Note the similarity with recommendations by Nida and Newmark which were discussed in chapter 3.

2   This forms the basis of the discourse analysis models discussed in chapter 6.

3   These functions originate in Bühler (1939/65) and are later developed by Halliday. See chapters 5 and 6 for a more detailed explanation.

4   See, for example, Fish (1981) or van Peer (1989).

5   In *The Royal River Thames: Westminster to Greenwich Cruise and Sail and Rail Guide* (1997), London: Paton Walker, pp. 7 and 14.

5 FUNCTIONAL THEORIES OF TRANSLATION

1   In Bühler (1934/65). These are: *Darstellungsfunktion* (the informative function), *Ausdrucksfunktion* (the expressive function) and *Appellfunktion* (the appellative function).

2   The phatic function figured in Roman Jakobson's influential typology (1960), along with two other functions: the metalingual and poetic.

3   Neither this book nor Reiss and Vermeer's *Grundlegung einer allgemeine Translationstheorie* in the next section are available in English; in this chapter, the quotations from both works are my own translations.

4   Vermeer (1989/2000: 224) states that the skopos can be considered in three ways: (1) the translation process; (2) the *translatum* itself; and (3) the translation mode and intention. A single text may have sections that exhibit various different aims or 'sub-skopoi'.

5   As Nord herself recognizes (1991: 72), this distinction is in some ways similar to House's (1977) 'covert' and 'overt' translation distinction, which is discussed in chapter 6.
6   The model is based on the so-called 'New Rhetoric formula', a series of *wh*-questions ('Who says what in which channel to whom with what effect?') quoted in Nord (1991: 36). Her text analysis model owes much to Beaugrande and Dressler's work (1981).
7   Roz Denny and Fiona Watt (1998) *Cooking for Beginners*, London: Usborne. The translation titles, also published by Usborne are as follows: (Dutch) *Koken voor beginners* (1999); (French) *La cuisine pour débutants*; (Italian) *Imparo a cucinare* (1999); (Spanish) *Cocina para principiantes* (2000).

6 DISCOURSE AND REGISTER ANALYSIS APPROACHES

1   The crucial role of systemic functional grammar is to provide a precise grammatical terminology for what is known as discourse analysis. That is, it builds a specific linguistic description into the more general framework of language as communication and as an expression of the sociocultural process. Discourse analysis itself is a wider term, employed differently by different scholars. In discussing the translation studies work below, we use it to mean a combination of (1) analysis of text at text level (using the tools of systemic functional grammar) and (2) the related analysis of social communication and power relationships as expressed in the text as a communicative act.
2   See the further reading section for suggestions of studies describing analysis from a functional sentence perspective angle.
3   Some of the pragmatic concepts discussed here were also seen as important in Nida's notion of dynamic equivalence (see chapter 3).
4   Here they are following Halliday's *Language as Social Semiotic* (1978).
5   The German original is entitled *Jeder für sich und Gott gegen alle* (ZDF, 1974).

7 SYSTEMS THEORIES

1   Published in 1997 by Bloomsbury (London).
2   Translated by Marina Astrologo, published in 1998 by Adriano Salane editore (Florence).
3   Translated by Alicia Dellepiane, published in 1999 by Emecé (Barcelona).

8 VARIETIES OF CULTURAL STUDIES

1   The book therefore continues the line followed by Bassnett in her earlier volume *Translation Studies*, where she urges a move away from the then fashionable 'narrowly linguistic approach' of translation (Bassnett 1980: 13).
2   Lefevere here adopts the definition of Fredric Jameson (1974) *The Prison House of Language*, Princeton, NJ: Princeton University Press, p. 109.
3   A recent example is the decision of the Loeb Classical Library (since 1989 part of Harvard University Press) to commission 'more accurate and less cautious' translations of Greek and Roman texts, including Aristophanes (Steven Morris, 'Classic translations let obscenity speak for itself', *Guardian* 23 August 2000, p. 7).

4 The accuracy of Lowe-Porter's translations became the centre of a heated debate in *The Times Literary Supplement* in the autumn of 1995. See Venuti (1998: 32–3) and Hermans (1999: 1–7).

5 Spivak has, amongst others, translated Derrida and texts by Bengali writers including Mahasweta Devi.

6 Gurdial Singh (1991), *The Last Flicker*, translated by Ajmer S. Rode, New Delhi: Sahitya Akademi.

7 From the webpage of the Sahitya Akademi, http://www.sahitya-akademi.org/sahitya-akademi/org1/.htm [accessed 28 August 2000].

8 *Chachi* or *Tayyi* are used depending on whether a younger or elder aunt is being addressed.

9 TRANSLATING THE FOREIGN: THE (IN)VISIBILITY OF TRANSLATION

1 I. U. Tarchetti (1977) *Racconti fantastici*, ed. N. Bonifazi, Milan: Guanda translated by L. Venuti (1992) as *Fantastic Tales*, San Francisco, CA: Mercury House.

2 John Mort, Untitled, *Booklist* 1 September 1993, p. 4.

3 Paul Gray, 'Twelve stories of solitude', *Time* 29 November 1993, p. 80.

4 John Bayley, 'Singing in the rain', *New York Review of Books* 17 February 1994, pp. 19–21.

5 Untitled, November 1993, p. 158.

6 John Sturrock, 'A wilder race', *Times Literary Supplement* 17 September 1993, p. 20.

7 Janette Turner Hospital, 'García Márquez: chronicle of a text foretold', *Independent* 18 September 1993, p. 29.

10 PHILOSOPHICAL THEORIES OF TRANSLATION

1 See Palmer (1969) for a standard introduction to hermeneutics from Schleiermacher to Gadamer.

2 *Tableaux Parisiens*, translated by W. Benjamin, originally published Heidelberg: Richard Weissbach, 1923, reissued Frankfurt-am-Main: Suhrkamp, 1963.

3 Ironically, the oft-quoted English translation of Benjamin's paper has itself come to be severely criticized for inaccuracies of meaning (see, for example, Randall's criticisms in Venuti 2000: 23–5).

4 *Beowulf*, translated by Seamus Heaney (1999), London: Faber & Faber.

5 Published in ¡*Cavernícolas!* (1985), Buenos Aires: Père Abbat editora, pp. 105–46.

11 TRANSLATION STUDIES AS AN INTERDISCIPLINE

1 See M. L. Pratt (1987), 'Linguistic utopias', in N. Fabb, D. Attridge, A. Durant and C. McCabe (eds) *The Linguistics of Writing: Arguments between Language and Literature*, Manchester: Manchester University Press. Harvey discusses how it is used by Rusty Barrett (1997) 'The homo-genius speech community', in A. Livia and K. Hall (eds) *Queerly Phrased: Language, Gender and Sexuality*, Oxford: Oxford University Press.

2 Published in 1992 by the Royal National Theatre and Nick Hearn Books, London.

3 Published by Panther Books, London. The translation, by Philippe Mikriam-mos, is *Un garçon près de la rivière*, Paris; Persona, 1981.

4 The term is coined by Fowler (1986/96).

5 Published in 1992 in the collection *Doce cuentos peregrinos* by Mondadori España, Madrid.

6 Published in 1993 in *Strange Pilgrims* by Alfred Knopf, New York, and Jonathan Cape, London.

7 Simpson (1993: 12–21) describes how spatial and temporal point of view determines and affects the narration by, amongst other things, the order of presentation of elements.

8 Published in Spain as 'Náufrago en tierra firme' ['Shipwrecked on dry land'], *El País* 19 March 2000: 6–7. This was translated anonymously into English as 'Torn in the USA', *Guardian Review* 25 March 2000: 1–2.

9 See Munday (in press) for analysis of the translation.

Bibliography

Alvarez, R. and M. Carmen-Africa Vidal (eds) (1996) *Translation, Power, Subversion*, Clevedon: Multilingual Matters.

Amos, F. R. (1920/73) *Early Theories of Translation*, New York: Octagon.

Arnold, M. (1861/1978) *On Translating Homer*, London: AMS Press.

Arroyo, R. (1999) 'Interpretation as possessive love: Hélène Cixous, Clarice Lispector and the ambivalence of fidelity', in S. Bassnett and H. Trivedi (eds) (1999), pp. 141–61.

Austin, J. L. (1962) *How to Do Things with Words*, Oxford: Oxford University Press.

Baker, M. (1992) *In Other Words: A Coursebook on Translation*, London and New York: Routledge.

—— (1995) 'Corpora in translation studies: an overview and suggestions for future research', *Target* 7.2: 223–43.

—— (1996) 'Linguistics and cultural studies: Complementary or competing paradigms in translation studies?', in A. Lauer, H. Gerzymisch-Arbogast, J. Haller and E. Steiner (eds) *Übersetzungswissenschaft im Umbruch. Festschrift für Wilss zum 70 Geburtstag*, Tübingen: Gunter Narr, pp. 9–19.

—— (ed.) (1997a) *The Routledge Encyclopedia of Translation Studies*, London and New York: Routledge.

—— (1977b) 'Translation studies', in M. Baker (1997a), pp. 277–80.

Bal, M. (1985) *Narratology: Introduction to the Theory of Narrative* (translated from the Dutch by C. van Boheemen), Toronto: University of Toronto Press.

Bassnett, S. (1980, revised edition 1991) *Translation Studies*, London and New York: Routledge.

Bassnett, S. and A. Lefevere (eds) (1990) *Translation, History and Culture*, London and New York: Pinter.

Bassnett, S. and H. Trivedi (eds) (1999) *Post-Colonial Translation: Theory and Practice*, London and New York: Pinter.

Beaugrande, R. de (1978) *Factors in a Theory of Poetic Translating*, Assen: Van Gorcum.

Beaugrande, R. de and W. Dressler (1981) *Introduction to Text Linguistics*, London and New York: Longman.

Bell, R. (1991) *Translation and Translating: Theory and Practice*, London and New York: Longman.

Benjamin, A. (1989) *Translation and the Nature of Philosophy: A New Theory of Words*, London and New York: Routledge.

Benjamin, W. (1923/2000) 'Die Aufgabe des Übersetzers', in H. Störig (ed.) (1963), pp. 182–95.

——(1969/2000) 'The task of the translator', translated by H. Zohn (1969), in L. Venuti (ed.) (2000), pp. 15–25.

Bennington, G. and J. Derrida (1993) *Jacques Derrida*, Chicago and London: University of Chicago Press.

Berman, A. (1984/92) *L'épreuve de l'étranger: Culture et traduction dans l'Allemagne romantique*, Paris: Éditions Gallimard; translated (1992) by S. Heyvaert as *The Experience of the Foreign: Culture and Translation in Romantic Germany*, Albany: State University of New York.

——(1985a/99) *Traduction et la lettre ou l'auberge du lointain*, Paris: Seuil.

——(1985b/2000) 'La traduction comme épreuve de l'étranger', *Texte* 4 (1985): 67–81, translated by L. Venuti as 'Translation and the trials of the foreign', in L. Venuti (ed.) (2000), pp. 284–97.

——(1995) *Pour une critique des traductions*, Paris: Gallimard.

Bhabha, H. (1994) *The Location of Culture*, London and New York: Routledge.

Biber, D., S. Conrad and R. Reppen (1998) *Corpus Linguistics: Investigating Language Structure and Use*, Cambridge: Cambridge University Press.

Blum-Kulka, S. (1986/2000) 'Shifts of cohesion and coherence in translation', in L. Venuti (ed.) (2000), pp. 298–313.

Broeck, R. van den (1978) 'The concept of equivalence in translation theory: Some critical reflections', in J. S. Holmes, J. Lambert and R. van den Broeck (eds) *Literature and Translation*, Leuven: Academic, pp. 29–47.

Brown, M. H. (1994) *The Reception of Spanish American Fiction in West Germany 1981–91*, Tübingen: Niemeyer.

Brown, P. and S. Levinson (1987) *Politeness: Some Universals in Language Usage*, Cambridge: Cambridge University Press.

Bühler, K. (1934/65) *Sprachtheorie: Die Darstellungsfunktion der Sprache*. Stuttgart: Gustav Fischer.

Buikema, R. and A. Smelik (1995) *Women's Studies and Culture: A Feminist Introduction*, London: Zed Books.

Bush, P. (1997) 'Literary translation: Practices', in M. Baker (ed.) (1997a), pp. 127–30.

Butler, J. (1990) *Gender Trouble: Feminism and the Subversion of Identity*, London: Routledge.

Caminade, M. and A. Pym (1995) *Les formations en traduction et interprétation. Essai de recensement mondial*, special issue of *Traduire*, Paris: Société Française des Traducteurs.

Campos, H. de (1992) *Metalinguagem e outras metas: Ensaios de teoria e crítica literária*, São Paolo: Perspectiva.

Carter, R. (1987, 2nd edition 1998) *Vocabulary: Applied Linguistic Perspectives*, London and New York: Routledge.

Catford, J. C. (1965/2000) *A Linguistic Theory of Translation*, London: Oxford University Press (1965). See also extract ('Translation shifts') in L. Venuti (ed.) (2000), pp. 141–7.

Chamberlain, L. (1988/2000) 'Gender and the metaphorics of translation', in L. Venuti (ed.) (2000), pp. 314–29.

Chesterman, A. (ed.) (1989) *Readings in Translation Theory*. Helsinki: Finn Lectura.

——(1997) *Memes of Translation*, Amsterdam and Philadelphia, PA: John Benjamins.

Cheyfitz, E. (1991) *The Poetics of Imperialism: Translation and Colonization from The Tempest to Tarzan*, New York and Oxford: Oxford University Press.

Chomsky, N. (1957) *Syntactic Structures*, Gravenhage: Mouton.

Chomsky, N. (1965) *Aspects of the Theory of Syntax*, Cambridge, MA: MIT Press.

Christ, R. (1982) 'On not reviewing translations: A critical exchange', *Translation Review* 9: 16–23.

Cicero, M. T. (46 BCE/1960 CE) 'De optimo genere oratorum', in Cicero *De inventione, De optimo genere oratorum, topica*, translated by H. M. Hubbell, Cambridge, MA: Harvard University Press; London: Heinemann, pp. 347–73.

Cronin, M. (1996) *Translating Ireland: Translation, Languages, Cultures*, Cork: Cork University Press.

—— (1998) 'The cracked looking glass of servants: Translation and minority in a global age', *The Translator* 4.2: 145–62.

Delisle, J. (1982, 2nd edition) *L'analyze du discours comme méthode de traduction*, Ottawa: University of Ottawa Press, Part I, translated by P. Logan and M. Creery (1988) as *Translation: An Interpretive Approach*, Ottawa: University of Ottawa Press.

Delisle, J. and J. Woodsworth (eds) (1995) *Translators through History*. Amsterdam and Philadelphia, PA: John Benjamins.

Derrida, J. (1972/82) *Marges de la philosophie*, Paris: Éditions de Minuit, translated by A. Bass as *Margins of Philosophy*, London and New York: Prentice-Hall.

—— (1974) 'White mythology', *New Literary History* 6.1: 5–74; original is 'La mythologie blanche', in *Marges de la Philosophie*, Paris: Minuit, 1972, pp. 247–324.

—— (1985) 'Des tours de Babel', in J. F. Graham (ed.), French original pp. 209–48, translation in the same volume by J. F. Graham, pp. 165–207.

—— (forthcoming) 'What is a 'relevant' translation?', translated by L. Venuti, *Critical Inquiry*.

Devy, G. (1999) 'Translation and literary history: An Indian view', in S. Bassnett and H. Trivedi (eds), pp. 182–8.

Dharwadker, V. (1999) 'A. K. Ramanujan's theory and practice of translation', in S. Bassnett and H. Trivedi (eds), pp. 114–40.

Di Pietro, R. J. (1971) *Language Structures in Contrast*, Rowley, MA: Newbury House.

Dolet, E. (1540/1997) *La manière de bien traduire d'une langue en aultre*, Paris: J. de Marnef, translated by D. G. Ross as 'How to translate well from one language into another', in D. Robinson (ed.) (1997b), pp. 95–7.

Dryden, J. (1680/1697/1992) 'Metaphrase, paraphrase and imitation'. Extracts of 'Preface to Ovid's Epistles' (1680), and 'Dedication of the Aeneis' (1697), in R. Schulte and J. Biguenet (eds) (1992), pp. 17–31.

During, S. (1999, 2nd edition) *Cultural Studies Reader*, London and New York: Routledge.

Easthope, A. (1991) *Literary into Cultural Studies*, London and New York: Routledge.

Eggins, S. (1994) *An Introduction to Systemic Functional Linguistics*, London: Pinter.

Enkvist, N. E. (1978) 'Contrastive text linguistics and translation', in L. Grähs, G. Korlén and B. Malmberg (eds) *Theory and Practice of Translation*. Bern: Peter Lang, pp. 169–88.

Even-Zohar, I. (1978/2000) 'The position of translated literature within the literary polysystem', in L. Venuti (ed.) (2000), pp. 192–7.

—— (1990) *Polysystem Studies*, Tel Aviv: Porter Institute of Poetics and Semiotics, Durham, NC: Duke University Press, special issue of *Poetics Today*, 11: 1.

Fawcett, P. (1995) 'Translation and power play', *The Translator* 1.2: 177–92.

—— (1997) *Translation and Language: Linguistic Approaches Explained*, Manchester: St Jerome.

Felstiner, J. (1980) *Translating Neruda: The Way to Macchu Picchu*, Stanford, CA: Stanford University Press.

Firbas, J. (1986) 'On the dynamics of written communication in the light of the theory of functional sentence perspective', in C. R. Cooper and S. Greenbaum (eds) *Studying Writing: Linguistic Approaches*, Beverly Hills, CA: Sage.

—— (1992) *Functional Sentence Perspective in Written and Spoken Communication*, Cambridge: Cambridge University Press.

Fish, S. E. (1981) 'What is stylistics and why are they saying such terrible things about it?', in D. C. Freeman (ed.) *Essays in Modern Stylistics*, London and New York: Methuen, pp. 53–78.

Fowler, R. (1986, 2nd edition 1996) *Linguistic Criticism*, Oxford: Oxford University Press.

Frawley, W. (ed.) (1984) *Translation: Literary, Linguistic and Philosophical Perspectives*, Newark, London and Toronto: Associated University Presses.

Fyodorov, A. V. (1968) *Osnovy obshchey teorii perevoda* [Foundations of a General Theory of Translation], Moscow: Vysshaya shkola.

Gaddis Rose, M. (1997) *Translation and Literary Criticism*, Manchester: St Jerome.

Gauvin, L. (1989) *Letters from an Other*, translated by S. de Lotbinière-Harwood, Toronto: Women's Press.

García Yebra, V. (1982) *Teoría y práctica de la traducción*, Madrid: Gredos.

Gentzler, E. (1993) *Contemporary Translation Theories*, London and New York: Routledge.

Gerzymisch-Arbogast, H. (1986) 'Zur Relevanz der Thema-Rhema-Gliederung für den Übersetzungsprozeß', in Mary Snell-Hornby (ed.), pp. 160–83.

Godard, B. (1990) 'Theorizing feminist discourse/translation', in S. Bassnett and A. Lefevere (eds), pp. 87–96.

Graham, J. F. (ed.) (1985) *Difference in Translation*, Ithaca, NY: Cornell University Press.

Grice, H. P. (1975) 'Logic and conversation', in P. Cole and J. L. Morgan (eds) *Syntax and Semantics*, vol. 3: *Speech Acts*, New York: Academic Press, pp. 41–58.

Guenthner, F. and M. Guenthner-Reutter (eds) (1978) *Meaning and Translation: Philosophical and Linguistic Approaches*, London: Duckworth.

Gutt, E. (1991, 2nd edition 2000) *Translation and Relevance: Cognition and Context*, Oxford: Blackwell; Manchester: St Jerome.

Hale, T. (1997) 'Publishing strategies', in M. Baker (ed.) (1997a), pp. 190–4.

Halliday, M. A. K. (1978) *Language as Social Semiotic*, London and New York: Arnold.

—— (1994, 2nd edition) *An Introduction to Functional Grammar*, London, Melbourne and Auckland: Arnold.

Halliday, M. A. K. and R. Hasan (1976) *Cohesion in English*, London: Longman.

Harvey, K. (1998/2000) 'Translating camp talk: Gay identities and cultural transfer', in L. Venuti (ed.) (2000), pp. 446–67.

Hatim, B. and I. Mason (1990) *Discourse and the Translator*, London and New York: Longman.

—— (1997) *The Translator as Communicator*, London and New York: Routledge.

Heidegger, M. (1962) *Being and Time*, translated by J. Macquarrie and E. Robinson, New York: Harper & Row.

—— (1971) *On the Way to Language*, translated by P. D. Hertz, New York: Harper & Row.

Henry, R. (1984) 'Points for inquiry into total translation: A review of J. C. Catford's *A Linguistic Theory of Translation*', Meta 29.2: 152–8.

Hermans, T. (ed.) (1985a) *The Manipulation of Literature: Studies in Literary Translation*, Beckenham: Croom Helm.

—— (1985b) 'Translation studies and a new paradigm', in T. Hermans (ed.) (1985a), pp. 7–15.

—— (1995) 'Revisiting the classics: Toury's empiricism version one', *The Translator* 1.2: 215–23.

—— (1996) 'Norms and the determination of translation: A theoretical framework', in R. Alvarez and M. Carmen-Africa Vidal (eds), pp. 25–51.

—— (1999) *Translation in Systems*, Manchester: St Jerome.

Hoeksema, T. (1978) 'The translator's voice: An interview with Gregory Rabassa', *Translation Review* 1: 5–18.

Holmes, J. S. (ed.) (1970) *The Nature of Translation: Essays on the Theory and Practice of Literary Translation*, The Hague and Paris: Mouton.

—— (1988a) *Translated! Papers on Literary Translation and Translation Studies*, Amsterdam: Rodopi.

—— (1988b/2000) 'The name and nature of translation studies', in L. Venuti (ed.) (2000), pp. 172–85.

Holub, R. C. (1984) *Reception Theory: A Critical Introduction*, London and New York: Methuen.

Holz-Mänttäri, J. (1984) *Translatorisches Handeln: Theorie und Methode*, Helsinki: Suomalainen Tiedeakatemia.

—— (1986) 'Translatorisches Handeln – theoretische fundierte Berufsprofile', in M. Snell-Hornby (ed.) *Übersetzungswissenschaft: Eine Neuorientierung*, Tübingen: Franke, pp. 348–74.

House, J. (1977) *A Model for Translation Quality Assessment*, Tübingen: Gunter Narr.

—— (1997) *Translation Quality Assessment: A Model Revisited*, Tübingen: Gunter Narr.

Hung, E. and D. Pollard (1997) 'The Chinese tradition', in M. Baker (ed.) (1997a), pp. 365–74.

Ivir, V. (1981) 'Formal correspondence vs. translation equivalence revisited', *Poetics Today* 2.4: 51–9.

Jakobson, R. (1959/2000) 'On linguistic aspects of translation', in L. Venuti (ed.) (2000), pp. 113–18.

—— (1960) 'Closing statement: linguistics and poetics', in T. Seboek (ed.) (1960) *Style in Language*, Cambridge, MA: MIT Press, pp. 350–77.

James, C. (1980) *Contrastive Analysis*, London: Longman.

Jauss, H. R. (1982) *Toward an Aesthetic of Reception* (translated from the German by Timothy Bahti), Brighton: Harvester Press.

Jerome, E. H. (St Jerome) (395 CE/1997) 'De optime genere interpretandi' (Letter 101, to Pammachius), in *Epistolae D. Hieronymi Stridoniensis*, Rome: Aldi F., (1565), pp. 285–91, translated by P. Carroll as 'On the best kind of translator', in D. Robinson (ed.) (1997b), pp. 22–30.

Kade, O. (1968) *Zufall und Gesetzmäßigkeit in der Übersetzung*, Leipzig: VEB Verlag Enzyklopädie.

Kelly, L. (1979) *The True Interpreter*, Oxford: Blackwell.

Kennedy, G. (1998) *An Introduction to Corpus Linguistics*, Harlow: Longman.

Kenny, D. (1997) 'Equivalence', in M. Baker (ed.) (1997a), pp. 77–80.

Kittel, H. and A. Polterman (1997) 'The German tradition', in M. Baker (ed.) (1997a), pp. 418–28.

Koller, W. (1979a) *Einführung in die Übersetzungswissenschaft*, Heidelberg-Wiesbaden: Quelle und Meyer.

—— (1979b/1989) 'Equivalence in translation theory', translated from the German by A. Chesterman, in A. Chesterman (ed.), pp. 99–104.

Komissarov, V. (1993) 'Norms in translation', in P. Zlateva (ed.) *Translation as Social Action: Russian and Bulgarian Perspectives*, London and New York: Routledge, pp. 63–75.

Kuhiwczak, P. (1990) 'Translation as appropriation: The case of Milan Kundera's *The Joke*', in S. Bassnett and A. Lefevere (eds), pp. 118–30.

Lambert, J.-R. (1991) 'Shifts, oppositions and goals in translation studies: Towards a genealogy of concepts', in K. van Leuven-Zwart and T. Naaijkens (eds), pp. 25–37.

Lambert J.-R. and H. van Gorp (1985) 'On describing translations', in T. Hermans (ed.) (1985a), pp. 42–53.

Larose, R. (1989, 2nd edition) *Théories contemporaines de la traduction*, Quebec: Presses de l'Université du Québec.

Larson, M. L. (1984) *Meaning-Based Translation: A Guide to Cross-Language Equivalence*, Lanham, New York and London: University Press of America.

Laviosa, S. (ed.) (1998) *The Corpus-Based Approach/L'approche basé sur le corpus*, special issue of *Meta* 13.4.

Leech, G. (1983) *Principles of Pragmatics*, London: Longman.

Leech, G. and M. Short (1981) *Style in Fiction: A Linguistic Introduction to English Fictional Prose*, London and New York: Longman.

Lefevere, A. (1981) 'Beyond the process: Literary translation in literature and literary theory', in M. Gaddis Rose (ed.) *Translation Spectrum: Essays in Theory and Practice*, Albany: State University of New York Press, pp. 52–9.

—— (1985) 'Why waste our time on rewrites?: The trouble with interpretation and the role of rewriting in an alternative paradigm', in T. Hermans (ed.) (1985a), pp. 215–43.

—— (1992a) *Translation, Rewriting and the Manipulation of Literary Fame*, London and New York: Routledge.

—— (ed.) (1992b) *Translation/History/Culture: A Sourcebook*, London and New York: Routledge.

—— (1993) *Translating Literature: Practice and Theory in a Comparative Literature Context*, New York: The Modern Language Association of America.

Leuven-Zwart, K. M. van (1989) 'Translation and original: Similarities and dissimilarities, I', *Target* 1.2: 151–81.

—— (1990) 'Translation and original: Similarities and dissimilarities, II', *Target* 2.1: 69–95.

—— (1991) 'The field of translation studies: An introduction', in K. van Leuven-Zwart and T. Naaijkens (eds), pp. 5–11.

Leuven-Zwart, K. van and T. Naaijkens (eds) (1991) *Translation Studies: State of the Art*, Amsterdam: Rodopi.

Levine, S. J. (1991) *The Subversive Scribe: Translating Latin American Fiction*, St Paul, MN: Graywolf Press.

Levinson, S. C. (1983) *Pragmatics*, Cambridge: Cambridge University Press.

Levý, J. (1967/2000) 'Translation as a decision process', in L. Venuti (ed.) (2000): 148–59.

—— (1963/69) *Umění překladu*, Prague: Československý spisovatel, translated by W. Schamschula (1969) as *Die Literarische Übersetzung: Theorie einer Kunstgattung*, Frankfurt: Athenäum.

Lewis, P. (1985/2000) 'The measure of translation effects', in L. Venuti (ed.) (2000), pp. 264–83.

Luther, M. (1530/1963) 'Sendbrief vom Dolmetschen', in H. Störig (ed.) (1963), pp. 14–32.

Lyons, J. (1977) *Semantics*, Cambridge: Cambridge University Press.

Maier, C. (1990) 'Reviewing Latin American literature', *Translation Review* 34.5: 18–24.

Malblanc, A. (1963, 2nd edition), *Stylistique comparée du français et de l'allemand*, Paris: Didier.

Malone, J. L. (1988) *The Science of Linguistics in the Art of Translation*, Albany: State University of New York Press.

Mason, K. (1969/74) *Advanced Spanish Course*, Oxford: Pergamon.

Matejka, L. and K. Pomorska (eds) (1971) *Readings in Russian Poetics: Formalist and Structuralist Views*, Cambridge, MA: MIT Press.

May, R. (1994) *The Translator in the Text: On Reading Russian Literature in English*, Evanston, IL: Northwestern University Press.

McCarty, W. (1999) 'Humanities computing as interdiscipline', Available online: http://ilex.cc.kcl.ac.uk/wlm/essays/inter/

Miko, F. (1970) 'La théorie de l'expression et la traduction', in J. S. Holmes (ed.), pp. 61–77.

Mounin, G. (1955) *Les belles infidèles*, Paris: Cahiers du Sud.

—— (1963) *Les problèmes théoriques de la traduction*, Paris: Gallimard.

Munday, J. (1997) 'Systems in translation: A computer-assisted systemic analysis of the translation of García Márquez', unpublished PhD thesis, University of Bradford, UK.

—— (1998) 'The Caribbean conquers the world? An analysis of the reception of García Márquez in translation', *Bulletin of Hispanic Studies* 75.1: 137–44.

—— (in press) 'Systems in translation: A systemic model for descriptive translation studies', in T. Hermans (ed.) *Crosscultural Transgressions. Research Models in Translation Studies II: Historical and Ideological Issues*, Manchester: St Jerome.

Newmark, P. (1981) *Approaches to Translation*, Oxford and New York: Pergamon.

—— (1988) *A Textbook of Translation*, New York and London: Prentice-Hall.

Nida, E. A. (1964a) *Toward a Science of Translating*, Leiden: E. J. Brill.

—— (1964b/2000) 'Principles of correspondence', in L. Venuti (ed.) (2000), *The Translation Studies Reader*, London and New York: Routledge, pp. 126–40.

Nida, E. A. and C. R. Taber (1969) *The Theory and Practice of Translation*, Leiden: E. J. Brill.

Niranjana, T. (1992) *Siting Translation: History, Post-Structuralism, and the Colonial Context*, Berkeley, CA: University of California Press.

Nord, C. (1988/91) *Textanalyze und Übersetzen: Theoretische Grundlagen, Methode und didaktische Anwendung einer übersetzungsrelevanten Textanalyze*, Heidelberg: J. Groos, translated (1991) as *Text Analysis in Translation: Theory, Methodology and Didactic Application of a Model for Translation-Oriented Text Analysis*, Amsterdam: Rodopi.

—— (1997) *Translating as a Purposeful Activity: Functionalist Approaches Explained*, Manchester: St Jerome.

Norris, C. (1991) *Deconstruction: Theory and Practice*, London and New York: Routledge.

Orero, P. and J. Sager (eds) (1997) *The Translator's Dialogue: Giovanni Pontiero*, Amsterdam and Philadelphia, PA: John Benjamins.

Osgood, C., G. Suci and R. Tannenbaum (1957) *The Measurement of Meaning*, Urbana, IL: University of Illinois Press.

Palmer, R. (1969) *Hermeneutics: Interpretation Theory in Schleiermacher, Dilthey, Heidegger and Gadamer*, Evanston, IL: Northwestern University Press.

Parks, T. (1998) *Translating Style: The English Modernists and their Italian Translations*, London and Washington: Cassell.

Peden, M. S. (1987) 'Telling others' tales', *Translation Review* 24.5: 9–12.

Peer, Willie van (1989) 'Quantitative studies of literature: A critique and an outlook', *Computers and the Humanities* 23: 301–7.

Popovič, A. (1970) "The concept "shift of expression" in translation analysis', in J. S. Holmes (ed.), pp. 78–87.

—— (1976) *Dictionary for the Analysis of Literary Translation*, Edmonton: Department of Comparative Literature, University of Alberta.

Pound, E. (1929/2000) 'Guido's relations', in L. Venuti (ed.) (2000), pp. 26–33.

—— (1951) *ABC of Reading*, London: Faber & Faber.

—— (1953) *The Translations of Ezra Pound*, London: Faber & Faber.

—— (1954) *Literary Essays*, ed. T. S. Eliot, London: Faber & Faber.

Pym, A. (1996) 'Venuti's visibility' (Review of *The Translator's Invisibility*), *Target* 8.1: 165–77.

—— (1998) *Method in Translation History*, Manchester: St Jerome.

Qian, H. (1993) 'On the implausibility of equivalent response (part IV)', *Meta* 38.3: 449–67.

Rabassa, G. (1984) 'The silk purse business: A translator's conflicting responsibilities', in W. Frawley (ed.) (1984), pp. 35–40.

Reiss, K. (1971/2000) *Möglichkeiten und Grenzen der Übersetzungskritik*, Munich: M. Hueber, translated (2000) by E. F. Rhodes as *Translation Criticism: Potential and Limitations*, Manchester: St Jerome and American Bible Society.

—— (1976) *Texttyp und Übersetzungsmethode: Der operative Text*, Kronberg: Scriptor Verlag.

—— (1977/89) 'Text types, translation types and translation assessment', translated by A. Chesterman, in A. Chesterman (ed.) (1989), pp. 105–15.

—— (1981/2000) 'Type, kind and individuality of text: Decision making in translation', translated by S. Kitron, in L. Venuti (ed.) (2000), pp. 160–71.

Reiss, K. and H. J. Vermeer (1984) *Grundlegung einer allgemeinen Translationstheorie*, Tübingen: Niemeyer.

Robinson, D. (1997a) *Translation and Empire: Postcolonial Theories Explained*, Manchester: St Jerome.

—— (ed.) (1997b) *Western Translation Theory from Herodotus to Nietzsche*, Manchester: St Jerome.

Rosenthal, F. (1965/94) *Das Fortleben der Antike im Islam*, translated (1994) by E. and J. Marmorstein as *The Classical Heritage in Islam (Arabic Thought and Culture)*, London and New York: Routledge.

Said, E. (1978) *Orientalism*, London: Penguin.

Saussure, F. de (1916/83) *Cours de linguistique générale*, Paris: Éditions Payot, translated (1983) by R. Harris as *Course in General Linguistics*, London: Duckworth.

Schäffner, C. (1997) 'Skopos theory', in M. Baker (ed.) (1997a), pp. 235–8.

Schleiermacher, F. (1813/1992) 'On the different methods of translating', in

R. Schulte and J. Biguenet (eds) (1992), pp. 36–54. Also in Robinson (ed.) (1997b), pp. 225–38.

Schulte, R and J. Biguenet (eds) (1992) *Theories of Translation*, Chicago and London: University of Chicago Press.

Shuttleworth, M. and M. Cowie (eds) (1997) *Dictionary of Translation Studies*, Manchester: St Jerome.

Simon, S. (1996) *Gender in Translation: Cultural Identity and the Politics of Transmission*, London and New York: Routledge.

Simpson, P. (1993) *Language, Ideology and Point of View*, London and New York: Routledge.

Snell-Hornby, M. (1988, revised 1995) *Translation Studies: An Integrated Approach*, Amsterdam and Philadelphia, PA: John Benjamins.

—— (1990) 'Linguistic transcoding or cultural transfer: A critique of translation theory in Germany', in S. Bassnett and A. Lefevere (eds), pp. 79–86.

—— (1991) 'Translation studies: Art, science or utopia?', in K. van Leuven-Zwart and T. Naaijkens (eds), pp. 13–23.

Snell-Hornby, M., F. Pöchhacker and K. Kaindl (eds) (1994) *Translation Studies: An Interdiscipline*, Amsterdam: John Benjamins.

Snell-Hornby, M., Z. Jettmarova and K. Kaindl (eds) (1996) *Translation as Intercultural Communication*, Amsterdam and Philadelphia, PA: John Benjamins.

Spivak, G. (1993/2000) 'The politics of translation', in L. Venuti (ed.) (2000) *The Translation Studies Reader*, London and New York: Routledge, pp. 397–416.

Steiner, E. and W. Ramm (1995) 'On theme as a grammatical notion in German', *Functions of Language* 2.1: 57–93.

Steiner, G. (1975, 3rd edition 1998) *After Babel: Aspects of Language and Translation*, London, Oxford and New York: Oxford University Press.

Steiner, T. (ed.) (1975) *English Translation Theory: 1650–1800*, Assen and Amsterdam: van Gorcum.

Störig, H.-J. (ed.) (1963) *Das Problem des Übersetzens*, Darmstadt: Wissenschaftliche Buchgesellschaft.

Stubbs, M. (1996) *Text and Corpus Analysis*, Oxford: Blackwell.

Švecjer, A. D. (1987) *Übersetzung und Linguistik* (translated from the Russian by C. Cartellieri and M. Heine), Berlin: Akademie.

Taylor, C. (1990) *Aspects of Language and Translation: Approaches for Italian–English Translation*, Udine: Camponette.

Thompson, G. (1995) *Introducing Functional Grammar*, London: Arnold.

Tirkkonen-Condit, S. (ed.) (1991) *Empirical Research in Translation and Intercultural Studies*, Tübingen: Gunter Narr.

Toury, G. (1978/2000) 'The nature and role of norms in literary translation', in L. Venuti (ed.) (2000) *The Translation Studies Reader*, London and New York: Routledge, pp. 198–211.

—— (1980) *In Search of a Theory of Translation*, Tel Aviv: The Porter Institute.

—— (1985) 'A rationale for descriptive translation studies', in T. Hermans (ed.) (1985a), pp. 16–41.

—— (1991) 'What are descriptive studies in translation likely to yield apart from isolated descriptions?', in K. van Leuven-Zwart and T. Naaijkens (eds), pp. 179–92.

—— (1995) *Descriptive Translation Studies – And Beyond*, Amsterdam and Philadelphia, PA: John Benjamins.

Tymoczko, M. (1999a) *Translation in a Post-Colonial Context: Early Irish literature in English translation*, Manchester: St Jerome.

—— (1999b) 'Post-colonial writing and literary translation', in S. Bassnett and H. Trivedi (eds) (1999), pp. 19–40.

Tynjanov, J. N. (1927) *Arkhaisty i novatory*, Moscow: Akademia, translated (1978) by C. A. Luplow as 'On literary evolution', in Matejka and Pomorska (eds), pp. 66–78.

Tytler, A. F. Lord Woodhouselee (1797, 2nd edition 1997) *Essay on the Principles of Translation*, Edinburgh: Cadell & Davies, extracted in D. Robinson (ed.) (1997b), pp. 208–12.

Vázquez-Ayora, G. (1977) *Introducción a la Traductología*. Washington, DC: Georgetown University Press.

Venuti, L. (ed.) (1992) *Rethinking Translation: Discourse, Subjectivity, Ideology*, London and New York: Routledge.

—— (1995) *The Translator's Invisibility: A History of Translation*, London and New York: Routledge.

—— (1997) 'The American tradition', in M. Baker (ed.) (1997a), pp. 305–15.

—— (1998) *The Scandals of Translation: Towards an Ethics of Difference*, London and New York: Routledge.

—— (1999) *L'invisibilitá del traduttore: una storia della traduzione*, translated by M. Guglielmi, Roma: Armando Editore.

—— (ed.) (2000) *The Translation Studies Reader*, London and New York: Routledge.

Vermeer, H. J. (1989/2000) 'Skopos and commission in translational action', in L. Venuti (ed.) (2000), pp. 221–32.

Vieira, E. (1997) 'New registers in translation for Latin America', in K. Malmkjaer and P. Bush (eds) *Rimbaud's Rainbow: Literary Translation and Higher Education*, Amsterdam and Philadelphia, PA: John Benjamins, pp. 171–95.

—— (1999) 'Liberating Calibans: Readings of Antropofagia and Haroldo de Campos' poetics of transcreation', in S. Bassnett and H. Trivedi (eds), pp. 95–113.

Vinay, J.-P. and J. Darbelnet (1958, 2nd edition 1977) *Stylistique comparée du français et de l'anglais: Méthode de traduction*, Paris: Didier, translated and edited by J. C. Sager and M.-J. Hamel (1995) as *Comparative Stylistics of French and English: A Methodology for Translation*, Amsterdam and Philadelphia, PA: John Benjamins.

Viswanatha, V. and S. Simon (1999) 'Shifting grounds of exchange: B. M. Srikantaiah and Kannada translation', in S. Bassnett and H. Trivedi (eds), pp. 162–81.

Warren, R. (ed.) (1989) *The Art of Translation: Voices from the Field*, Boston: Northeastern University Press.

Wilss, W. (1977) *Übersetzungswissenschaft. Probleme und Methoden*, Stuttgart: E. Klett, translated (1982) as *The Science of Translation. Problems and Methods*, Tübingen: Gunter Narr.

—— (1996) *Knowledge and Skills in Translation Behavior*, Amsterdam and Philadelphia, PA: John Benjamins.

Index

Figures in **bold** indicate a major entry; <u>underlinings</u> indicate a reference in a case study.

Index

- systemic study
- hermeneutics modern.

- idiosyncratic
- preface 32
39 - generative- transformational

43 - Nida's systematic linguistic approach.

- tertium comparationis = interlingual comparison.
77 - translational action.
171 - deconstruction